RUFF FORECASTS
FOR THE
INFLATIONARY EIGHTIES

- Gold will be over $2,000 an ounce and silver over $100.

- Rising gold prices will cause dividends from gold stocks to be greater than 1980 share prices.

- Interest rates will exceed 40%.

- Social Security pension benefits will exceed $100,000 a year—and still not be enough to live on.

- After 1982, there will be no more fixed-rate, fully amortized thirty-year home loans.

- Inflation will cause a Constitutional crisis before 1987.

Ruff tells you how:

"YOU CAN BEAT INFLATION, TAXES, RECESSION AND THE ENERGY CRISIS. YOU CAN EVEN BEAT THE DEPRESSION THAT WILL FOLLOW."

Books by Howard J. Ruff

How To Prosper During
The Coming Bad Years

Survive & Win in the
Inflationary Eighties

Published by
WARNER BOOKS

SURVIVE & WIN IN THE INFLATIONARY EIGHTIES

Howard J. Ruff

With a Foreword by Senator Orrin Hatch

WARNER BOOKS

A Warner Communications Company

This publication is designed to provide the author's opinion in regard to the subject matter covered. It is sold with the understanding that the publisher or author is not engaged in rendering legal, accounting, or other professional service. If legal advice or other expert assistance is required, the services of a competent professional person should be sought.

The author specifically disclaims any personal liability, loss, or risk incurred as a consequence of the use and application, either directly or indirectly, of any advice or information presented herein.

WARNER BOOKS EDITION

This Warner Books Edition is published by arrangement with TIMES BOOKS, a division of Quadrangle/The New York Times Book, Co., Inc., 3 Park Avenue, New York, N.Y. 10016

Warner Books, Inc., 75 Rockefeller Plaza, New York, N.Y. 10019

 A Warner Communications Company

Printed in the United States of America

First Printing: May, 1982

10 9 8 7 6 5 4 3

With Thanks

I've been accused of not writing my own books, and I wish it were true. Writing a book is like giving birth to a litter of hippos—before Lamaze. Fortunately, I was surrounded by midwives, those hitherto anonymous people without whom this book would never have seen the light of day.

Judy Kimball, my personal assistant was as usual, invaluable. Bob Bishop and George Resch from my research staff at *The Ruff Times* provided research, some prose, and lots of update revisions for this paperback edition.

Erin Goldstone, way back when the hardcover edition was in the gestation period, helped me break through a world-class case of writer's block with some cogent insights. Linda Parker and the word processing staff at *Target* processed every word.

Last of all, Kay, my bride of twenty-seven years, tolerated the whole beastly process and kept the home fires burning brightly.

Foreword
by the Honorable Orrin Hatch,

U.S. Senator from Utah

Howard Ruff is an honest and courageous man, and is fast becoming one of America's most influential opinion-makers. His book, *How to Prosper During the Coming Bad Years*, is now the biggest selling financial book in history, and many millions of people have been helped by his radio and TV shows.

I know him best as a friend and a public-spirited American who, at considerable financial and personal risk, got involved in the American political process in 1980, and as much as any individual, helped to give the Congress a free-market majority.

Howard stuck his neck out ten miles when he decided in March, 1980, to risk his reputation and his subscription revenues to use his influence to help stem the tide of inflation and the growth of government power. He knew that many subscribers to his financial newsletter, *The Ruff Times*, would disapprove of his partisan political activities and refuse to renew their subscriptions, and he was right. He cheerfully lost about $1 million in revenues.

When he accepted Senator Harrison "Jack" Schmitt's call to become National Finance Co-Chairman for Americans for Change, the independent Political Action Committee that raised and spent $1.5 million on behalf of Ronald Reagan, it was at great personal risk. His publishing business is vulnerable to harassment by overregulation by the SEC, the FTC, the IRS, and the postal authorities, and if President Reagan had lost the election, who knows what a long memory the Carter White House would have had. As it was, due to pressure from the Carter-Mondale Committee, twenty radio stations dropped his radio commentary after a broadcast criticizing the administration's unsuccessful Iranian hostage rescue mission.

Howard comments that his own Independent Action Committee rallied his subscribers to provide what may have been the decisive financial and advertising support for at least two Senate and two House races, and it demonstrated that one concerned American, if he has the courage to try, can make a real difference within the spirit and the letter of our Constitutional Democratic Republic.

This book is different from most "how to make money" books, in that it moves beyond selfish concern for one's personal financial well-being, to present a workable political program for turning this great country around. If it enjoys the same success as *How to Prosper During the Coming Bad Years*, it could be one of the most influential books of our times. Howard's love of the Constitution and the free enterprise system shines through every page, and belies the image of him, concocted by a hostile media, of being a gloomy pessimist. He is anything but. I think he's a great American, and I am proud to call him my friend.

The next four years could be as crucial as any period in the history of the Republic. Either we reverse the direction of the last thirty years of political and fiscal philosophy, or we continue down the road towards inflationary ruin, with a high risk of losing our system of government. As Howard says, what good would it do you to get rich following his advice if, through our political neglect, we lose the free enterprise system to the taxing, inflating, and regulating power of government. Your wealth would turn to ashes in your hand. You wouldn't have the freedom to enjoy it.

Let's hope this book is read, believed, and acted upon. If it is, this just might be a better world for your children and grandchildren.

Contents

PART III:
Free the Eagle

PART I

The Failing Systems of the Inflationary Eighties

CHAPTER 1

The End of
the American Cycle?
Or a New Start?

In April 1980, Kay and I became the proud grandparents of a 5 pound 8 ounce baby boy, Ryan Lawrence Ruff. Maybe it was because he was born on April 15, but as I held Ryan's impossibly tiny body for the first time, the sickening thought hit me: "This kid is less than two days old and he is already $3200 in debt." That's his share of the national debt. By the time he is twenty-one, if we continue to accumulate public debt at our present rate, his share of that debt will be over $31,500,000.

Taxation without representation is supposed to be unconstitutional. We fought a revolution and founded a new country over this principle. Taxing our children and our grandchildren by piling up public debt to pass on to them is being done without consulting them. If that isn't taxation without representation, I don't know what is.

Ryan's share of the national debt evolved out of the historic cycle of a democracy. When everyone has the vote, most everyone, clear across the economic and social spectrum, sooner or later discovers he can vote himself benefits from the public treasury.

The following was written by the great Scottish economist Alexander Fraser Tytler shortly after our original thirteen colonies gained their independence from Great Britain. He was speaking of the Athenian Republic some 2,000 years before, but it has application today.

A democracy cannot exist as a permanent form of government. It can only exist until the voters discover that they can vote themselves largesse (generous benefits) from the public treasury.

From that moment on, the majority always votes for the candidates promising them the most benefits from the public treasury, with the result that a democracy always collapses over loose fiscal policy, always followed by a dictatorship.

The average age of the world's greatest civilizations has been 200 years. These nations have progressed through this sequence:

From bondage to spiritual faith; from spiritual faith to great courage; from courage to liberty; from liberty to abundance; from abundance to selfishness; from selfishness to complacency; from complacency to apathy; from apathy to dependence; from dependency back again into bondage.

Can this cycle be broken? Yes, it can, and it must. Nothing less than your freedom, your three bedrooms and mortgage, and your basic way of life are at stake. Cycles are not decreed in Heaven. They are man-made. What is made by man can be unmade by man, but to change it we must understand it and recognize it and admit it when it happens to us, as it is now happening. If we don't, this nation's political and economic institutions won't survive the Inflationary Eighties, and their failure will drag you down with them.

Let's see how far we have traveled down the Tytler Cycle.

The first benefits from the public treasury were financed by taxing the rich. We got away with it because there weren't enough of the rich to fight back effectively. In a few years, the "dumb" rich were being gradually liquidated through income taxes, capital gains taxes, and finally the estate tax, based on the assumption that "You can't take it with you, so we might as well take it from you." The "smart" rich, however, found tax preferences or legislated them into existence so that no more of their wealth could be confiscated.

When this revenue source proved inadequate, the tumorously expanding bureaucratic class that had been created by this tax money, and the politicians who had discovered the "Tytler principle," went after the middle class, starting with a tiny tax rate that was hardly worth complaining about. They escalated it to high levels during the patriotic fervor of World War II, and the high tax rates became an ever-rising permanent fixture through the 1960s and 1970s.

When the middle class would no longer accept higher and higher direct tax rates, the taxing power of inflation was discovered. It was perfect, because inflation taxes the middle class without them understanding what is happening to them.

First it was a simple transfer of wealth through government to the favored classes of tax recipients, whether they were the welfare crowd, or professors seeking "grant money" to conduct studies, or defense contractors, farmers, or whoever. The government would simply create the money out of nothing and spend it into circulation, which would dilute the value of everyone's "stored money," making it a tax on savings accounts, insurance cash values, bonds, etc. As long as inflation was low or moderate, the phony money would stimulate economic activity, making everyone feel more prosperous. The bureaucrats, politicians, and planners also made sure that there was enough money available through the banking system so that people could be encouraged to go into debt, and through the principle of leverage, buy more things,

15

creating more jobs. They also made interest tax-deductible, thus subsidizing, legitimatizing, and encouraging debt. Then rising incomes would move people into higher tax brackets so they could pay more taxes. This "bracket creep" meant that politicians could keep tax rates the same, or even vote for "tax cuts," while extracting more money from the same people until, now, *the lower middle class is paying income tax rates originally intended only for the rich.* The new 1981 tax law ends bracket creep in 1985 but with the inflation I anticipate that will be too late to do you any good.

Simultaneously, that formless, shadowy coalition of politicians, economists, and tax collectors I shall refer to as government had figured out another sneaky technique. They would tax businesses, a technique which years later would ultimately be elevated to the level of a fine art by whipping up a resentment of "obscene corporate profits" to assure that technique would remain politically popular. They knew that corporations don't pay taxes, that they only collect taxes from the consumer at the sales counter. They knew that if they could make the corporations their tax collectors, our anger would be misdirected toward the corporation because of the higher prices they would have to charge to cover the taxes they pay, as taxes are merely another cost of doing business, like commissions, license fees, rent, etc. Some day, future Econ. 101 students will study the so-called windfall profits tax on domestic oil as the quintessential prototype of the fine art of taxpayer seduction, as I will explain in Chapter 5. Direct tax rape through higher tax rates is probably no longer possible, as the victim won't hold still, but taxpayer seduction is a deceptive, safe, and profitable step-by-step process. When the victim finally discovers the intentions are not honorable, there is nothing left to be surrendered. The art of taxing is much like the art of plucking a goose. You've got to get the maximum amount of feathers with the minimum amount of honking.

The debt we are accumulating is now supporting a vast

army of bureaucrats who are multiplying madly like the Sorcerer's Apprentice's brooms, ravenous for money, fiercely protective of their jobs, defying the efforts of every administration to reduce their size and influence. The costs are unimaginably huge and growing at an exponential rate, and are passed on to the next two generations.

Little Ryan will pay the price in one of two ways. Either we will manage to evade the moment of truth of debt repayment by continuing to inflate, piling the debt even higher and higher, until Ryan finds himself paying 50%, 60%, 70% of his income to support our Social Security pensions and service the debt, or the whole jury-rigged house of cards will come down in a horrendous crash, not only bringing civilization to a halt but sending it back generations, and Ryan will grow up in a world that is trying to drag itself out of the fall of the American empire. However it turns out, Ryan will pay the debt.

Will Ryan and his generation revolt against us? Will he sit still while horrible chunks are ripped out of his paycheck to pay our retirement check? Will he love, appreciate, and support us in our old age when it dawns on him what we have done to him? Will he be thrilled to know that he started off swimming through the sea of life weighted down with $4,545 of debt shackles?

Bringing a child into the world at a time like this is an affirmative act that expresses everything that is soaring in the human spirit. We owe it to Ryan and his generation to solve our problems now. We owe it to him to pass on our estates to him, enhanced in value so he can handle his inadvertent share of this debt which is our legacy to him. We owe it to him to work for a world in which this cannot happen to his children and his grandchildren. We owe it to him to hand him a world better than the one that welcomed us, not worse. And this book is my small effort at achieving those ends.*

---

*A year and a half after Ryan was born along came Melissa Kay. Her debt burden is $4,545 and rising.

How to Prosper During the
Coming Bad Years—Revisited

My last book, *How to Prosper During the Coming Bad Years*, is now the biggest best-seller on money in the history of American publishing. The financial and economic establishment generally ignored it, although *Forbes* did a three-part series on alleged "financial cults" and called me the "Jim Jones of the financial world," which I thought was a bit excessive. The book received no serious reviews from major reviewers, even including the book review section of *The New York Times*, the parent corporation of my publisher. It did get me a lot of editorial attention from the press, who, for the most part, castigated me, characterizing me as a "prophet of doom," raking in ill-gotten gains by scaring people to death and pretending to be able to save them from purely ficticious disasters which I had erroneously forecast. For the most part, they refused to debate the merits of my case. But hundreds of thousands took the advice in that book and have enjoyed exceptional profits and a reassuring sense of personal security.

While traveling through the Midwest in early 1979 to promote the hardcover edition of *How to Prosper*, I appeared on a local television interview show and the host introduced me as follows: "Today we are studying psycho-ceramics, and we have with us a crackpot from California." A year later I came back to the same show to promote the paperback edition. In the meantime, the same man had read my book and had apparently bought some gold and silver based on my recommendations. This time when he introduced me he said, "Today we will be talking to America's most respected financial advisor." I hadn't changed, he had. Because of my track record, he perceived me as at least a bit more respectable.

The basic premise of *How to Prosper During the Coming Bad Years* was that inflation is endemic and epidemic and here to stay for the foreseeable future. I also stated my case that inflation would get much worse and that we would look back on 10% inflation with nostalgia as "the good old days." That, of course, has already happened, hitting 18% in the most recent cycle, proving that nostalgia ain't what it used to be—and it never was. I pointed out the great strains in society created by inflation and that because of it, cracks could appear on the face of institutions that we have taken for granted, most notably, Social Security, the banking system, and big city finances, and that these institutions would fail to consistently deliver their expected benefits and services.

I said that financial crises among the large cities would cause reductions in essential services and a rise in crime and social disorders, making our cities less and less tenable places for Americans to live and educate their children in. Since *How to Prosper* was published, Cleveland has defaulted on some of its debt, Chicago is close to broke. Despite some short-term optimistic developments, New York is edging back into the headlines. It is dirtier, and services are visibly eroding; about twenty other cities are on the sick list. This, I said, would accelerate an already established demographic shift of the American middle class from the big cities to small towns in America, and it has. After the 1980 census, New York, Illinois, and Pennsylvania have lost seats in Congress and electoral votes. Sun Belt states like Florida and Texas have gained.

I said the banking system would run into serious problems during "the next recession which will begin shortly after the publication of this book," and your bank might deny you access to your money, as the banks and the government try to save the banking system from the onslaught of depositors withdrawing money trying to find higher yields than the interest paid by the bank. This is because inflation would have risen to the point where it would become obvious that the amount of interest earned on bank deposits would not be sufficient to make up for the rate at which money is losing purchasing power.

19

The recession showed up on schedule, and in mid-1980, ten savings banks refused to allow early withdrawal on DCs, even with an interest penalty, because the flood of withdrawals threatened their solvency. That's not a lot of banks, but it is a startling precedent, because they got away with it. Tens of millions of Americans have watched their savings shrink in purchasing power, as the rate at which their money was losing purchasing power (inflation) rose to as high as 18%, while their CDs were yielding an average of only 8%.

I forecast that the Social Security System would become such an immense burden that it would finally have to be funded from the general fund and paid with printing press money. I said that the system would not go broke and that everyone would receive their pension checks, but they wouldn't buy much. The shrinking of Social Security-check purchasing power is now a matter of public record and common knowledge, and has only begun. You ain't seen nothin' yet.

For protection against inflation, I suggested that you buy gold and silver, preferably in the form of coins. Gold was then under $200 an ounce and silver was $6. Since then gold has been as high as $850 an ounce and silver as high as $50. Most of those who took my advice are enjoying increases in market value of their inflation-hedge holdings of 100% or more, even after substantial corrections.

I forecast that inflation would rise to unimaginable heights. It has soared to 18%, and if that doesn't boggle the brain, I don't know what will. And although it is retreating as this book is written, and will fall much lower than anyone anticipates during this recession (a development I also forecast), it will take off again to much higher levels, probably starting late this year (1982). Our recessions are only temporary interludes in an accelerating inflationary trend.

I said that interest rates would go to unimaginably high levels, causing a collapse of the bond and mortgage markets, creating a brief opportunity near the bottom of the recession to buy bonds at terribly depressed levels and ride the recovery cycle upward as interest rates go down. The bond markets collapsed twice, bottoming in March and December 1980, and the buying opportunities arrived much earlier than expected. We switched from some of our gold and silver into bonds, as interest rates touched 18% and the blood was "running in the streets" in the bond markets. Our profits have been spectacular, as interest rates plummeted, contrary to everyone's expectations.

I said that real estate prices, particularly in the big cities, would peak, plateau, and slide. They peaked in late 1979, and plateaued in 1980 and slid in 1981, especially in the suburbs of big northeastern and midwestern cities such as Boston, Cleveland, and Detroit. Some areas have even shown declines in mid-range home prices of as much as 20% in 1981. The tremendous interest rate surges in 1980-81 brought sales of income properties to a halt over most of the country, creating some mouth-watering buying opportunities for those who understand creative finance.

I forecast the 1980-81 recession in no uncertain terms. I also said that, for a while, those who have forecast that a great deflationary depression is at hand would look as if they were right, but that government would abandon the inflation fight and go to work to inflate us out of it, and it would work—one more time. During the 1980 election campaign, the inflation fight was abandoned, and politicians fell all over themselves to cut taxes and spend money at the same time, in the interest of being elected. The "balanced" 1981 budget was abandoned as the myth it always was.

I forecast that wage and price controls would come. We seem to have escaped them in this phase of the inflationary spiral, and President Reagan will probably resist them as long as it is politically possible to do so, so we will probably not get controls, until at least 1982, after the recession, when the fiscal stimulus begins to have its renewed inflationary impact.

There's not much I would change in *How to Prosper*, even with 20-20 hindsight, except that bond prices bottomed and interest rates peaked twice, near the beginning of and again quite early in the recession, rather than at the bottom, but my newsletter subscribers were notified of the change in timing. In fact, both times, almost at the exact bottom, I sent out a red alert saying, "Throw caution to the winds. Buy bonds."

Other than that, I wouldn't change a darn thing. Anyone who took my advice on the publication date of *How to Prosper* would have enjoyed more than 100% per annum appreciation on his assets, and that "beats inflation plus a little bit"!

For example, if you had bought a bag of "junk silver" coins one month after the publication of *How to Prosper During the Coming Bad Years* (February, 1979) and sold it in December, 1980 when this book was written, here's how it would have worked out.

	$13,572	Sale price
less	4,795	Purchase price per bag in 1979 dollars (720 oz. @ $6.66 ea)
	$ 8,776	Gross profit
less	1,755	Tax on profit (20% estimated)
	$ 7,021	Net before inflation
less	4,071	Two-year inflationary loss of purchasing power on capital (30% of sales price)
	$ 2,950	Net profit (increases in purchasing power) in 1979 dollars
		A 61.5% real after-inflation-and-taxes profit in two years

Here's how 100 ounces of gold would have looked.

	$64,100	Sale price
less	23,000	Purchase price in 1979 dollars (100 oz. @ $230 ea)
	$41,100	Gross profit

less	8,220	Tax on profit (20% capital gains)
	$32,880	Net before inflation
less	19,230	Two-year inflationary loss of purchasing power on capital (30% of sales price)
	$13,650	Net profit (increase in purchasing power) in 1979 dollars A 59% real after-inflation-and-taxes profit in two years.

If, on the other hand, you haven't taken my advice because (a) you didn't read the book in the first place, (b) I wasn't persuasive enough, or (c) you were convinced but for some reason didn't act, here's what your picture would be like. The most common example would be the person who has a $10,000 two-year CD, which at that time was probably yielding around 8%, if you were lucky.

	$10,000	Principal balance in 1979 dollars
plus	1,600	Interest earned
	$11,600	Total after two years
less	3,000	Two-year inflationary loss of purchasing power (30%)
	$ 8,600	Before-tax net worth in 1979 dollars
less	480	Tax on interest (30% ordinary income tax)
	$ 8,120	Remaining purchasing power in 1979 dollars
	<$ 1,880>	Net loss (*decrease* in purchasing power)

You are now poorer by $1,880 in terms of purchasing power, a loss of 18.9%, or 9.45% per year. And that ain't no way to get rich.

I guess the reason I went through that whole exercise was to demonstrate that knowing what to do doesn't do you a bit of good unless you do it. As a well-known American once commented after hearing someone say, "I know I should have done that, but . . . ," "Most people are sliding to Hell on their 'buts.' "

This postmortem on *How to Prosper* is not just an ego trip, but an effort to show you that the philosophy is sound. You have a right to know that before you follow the advice in this book. I feel very secure in building further on the foundation laid in *How to Prosper*.

The bottom line is that if you do not take the actions outlined in this book, or follow other strategies based on the same principles, you will be impoverished, and the date on which you arrive at that indefinable state called "poverty" is probably less than seven years ahead, no matter how much money you have. This is a last call to action, not just my axe to grind. It doesn't help me at all if you take my financial advice. It doesn't hurt me if you go broke. And you probably wouldn't be too impressed by my protestations that I care about you, even if I do. Just remember that your inaction will affect the lives of all those who depend on you or who shall come afterwards. So if you don't care about yourself, care about them.

After *How to Prosper During the Coming Bad Years,* what can I do for an encore to help you survive the Inflationary Eighties?

A lot, I hope. There were many things I was not able to cover in *How to Prosper,* and I've learned a lot since it was written.

Avoiding Failure

The systems and institutions we trust to preserve our hard-earned savings and investment capital are now failing to perform their appointed missions.

The money is failing, and inflation, which is the index of that failure, also threatens the banks and savings institutions.

Anyone who "owns money" will be caught up in that inflationary wipeout.

American corporations and their stocks are failing to beat inflation and free enterprise itself is on the ropes, and if it fails, will take stock and bondholders with it.

Our energy-dependent economic and social system is threatened by the failure of government to unleash the power of the free market to produce energy to meet our needs.

Our cities are failing to keep their promises to deliver a safe and clean living place, and they are starting to fail to pay their debts when due.

Our own government is failing to defend the freedoms it is constitutionally bound to protect, and has become, too often, the enemy of those freedoms.

This book is my effort to explain all of these failure areas in terms you can understand, show how they affect you, and give you explicit offsetting strategies for you to apply to your own life so that these failures have minimum effect on you and those you care about.

In fact, you can anticipate all of these failures and increase your chances of personal success. The assumption is that if you reduce or eliminate the chance of failure, the odds for success rise proportionally.

I have also prepared a political strategy with real clout, and a real chance of success, that can prevent the above-described failures from dumping on our heads the only failure that would overwhelm every failure-avoidance strategy—the total collapse of freedom and a national yearning for a "strong man" of the totalitarian left or right to "do something," as the coming runaway inflation churns its disruptive path through your hitherto orderly world in the next four to seven years.

You *can* beat inflation, taxes, recession, and the energy crisis. You can even beat the depression that will follow.

In the 1982 and 1984 elections, we together can make a political difference in the arena where the decisive battles will be fought—the Congress of the United States. Part III tells you how, and is a trumpet call to battle.

Crowded Theaters

Now I'd like to raise a question laid on me over and over again on radio and television shows. It usually starts out, "If everyone took your advice ...," and then follows with a list of all the bad things that could go wrong, such as banks failing because of everybody withdrawing their money, food shortages from everybody stockpiling food, etc., etc. The analogy is used of "yelling 'Fire' in a crowded theater."

There's nothing wrong with shouting "Fire" in a crowded theater, if you are sure that all but two or three people are deaf, and there really is a fire. If I thought everyone would try to take my financial advice, I'd stop giving it publicly, because it would no longer be valid. The kind of instructions I'm giving can only be followed by a minority, otherwise they would turn the markets upside down, driving up the prices of the inflation-hedge investments, making them useless, as everyone tries to get through the same door at the same time. Whether or not what I say could be harmful if everyone took my advice is an interesting theoretical exercise and lots of fun to debate, but in the real world, only a tiny segment of society will take my advice, because even the most monstrous best-seller only touches a small segment of the population. I'm even going to limit my newsletter subscriptions to 200,000 to be sure my advice is effective, and because, given our high levels of personal service, I don't think we can effectively counsel more than that. We're at 150,000 now.

But let's look at whether or not my advice is good or bad for the nation. It's a legitimate question.

If inflation caused the monetary situation to come unglued, and significant numbers of people lost their incomes, how would *How to Prosper* fans make out if they had stockpiled food, increased their self-sufficiency, bought gold and silver,

26

reduced their consumer debt, and pulled their money out of lending situations?

1. They wouldn't need welfare, so they would not be a burden upon the public purse.
2. They could eat the food they have stored, and would not be competing with others for scarce goods.
3. They would probably have a wood stove and would not suffer from heating and cooking fuel shortages, because wood is still (except in major metropolitan areas) a widely available and relatively inexpensive source of energy and it's renewable.
4. They would have some liquid reserves, probably in the form of gold coins, the prices of which would go through the ceiling with that kind of trouble. They would be able to service their debts and wouldn't run the risk of losing their homes and hurting creditors because of their bankruptcies.
5. They would have investments that are growing, not shrinking, because of inflation.
6. They would not be part of any banking panic when it occurs. They would be mostly out of the banking system, well in advance of any such troubles, so they would not be contributing to a domino collapse when the first domino falls.
7. They wouldn't be hurt by loan defaults, because they are not lenders.
8. They wouldn't lose their big city equities if the urban real estate market breaks, because they would have sold their big city real estate.

In sum total, my advice is stabilizing, not destabilizing. It is anti-panic, not panic-inducing. The nation is nervous and apprehensive, but fear of the unknown is a lot worse than knowledge of a finite known factor that can be hedged against. I will continue to say all the things I'm saying, as long as I know I am talking to a minority that can, in the real world, act upon my recommendations. If I reach the point where the majority might act on my financial advice, I'll probably shut up.

Roger Babson, one of the great early securities analysts, was the first of my breed to be called a Prophet Of Doom by the press, when before a meeting of the New York securities analysts early in 1928, he said the nation was headed for a stock market crash and a depression. He was vilified, but he was right. He was called a "Cassandra." If you will remember, Cassandra was the oracle who made gloomy forecasts that nobody believed, but that always came true. I have also been called a Cassandra. Perhaps, however, the titles of "Prophet Of Doom" and "Cassandra" should be worn as a badge of honor.

Realism is much more useful in economic matters—realism tempered with hope and a willingness to fight against odds. Pollyanna thinking ignores reality. If you ignore reality, you will never recognize problems and work to solve them. The world needs gadflies to point out problems so they will get our attention. Neither freedom nor financial stability happen all by themselves.

The natural drift of societies is away from freedom towards tyranny. To simply say, "There is no way that the prophets of doom could ever be right, just because we are America," is simply to stick our heads in the sand and fail to recognize reality. There is a heck of a lot more chance that the prophets of doom will be wrong if they are listened to, than if they are rejected out of hand. Nineveh would have been destroyed if Jonah had not made his prophecies. Positive thinking which ignores truth is ultimately negative. The truth is that we are in bad trouble. We have suffered severe structural damage, caused by inflation and high interest rates. The ultimate solutions will be political and they will be very difficult if not impossible to make. Failure to recognize this by merely saying "We must have faith in America" is foolish. We must love America, but we must have faith in it only when it is

28

right and facing reality. I want to be called a Prophet of Reality.

All I can say, my friends, is that I truly believe that this nation is in desperate straits that will become more and more apparent as the months and years go on.

I am the father of nine children and six foster children, the grandfather of three with one more grandchild on the way, and I am desperately concerned about the kind of world they will live in. I am also an active practicing Mormon (I'll keep practicing until I get it right), and that implies a lot of things about my personal philosophy. I have been taught that integrity is the highest of values and I have tried to live my life with integrity. I have sometimes failed to live up to my own standards, and like any other conscientious human with strong religious convictions, I struggle with my weaknesses. I have worked hard to bring my personal life into consistency with what I publicly profess to be, as a matter of principle and example to my children.

I have been taught, as have all Mormons, that America is a choice land above all other lands, especially favored by God, and that those who have come here, including Columbus and the immigrant groups who fled religious persecution, have literally been led here by God, and that this land will always have God's special protection as long as the people are righteous and serve God.

I have been taught that the Free Agency of man is a precious gift, and that this marvelous American experiment in freedom under the Constitution is a God-ordained exercise of that precious Free Agency, consistent with His plan for man, (and woman too, lest I be thought sexist).

Most important of all, I have concluded that if you are successful at beating inflation and taxes, but we lose the American Dream, your wealth will all turn to ashes in your hands. If we don't have the markets, the freedom, and the social stability to be able to enjoy the fruits of our wise decisions, what have we gained? It isn't enough to have personally beaten the inflation game. You owe it to this nation which has blessed you so abundantly to work to save this political and economic system so that, rather than passing a mountain of debt on to little Ryan, we will also pass on to him an American Dream which is still bright and vibrant and provides him the freedom and opportunity for the realization of all of his dreams.

If we don't make major political and legislative changes between now and 1984, the Ship of State could well sink as we sail through the inflationary storms ahead. This is a last ditch effort. *Survive and Win in the Inflationary Eighties* is my opening salvo on the ignorant and often venal clods in Washington and the State Houses and capitals of America who are still playing on your ignorance and inertia to buy your votes or seduce us all into alien social ideologies. This book contains a positive political and legislative program that I believe is politically feasible and creates a new mechanism for you to be heard and felt. We can't stop the runaway inflation from running its course, but we might save the nation from ending up on the historical scrap heap of failed dreams because of it. Part III, "Free the Eagle," is devoted to these tactics and strategies.

How to Read This Book

This book is organized in three sections.

Part I discusses the problems posed by this new world in which the rules have changed and in which we are threatened by failure. It deals with the liquidation of American capital, both corporate and savings, and explains why our institutions are likely to fail to serve you, protect you, and enhance your wealth as they have done in the past. It details who is responsible, and explains how this whole mess came about, in terms you can understand.

Part II tells you in simple, and detailed terms how to personally avoid the effects of the failures described in Part I.

The concept of Failure Avoidance is applied to each of the problems which we have posed.

We will teach you how to avoid the failure of the money so that even if what happened in Germany in 1923 should come true here—wheelbarrows full of money to buy loaves of bread, etc.—you will keep your purchasing power intact.

I will also discuss some unique, hard-money-oriented techniques for legal tax avoidance in an inflationary world so you and I can pass our hard-earned assets on to the Ryans of the world. The great American dilemma is that if you beat inflation with astute investments, you end up with capital gains taxes to pay on your profits, and estate taxes when you die, so you may end up giving back to Uncle Sam everything you gained through your astute application of a "beat inflation" strategy. Although most conservative, passive, tax sheltered investments, such as tax deferred annuities, Keogh plans, trusts, etc., help keep the tax man's sticky fingers off your money, they expose you to the ravages of inflation, so you get whipped either way.

My attorney, B. Ray (Bill) Anderson, and I have developed a total "beat inflation and taxes" strategy which enables you to keep your money out of the clutches of government with some novel but perfectly legal tax avoidance methods.

Part III maps out a program of political action so that we can avoid and prevent the most horrendous failure of all—the failure of this nation to preserve its freedoms as the nation is traumatized by the consequences of inflation and taxes and the deterioration of the money and market systems as they rot from within.

This political action program will increase the odds that the nation will be sufficiently stable that when the moment of truth arrives and the nation is searching desperately for answers, we will be ready to show the way within the spirit and the letter of the Constitutional Democratic Republic our founders envisioned.

The climactic crisis will come when inflation has devastated the hopes of the great middle class, and it cries out for a strong leader to "Do Something," even at the cost of freedom. Part III will get us organized to counter and defeat the totalitarian elements on the left and the right who always become a threat to seize power at such times, generally at the pleading of the people they want to dominate. We can and must become a mighty political force, electing and rewarding those politicians who have the guts to defy the individuals, corporations, public employees, cities, etc., that are swilling at the public trough and demanding more controls and regulations, and we must punish those at the polls who vote to hand out the swill. If enough of you catch the spirit of Part III, we can weld such a force.

Your journey through Part I may frighten you, because the facts are scary, but don't stop reading. I believe the answers are real and practical, and just as those people who read *How to Prosper During the Coming Bad Years* and followed its advice are sleeping a lot better now, I feel that the ultimate impact of this book should be reassuring as long as you read to the end, and accept and implement the advice that is offered.

Why The Reagan Program Will Fail

The paperback edition of this book will be on sale during a time of recession when the inflation rate is relatively flat and way below the terrifying levels of 1980 and early '81. It puts the author in a difficult position to try to persuade people they should act as though inflation were still epidemic when it is making one of its periodic retreats.

There's been a lot of euphoria for Ronald Reagan and many people have been assuming that the Reagan program will save America, although probably by the time you read this a lot of that euphoria will have eroded.

Nevertheless, the Reagan program is a new element since

this book was first published in hard cover and warrants discussion here.

To assess the Reagan program and its impact on America and your investments, let's cut through all the garbage and find out what it really is and isn't.

1. The Reagan tax cut is not a cut in taxes. It is merely a reduction in the rate of tax increase. It is a cut in the tax rates, which means that each bracket pays a slightly lower income tax. The reason why it isn't a cut in actual taxes paid is that "bracket creep" subjects people to higher tax percentages at least until 1985. Inflation is a tide which raises all boats, moving us all into higher tax brackets, so the lower middle class is now paying tax rates that were originally intended only for the rich. The "windfall profits tax" paid at the gas pump, the higher Social Security tax, and "bracket creep" have all guaranteed that the government will be taking a bigger percentage of the national income, even if all of the Reagan tax cuts are implemented.

2. The Reagan program is not a cut in spending. As Reagan himself pointed out, Federal spending in the next fiscal year would be $40 billion higher than the previous year. It is only a small reduction in the proposed Carter budget.

3. The Reagan program does not balance the budget.

4. The Reagan program is not an overall reduction of benefits from government. The increase in entitlements still goes on.

5. The Reagan program, even if enacted in its entirety, will not even begin to make a dent in the rate of inflation, so it alone is not the answer. There are two principal reasons why Ronald Reagan will not whip inflation, and your inflation hedge investments will prosper in the Dangerous Decade of the '80s.

Interest on the National Debt, Public and Private

The following excerpt from Robert Kinsman's outstanding

Low Risk Advisory Letter, March 6, 1981, (1700 South El Camino Real, Suite 408, San Mateo, CA 94402) says it best:

"At the beginning of this year, with the total federal government debt running about $930 billion, the interest payments alone were projected for the year at just over $93 billion (10.1%). Remember, that's interest alone.

Now, if there is no increase in the federal debt, except for accrued interest on it, and interest rates on it don't increase at all (an impossibility since even Reagan is projecting a debt increase of $125 billion by fiscal year 1984), the interest payments alone will increase to over $185 billion per year by the spring of 1988. (This still understates the problem, as it makes very low inflation assumptions. HJR)

I realize that these numbers are so large we can't grasp them fully. But, perhaps this will help. The total currency in circulation in the U.S. right now is just under $132 billion. If the government had to use cold cash to pay the debt interest this year, it would use up 70% of the greenbacks in circulation! By 1988, it will need 40% more than the cash now available. Fortunately for the government (and unfortunately for us), the debt interest is paid by credits to bank accounts which involves a broader definition of money than just currency. The money is inflated, even without printing it.

The government debt is just a goodly fraction of the total debt of the nation. That figure totals $4.3 trillion now. And the interest on it is above $430 billion per year. That amount is more than the definition of total current U.S. money supply known as M1B ($418.5 billion)!

In other words, if all of M1B was used to pay the interest on the debt in the country, we'd still come up short.

Now, are you ready for this? Without paying off some of that debt, and again assuming no increase in it except for the borrowed interest, and assuming a constant interest rate paid on the debt, the interest alone on the total debt, public and private will double to at least $860 billion per year by 1988. Most importantly, if the Fed doesn't increase our total liquidity (L, in their definition), by then we'll be using more than $1 of every $3 available in the country to pay that interest! (We're already using $1 of every $5.)

The Reagan program will have no effect on the numbers I've quoted, because it doesn't approach a balanced budget until 1984, and that's what's required to alter these figures. Without it (a balanced budget), the government corporations, municipalities, and you and I have to borrow to pay debt interest. That's what causes those figures to explode.

It is now certain that we'll have the same basic risks to our investments that we've had for the past couple of years: a collapse of the credit markets due to government borrowing, a runaway inflation, or a collapse of the debt, known as a depression.

The reason I say that we're still facing disaster risks, and believe that they'll be with us for another couple of years, at least, is a derivation of the above numbers. The way that the Fed has staved off disaster thus far is to monetize part of the debt: print more money. That is the irresistible temptation to avoid the ultimate disaster—a debt collapse followed by an economic collapse. The new money partly pays the interest on the debt. In the five years through 1980, the federal debt was up 61%, but total money available, liquidity (L), was up 71%.

The Fed will have to resort to a similar plan over the next several years, no matter what it says it will do. It cannot allow the debt or the interest on it to rise more rapidly than it can be financed. That means more money printing. That means more inflation. The financial roller coaster is still running. That means more of the same problems we've had.''

The only way to postpone the day of reckoning on that kind of debt is to print money or create money through the banking system. We have lots of wild and wonderful ways of manufacturing money other than printing it and, if necessary, I am sure we will come up with other ways of creating money using good old American ingenuity and know-how.

Just remember that figure—by 1988 $860 billion will be required just to service our debt. That money when pumped out by the Federal Reserve guarantees a wild runaway hyperinflation. The only other alternative is a repudiation of debt and a refusal on the part of government and other debtors to pay interest. That will not be permitted to happen. People who don't make interest payments can't borrow again. They must inflate or die, and they will inflate.

Social Insecurity

The second factor out of Reagan's control is Social Security.

Here are the facts of life. This program, if sold as an insurance plan by private enterprise, would have its perpetrators in jail. The Social Security plan was a hoax and a fraud from its very beginning. Sometime in the Inflationary Eighties, the total money you will be paid from the Social Security System in one year will grossly exceed the total amount of all contributions you made during your lifetime. Where will all the extra money come from?

The increases in Social Security payments will offset more than tenfold every Reagan budget cut. It is beyond and outside his control.

Even when President Reagan proposed the mildest of reforms to Social Security our "conservative" senate voted 96 to zip to tell the President to cool it on his proposed cuts. 96 to nothing is a tally usually reserved for declaring Mother's Day (as long as you're not in favor of excessive motherhood). Even Roosevelt only got 95 to 1 for a declaration of war on Japan after Pearl Harbor.

The President is the victim of a Catch-22. If he cuts Social Security, he will incur the hatred of his natural constituency and will wave bye-bye to his re-election. If, however, he does not cut Social Security, by the end of his first term the rate of inflation will be scaring the wits out of us. There is no way the President can win on the Social Security issue.

We haven't even discussed the monetary inflation potential of the Fed bailing out Brazil when it comes close to defaulting on its loans to the New York banks or ultimately bailing out Chrysler or Chicago. And how about Boston, being torn apart politically by Proposition 2½, which limited property taxes as Proposition 13 did in California, and almost shut down the police and fire departments?

Then there is the money that will be required to finance all of the mergers and realignment and rescue operations for the S and Ls that are already mortally damaged by the high interest rates of 1981. You will see the FSLIC exhausted. When they run out of money, newly printed money will be sent to the rescue, and this will be "off-budget financing," but it is just as inflationary, if not more so, than formal budget deficits.

Realistically, all of this points to this one conclusion: there will be a heck of a lot more inflation and RONALD REAGAN will probably go down in history as a well-loved, valiant and courageous loser.

Ronald Reagan was elected President of the Titanic. The only question is whether or not we will hit the iceberg before we have a change of crew.

Now I ordinarily don't like to expend any energy in lost causes, but I am going to fight for that brave man. When and if he goes down the tubes of history, I may go down with him, but I hope that some day my children and grandchildren will be proud that I made the effort. Regardless of my admiration for President Reagan, I'm betting my money, my reputation and a good many pages of this book that we will be having much more inflation.

CHAPTER   2

An Open Letter to
Your Investment Advisor

If you are advising people what they should be doing with
their money, the odds are that most of the things you are
suggesting for them will destroy them financially over the
next few years. The consequences of being wrong are awesome in the current inflationary environment, both in terms of
preserving the wealth of your clients and for the welfare of
the country, to say nothing of your future reputation.

Whether you are involved in estate planning, insurance
sales, brokerage, trust management, or whatever, you have a
fiduciary responsibility to be sure that what you do for your
clients is right for the present and future financial environment. If you persist in selling them cash value insurance, or
advise them to put money in CDs, bond for the long term, or
the stock market, and leave their portfolios unhedged with
beat-inflation investments and appropriate tax strategies, you
will someday have to account to wrathful clients for the total
loss of their purchasing power.

The only valid measurement of wealth is what it can be exchanged for in terms of goods and services—purchasing power! The inflation rate has been destroying purchasing power at a rate which is unprecedented within our lifetimes, even taking the recession into account.

We have seen 18% inflation, and this time around was just a rehearsal. We shall look back on 18% inflation and 18% mortgage rates with nostalgia as the "good old days." For the first time in my lifetime, prices are outracing income. Until 1979, the statistics indicate that most people's purchasing power, as measured in terms of their personal income, stayed even with rising prices. However, the value of the stored money that they sent ahead into the future to take care of them in their old age has shrunk, but the average American is not aware of that because he hasn't had the shock of trying to spend that money yet. It's only when he attempts to live on the income from that stored money that he will find, with a rude shock, that his purchasing power has been confiscated by government through the inflation tax. More and more people are forced to go into debt to maintain their standard of living, which means that more and more of their daily paycheck will be eaten up in loan payments, paying for dead horses—depreciating consumer goods such as cars and TV sets. Whatever is left to spend will be rapidly shrunk by money depreciation (inflation), forcing them to borrow more to maintain the same standard of living, etc., in a vicious cycle, like a snake eating its tail. Each new loan increases the money supply and is inflationary for all of us. When this incredible fact of life dawns on people, they will flee traditional investments, probably with large losses, and exchange their savings for precious metals, diamonds, colored stones, and real estate, in a frantic effort to keep up. For many it will be too late as the wise and perceptive minority will have already bought much of the available limited supply and will be reluctant to sell, forcing prices out of sight by the time most of your clients and colleagues wake up.

Take for example that Certificate of Deposit. If your client has an 8% CD and the inflation rate is 15%, and he reinvests his interest, he has a 7% loss of purchasing power. If you factor in the tax on the earned interest, his loss is probably closer to 10% or 11%. If he spends the 8% to live on, as many retirees, widows, and orphans do—precisely the people who are trusting you to make judgments for them—it's gone forever, and the principal is exposed to the entire onslaught of inflation at the rate of 15% per year. It only takes a few years at that rate to get wiped out. And that rate will increase!

Any time you put a client into a fixed-return investment—meaning that he will be paid back the same number of dollars he loaned—if the interest return *after taxes* is not at least three points higher than the anticipated inflation rate, his wealth is being systematically destroyed.

Now you tell me how, in good conscience, you can commit somebody's money out into the future to be returned in fixed dollars, even at compound interest, at anything less than the future rate of inflation, after taxes? If you can sleep well after that, you just don't understand the problem. The search for income must be subordinated to the quest for capital growth to keep up. If you can get both, so much the better, but that requires unorthodox investments.

Up until now, we "crackpots" in the hard-money crowd have been pretty much alone in taking this position. One of the targets of my skepticism has been Federal, city, state, and private pension funds, which I contend will do the workers little or no good when they retire because of the impact of inflation on the kinds of investments that these pension funds are making.

The state of Alaska has caught on. It is investing its pension funds in gold, real estate, and foreign securities. Peter Bushe, the state's Deputy Commissioner of Revenue, says, "It's the only way left we know of to protect beneficiaries of our public pension plans against continuing inflation." New legislation permits the state's public employees' retire-

41

ment fund and teachers' retirement fund, with a total of over $520 million, to invest in gold bullion or Certificates of Deposit denominated in foreign currencies, and in real estate. Before then, their funds were invested entirely in mortgages, bonds, money market funds, and common stocks, yielding an average return of about 8%. "These traditional outlets simply can't maintain the purchasing power of the pensions' dollars," says Michael J. Riley, state Investment Officer.

This is the first public pension fund to try to move into the hard-money camp. However, they ran into some trouble with the Municipal Financial Officers Association, which questioned how far they can move in this direction and still remain "prudent." Under the "prudent man rule," you aren't supposed to depart from the common herd, but the common herd now consists of prudent lemmings, plunging mindlessly but prudently over a cliff into a sea of inflation.

The bottom line is that, because of inflation, traditional conservative investments have been invalidated. Any fixed-dollar investment will be devastated by inflation.

Let's look at each of the investment markets and examine their future in an inflationary environment.

1. BONDS. Bonds clobber you two ways in rising inflation. First, long-term interest rates will rise along with the rate of inflation. That means declining bond prices, so you have capital losses. Second, the interest income is nowhere near enough to compensate for the loss of purchasing power, even if there was no dollar decline in the face value of the bonds. Anyone buying bonds and holding them to maturity in a period of rising interest rates and rising inflation rates is crazy or irresponsible or both. Bonds have become a trading vehicle only, to be bought when depressed by high interest rates, and sold when interest rates bottom out. They are no longer widows' and orphans' buy-and-hold-forever investments.

2. STOCK MARKET. The Blue Chips are being destroyed by inflation several ways. Don't you think there's some reason why the Dow Jones hasn't gone anywhere since 1966?

That's when inflation started taking off. That's when the money creation process began getting out of hand, forcing Nixon to close the gold window in 1971 because we were losing our gold hoard to foreign interests holding our dollars and demanding gold in exchange for them. And that's when the stock market peaked and started going nowhere at a rapid rate. If you adjust the Dow Jones Industrial Average for inflation and state it in 1966 dollars it's under 302. It will have to go to around 3000 in 1982-dollar terms just to break even, and that break-even point will recede even farther into the dim reaches of the 3000s as the inflation rate accelerates in the 1980s. I will show you that status is unlikely to change in the near future.

Until accounting rules are changed and inflation reverses, the stock market is going nowhere for a long time. Even if it goes sideways, stocks will lose real value at the rate of at least 15% to 20% a year at the expected inflation rate and much more in 1982–1985. If you persist in attempting to beat that rigged game with your clients' money, you are betting them into the longest of long shots.

3. CERTIFICATES OF DEPOSIT. I've already touched on that. A CD is a long-term loan to a financial institution. A long-term loan rips off the lender, because the borrower pays off in cheap dollars. When the inflation rate is only 7% or 8%, it is like being nibbled to death by ducks. When it is 15% or 16%, it is like being eaten by alligators.

4. KEOGH AND IRA PLANS. They are a little better, but not much. Some of the inflationary bite is offset by the tax savings. The higher your tax bracket, the more valid it is to have a Keogh or IRA. But most Keoghs or IRAs are invested in precisely the same kind of investments that will be destroyed by inflation. Inexorably those funds will be chewed up. It just takes a little longer, because of the tax saving offset. If you have a 30% tax saving, and you are talking about an inflationary loss of 15% a year, then it takes a couple of years longer before the losses begin. But the very nature of a Keogh or

IRA is a bet on a long-term future, using fixed dollars, receiving a fixed rate of return. Eventually inflation will destroy the typical Keogh and IRA.

I could sum it all up by saying, "The money is going broke." I don't know for sure whether the insurance company that holds your money, or the company whose stock you bought, or the city, state, or government who issued the bonds, is going broke. All I know is that the money is going broke and they will pay you off in cheap dollars.

Please examine your motivation in the selection of investments for your clients. Unfortunately, most of the income of the typical estate or financial planner comes from commissions on the investments. I believe this creates a difficult conflict of interest, because in this financial environment, the best commission rates often come from the investments which have the poorest long-term utility, such as cash value insurance and annuity programs.

The only basis on which you dare continue to make these kind of recommendations is if you are prepared to disagree with me about the future of inflation, and defend your stance. If so, proceed as you have done in the past, not at your own risk, but at the risk of your clients. I submit as my credentials that the terrifyingly high inflation and interest rates that we have experienced are as I forecast, loudly and publicly. You don't have to wait for the future to see inflation destroy your money. It's doing it now. The collapse of the money is not a sudden future event. It's a process. The money collapsed 12% to 15% last year and 15% to 20% the previous year. That's inflation. Don't expect government or the tax revolt or a "conservative ground swell" to bail you out. Inflation is out of control. What this world needs now is men and women of principle who put their clients first, and who advise them properly for an inflationary environment, without regard to the financial welfare of the adviser. There are many good honest advisors who have acted contrary to their own financial self-interest, if the client's welfare required it. It takes a lot of guts to say "I was wrong." If you simply don't agree with me, that's an honest difference of opinion. Just be sure that your motives are right, and please, please, please give serious consideration to the arguments in this book. It may have some constructive lessons for you.

What should you be recommending? Let's put in capsule form the basic Ruff Recommendations.

Ruff's Recommendations

1. Prepare for shortages due to inflation-induced labor problems, price controls, and credit market disruptions. Store an emergency supply of food, and a stockpile of basic commodities, as detailed in *How to Prosper*, so that you are not dependent upon trucks rolling into the city each day. When I was in Houston, a metropolitan area of 4 million people, I asked a question of an audience: "How many trucks do you think have to roll into this city every day in order to feed these people?" Nobody ventured a guess. I don't know the exact number, but it is awesome. Will they roll if inflation causes the credit system to breakdown, or gives us massive labor troubles, or workers don't trust the money in which they are to be paid, or our energy supplies from the Mid-East are cut off?

2. Buy approximately $5,000 worth of "junk silver" coins from a coin dealer for every member of the family. A bag costs about $7,500 now, and I have no idea what it will cost by the time you read this, but, if you bought one in 1964 when they stopped making silver coins, it would have been only $1,000, as that was the face value of the 90%-silver coins in the bag. If you bought one when *How to Prosper* was published, you would have paid $4,800. The time will come, probably in less than three years, when it will be worth $50,000 or more. Silver has risen in value because of inflation and the depreciation of paper money. As long as that

45

trend is intact, silver will rise, with occasional dramatic retreats. It also could serve for a while as the only spending money that will be universally accepted if we should have such a runaway inflation that we have a total collapse of the currency, which is possible.

3. Have an equivalent amount of gold coins (preferably Krugerrands, the various Mexican pesos, the Canadian Maple Leaf, or the Austrian 100 Corona). They are bought and sold strictly for their bullion value. You can safely deal with the firms listed in the Appendix, but compare prices among dealers.

4. With your discretionary funds, diversify among more gold coins, gold stocks, investment grade diamonds (bought at true wholesale prices), colored precious and semi-precious stones, and small-town, income-producing real estate. By small-town, I do not mean bedroom communities which are merely satellites of large metropolitan areas. I am referring to small towns where the traffic flows into that town in the morning, not out of it toward some megalopolis. A diversified agricultural economy, a growing middle class, a good community feeling, and a sense of small-town pride are all important in your selection. It could be anywhere in the country and could be as large as Portland, Oregon, or as small as Delta, Utah.

Buy income-producing real estate, such as commercial or residential properties, rather than speculating in raw land. Even small, single-family homes for rent will fit the plan nicely. If you compute the rate of return after holding a piece of raw land and pumping your pocket money into it in installment payments, taxes, and other expenses, you will realize you could have had far better rates of return if the property had produced income to service the debt. It's one of the few ways I know, other than running a business or buying stocks, to get investment income without loaning money at a fixed return. Using "creative finance" (a purchase by assum-

46

ing existing low interest rate mortgages), properties with assumable loans will be much more liquid and valuable, as lenders are becoming so gun-shy about rising inflation and interest rates that new fixed-rate, long-term mortgages will be dinosaurs by 1983. Buy apartment buildings in a small town somewhere, and inflation will ultimately cover most of your amateur mistakes. Most other income choices will result in the destruction of purchasing power through inflation.

5. Buy collectible items, such as stamps, baseball cards, comic books, antiques, old cars, fine art, and rare coins during a recession and sell them when the inflationary fever is at its height, four to seven years from now. To do well at this game, you must become a hobbyist. Don't do it unless you are either prepared to enjoy it enough to spend a lot of time at it, or unless you have an advisor whom you can trust completely to make your buying and selling decisions for you. Otherwise, leave it alone. Don't just go out and buy some stamps or comic books because someone says it's a good deal. You can get hurt paying too much for inferior merchandise unless you know what you are doing.

Inflation is an evil so monstrous as to almost defy description. It's immoral and dishonest. It's forcing me to teach my children to be speculators rather than prudent savers, and I find this immensely offensive. If your advice to your clients does not take this monster into account, and if you underestimate it or do not understand how it gets out of control, you are merely contributing to the inflationary disintegration of the nation's wealth in the eighties, as you shall see if you read on.

Last of all, don't take this letter as a hostile challenge. I'd like to work with you. I have literally tens of thousands of newsletter clients who need the services of enlightened financial planners. We want to help them. We will even be holding seminars to train and certify you so we can safely refer our clients to you. If you call or write, we will let you know where or when. We want to be on your side. Please refer to the Appendix under "Financial Planning Services."

Unfortunately, the advisors who most need the foregoing advice are probably not reading this book. Those of you who are probably don't need the advice.

Sincerely,
Howard J. Ruff

CHAPTER 3

The Liquidation
of America

If the present trends are not arrested, when the history books of the twentieth century have been written the great event of our times will be the Liquidation of America, an event of such magnitude as to dwarf in importance any other economic happening in the last fifty years.

It isn't really accurate to call it an event. It's a process. It's been going on for years, it's going on now, and unless major changes can be forced on an unwilling political and bureaucratic establishment, it will continue until the world you now know will slowly collapse onto the junk heap of history as a noble experiment that finally failed.

What do I mean by liquidation?

When a corporation dissolves its operations, it "liquidates" itself by selling off assets and distributing the proceeds to the creditors, and, if there is anything left, to the stockholders.

When you die, if you have not planned your estate properly, much of it will have to be "liquidated" to pay death taxes, with the remaining proceeds, if any, distributed to the heirs.

When I was forced into bankruptcy back in 1968, all of my assets were taken over by the court, "liquidated," and distributed among the creditors. That was the "liquidation" of Howard Ruff. (See *How to Prosper During the Coming Bad Years*.)

The capital base of capitalist America is being "liquidated" at an accelerating rate. Unless we do a 180-degree reversal, the process could be completed as soon as 1985, certainly by the end of this decade.

This liquidation by inflation and taxes goes on quietly, secretly, and unobtrusively in three arenas of liquidation: the savings of middle-class America, our precious pension and retirement funds, and corporate America.

The Fleecing of the Prudent

The first part of our liquidation scenario affects most directly the savers of America: the prudent, unsophisticated people who don't feel they have the time, money, or temperament to take chances in the stock market or the commodities market, but who are looking only for a nice, simple one-time-only decision. They want to loan their money to some institution which will give them a safe interest return, which, if allowed to compound, will allow the investment to grow, or which will give them the income they need to supplement their Social Security checks when they retire. This is the time-honored, conservative, traditional American thing to do, and the majority of Americans still play the game that way.

These people are the backbone of society. They provide the huge pools of capital through the banks, the insurance companies, and the savings institutions, which are necessary for the forward march of American growth and industry. If American savers cease saving, it's the end of the capitalist system. However, if they continue to save, it's the end of their capital, and the result is the same.

American savers are lenders to banks, savings and loans, and insurance companies, who will pay them back with cheap or worthless dollars which are diminishing in purchasing power through inflation. To add injury to insult, despite the fact that they are showing actual losses in purchasing power, they are submitted to the ignominy of paying taxes on their nonexistent income.

Inflation makes the income tax an even more effective liquidator. Let's say you are receiving a yield of 14% on a CD, and let's be charitable and assume that the inflation rate is only 13%. That means that after adjusting for the drop in purchasing power of your money, your true profit is only 1%. However, your tax will be based on the entire 14% interest received meaning, of course, that if you are in the 25% bracket, you would pay out in tax approximately one-quarter of your total interest income, or 3.5%. Now you don't have to be a genius to see that if you have a real net profit of 1%, and you are paying 3.5% of your gross earnings in taxes, the true tax rate for you is 350%, and that ain't no way to get rich. You are being liquidated by inflation and taxes. To check out how well you are doing, you may have to recalculate based on the current tax and inflation figures when you read this, as they will change, but I bet it will still be negative.

Added to these inexorable numbers is the fact that many Americans have perceived the truth and stopped saving. Our savings rate has been cut in half in the last ten years. It is the lowest among the industrialized nations, and the downward trend is continuing. You can't have a capitalist, free enterprise system without capital and capital markets. Not only that, but this trend could lead to the nationalization of our banking and savings institutions, which could not withstand a determined onslaught of savers pulling their money out, looking frantically for something better, somewhere else. The institutions' only hope will be to freeze the funds, and I'm sure that is precisely what the government will do through the device of a bank holiday, or by simply invoking the statutes which allow the banks to refuse early withdrawal requests on certificates of deposit, even with an interest penalty. If you think that sounds like an extreme expectation, take a look at this recent *Wall Street Journal* story:

NEW YORK—When the Roslyn Savings Bank on Long Island offers a six-month Certificate of Deposit, it really means it:

The Roslyn Bank is no longer allowing any early withdrawals of savings certificates of any maturity following the massive outflow of funds that has afflicted the entire thrift industry.

. . . Floyd N. York, the bank's president, blames "snowballing" amounts of premature withdrawals by customers who are rushing to put their funds in higher-yielding money-market investments.

Bank customers usually ignore the fine print on their accounts that leaves the financial institution the option of denying any early withdrawals on CDs, which are funds left by customers for specific periods of time. Federal banking regulations give banks this right, . . . however, banks have regularly allowed early withdrawals but have charged interest penalties as required by law.

Under banking rules, *banks have the option to demand advance notice for withdrawals from regular savings accounts,* too. [Emphasis mine. HJR]

Roslyn Savings has had a net outflow of deposits "in excess of $10 million" since June 30, Mr. York said. It lost $750,000 in deposits in a single day last Tuesday, the day before the bank instituted its ban.

But some bankers caution against a ban on early withdrawals, saying it threatens to erode consumer confidence in the thrift industry and could accelerate the switching of funds out of regular day-to-day savings accounts.

Some of these outstanding CDs take as long as twelve years to mature. If current inflation rates continue, I wonder what those frozen deposits will be worth. They won't "mature"; they will decompose.

There are those who have thought my warning in *How to Prosper* stating that banks can be dangerous to your financial health was a bit overblown, but I don't think the nervous depositors of Roslyn Savings Bank would think so now. Obviously, one savings bank isn't a whole industry, but shortly after Roslyn got away with it, nine other banks, mostly in New York, have taken the same steps. In the next higher round of inflation and interest rates, or the one after that, it could be hundreds.

The Death of the Pension

The second and perhaps cruelest manifestation of the Liquidation of America is the liquidation of the public and private pensions of middle-class America.

As stories such as that of the Roslyn Savings Bank become more common, it will increase the disincentives to saving. But an even more powerful savings disincentive is provided by the Social Security program, which, ironically, is thought of as the basis of most people's savings. The liquidation of capital is not just the loss of value through inflation and the rape of your pocketbook through taxes. It also is the reduced and falling savings rate which is among the lowest of all in Western civilization, and it isn't because people have unaccountably lost their inclination toward thrift. There are some real reasons why people no longer set aside money for a rainy day or for the old age monsoon.

When an individual makes provisions for old age by setting

53

aside part of his or her income in a bank, an annuity, or a retirement program, these funds become part of the capital stock of the economy. This helps to create new jobs, upgrade existing ones, finance industrial innovations and the development of new technologies, fund the discovery and development of new energy sources, and generally finance the production of all the goods and services that Americans want.

The tax burden which Social Security imposes on lower- and middle-income taxpayers absorbs much of the funds they could have invested for retirement. Even in the case of those individuals with higher incomes, the fact that the government will supposedly provide a significant retirement income provides a powerful disincentive to save. The best estimate by economists is that Social Security has reduced personal savings by between 40% and 50%, and has reduced total savings (including corporate savings) by about 40%. This disincentive has had a disastrous impact on our national income and on economic growth. With less capital, fewer resources are devoted to production of the things we need. Martin Feldstein, professor of economics at Harvard University and Chairman of the National Bureau of Economic Research, estimates that, in the long run, if it were not for Social Security, our capital stock would be 80% higher than it is today, and that our Gross National Product (GNP) would be almost 20% higher. What does this mean for the individual or the family? Well, in 1975, had it not been for the Social Security disincentive, the GNP would have been more than $285 billion higher! This amounted to nearly 30% of total consumer spending that year. The total loss amounted to $1,300 per person, or $3,500 per family. Feldstein estimates that from 1973 to 1978 Social Security cost the American public $1,367 billion, or about $6,200 per person and $16,800 per family! It left us collectively much poorer, even after allowing for the benefits received by the elderly.

Social Security weaknesses were explored at great length in *How to Prosper During the Coming Bad Years,* but if we are going to survive the Inflationary Eighties, we must see the liquidation problem in a new context, so a brief review and update would be helpful.

Just recently the chairman of the President's Commission on Pension Policy commented in a speech that the commission is "concerned" about "increasing dependency on...Social Security," and he added that the commission was also "extremely concerned" about population trends that could have a dramatic effect on Social Security: "We realize that the dependency ratios between active and retired workers will be critical to the future of the pay-as-you-go Social Security System—we must also come to grips with Social Security's long-range crisis. It threatens to imperil the system after the turn of the century."

Actually, if my inflation predictions are accurate, it will be a lot sooner than that. The commission suggests that it will be necessary to somehow cut back on the benefits before long, and that they would like to prepare the private sector to take up the slack. Specifically, the commission is concerned that only 42% of the work force is currently covered by a private pension plan, and their studies suggest that the proportion of the "work force that will be covered by a [private] pension plan in the future will not increase significantly under current policies." The likely outcome will be pressure for legislation for all employers to provide pension coverage.

Well, I suppose it's progress when someone in Washington recognizes and admits there's a problem, even if they are a decade or two late. It's a start. The private pension system, however, isn't in such great shape either, largely as a result of inflation. Before we get into the ailments of private pension plans, let's review briefly the factors that make Social Security an actuarial monstrosity.

When your employer deducts a Social Security tax from your paycheck and matches it with an "employer contribution," this money goes directly into the general fund of the government. Therefore, it is used to pay for all the wild and wonderful things government manages to spend money on. It's just one more means of raising government revenue. Your FICA payroll deductions pay for the FTC, EPA, DOE, and OSHA, as well as for Social Security benefits. The so-called trust fund amounts to little more than bookkeeping sleight of hand. Your FICA "contribution" is not saved for your golden years. It is paid this year to current retirees. Your kids will pay for yours. The real problem is the growing unwillingness of current and future taxpayers to shoulder this burden. At present, the combined employer and employee FICA deduction amounts to 12.26% of the first $25,900 of income or $1,588. Next year, the combined tax will go to 13.3% on the first $29,700. This amounts to almost $4,000 for a middle-income working couple. Social Security taxes today average 10% of payroll, but if the present trends continue, the Social Security Administration projects the tax could soar to 45% of payroll by 2050.

This increase in the tax burden is the result of not only the escalation of benefits (now that payments are indexed to the Consumer Price Index), but of the continuing decline in the ratio of workers to retirees. When the program began, there were thirty worker employed Americans supporting each retirement-age person. Right now there are about three. If the birth rate continues as at present, in forty years there will be only two workers to support each potential retiree. The result is an impending demographic disaster: a huge and growing group of elderly people dependent on fewer and fewer workers, with inflation-mandated benefits climbing higher and higher.

In addition to the burden on the individual employed taxpayers, Social Security also takes its toll on the economy as a whole.

This present Social Security System leaves us nothing but painful choices. If the system goes broke, we face the prospect of our parents starving if we can't personally care for them. On the other hand, if we raise taxes sufficiently to maintain the appearance of solvency, it will place a burden on

56

the economy that it simply cannot endure. The Social Security System is well on its way to bankrupting the economy because there is a third, more likely choice—the printing press, guaranteeing a ruinous inflation. Given the political clout of the elderly, that is probable, making the benefits worth less and less, even as they are increased.

Private Pension Plans

The future of the private pension plans on which many of you are relying isn't much brighter. The principal culprits are (1) inflation, (2) outdated regulations, (3) the refusal of the financial planning and pension management community to recognize the impact of inflation on their investment decisions, and (4) unfunded liabilities.

If you are already receiving a pension, the toll inflation is taking isn't any news to you. Even with an unrealistically low inflation rate of 6%, the value of your pension is cut almost in half in a decade. A 12% rate would reduce the pension's value by more than two-thirds in ten years, and, at the 20% inflation rate we experienced recently, by about 80% in just seven years!

When this silent theft by the inflation tax is combined with current life expectancy projections, the picture gets even darker. The typical sixty-five-year-old man can now expect to live to age eighty, and a sixty-five-year-old woman can expect to live to eighty-four. We are getting to be an older population. This, combined with the post–World War II baby boom and the drop in the birth rate, is producing that potential demographic disaster. Calculations by the Urban Institute project that the proportion of the Federal budget spent on the aged will explode from the present 26% to 63% in forty-five years. And who pays the bill?

Inflation has also been gnawing away at private pension capital. Because of the "prudent man rule," and probably a good measure of ignorance on the part of pension-fund managers, most fund assets have been invested in such traditional, conservative investments as mortgages, bonds, money market funds, securities, and common stocks. New York City employee pension funds are invested in New York City debt paper. They might as well have been shredded and scattered to the wind. While some of these things were conceivably good long-term investments when inflation was minimal, they are guaranteed instruments of purchasing power confiscation in inflationary times such as these.

It is easier to point out the damage done by the inflation tax than it is to find ways to live with it. One remedy that has been suggested to protect the purchasing power of pension benefits is to build cost-of-living escalators into benefit packages. That's really nifty! I have one small question: Where do we get the money? Indexing pension benefits to inflation actually increases pension costs about 10% for each percentage point of the long-run inflation rate. Obviously, this isn't a solution, as it would only hasten the collapse of the entire pension system.

Probably the most ominous aspect of the private pension problem is the huge amount of unfunded liabilities overhanging the system. "Unfunded liabilities" means that private businesses haven't set aside enough money to pay for the pensions that will legally have to be paid. These obligations currently amount to upwards of $30 billion! The total unfunded "prior service" costs of General Motors alone amount to about $12 billion. The unfunded pension liabilities of Lockheed, for example, amount to 117% of the firm's net worth. These obligations at LTV (Ling-Temco) amount to 87%. The principal reason Uncle Sam has bailed out Chrysler thus far is that he has already guaranteed Chrysler's pension fund, which is unfunded to the tune of $1.5 billion. If it goes broke, Uncle Sugar is on the hook.

What would happen if several large firms should go under? Chrysler isn't the only one in danger. The Pension Benefit Guarantee Corporation (PBGC) is supposed to assume any unfunded liabilities. Your Uncle Sam has agreed to bail out most pension funds if a company goes bust. Big deal! It would be a Band-Aid on a gaping wound. The failure of several pension funds—or even one large one—would bankrupt the PBGC. This agency, like the FDIC, or the pension system itself, only provides adequate protection in a stable and orderly economy. They are utterly inadequate for the Disintegrating Eighties.

Remember, the firms with all these unfunded liabilities will be facing the same "demographic disaster" that the Social Security System faces: a shrinking portion of the population working to support an expanding, longer-living group of retired workers. And those workers will be straining under the burden of higher Social Security taxes while inflation liquidates their purchasing power, rocketing them into higher and higher tax brackets. The strains of recession, rampant inflation, and escalating energy costs are likely to cause the failure of many companies. When the time comes for Uncle Sam to step in and pick up the wreckage of these firms, he will have no choice but to print money to fulfill these unfunded pension obligations. These unfunded obligations must either be paid off in inflationary funny money, or they will have to be written off altogether. Congress will assure that Good Old Uncle will pay off. He will print money. Anything else is politically unthinkable. The resulting inflation will raise demands for cost-of-living escalators, and here we go again.

If your retirement to that Adult Community in Sarasota is dependent on Social Security or a private pension plan, and is more than two or three years away, a better bet is to plan instead on a third-story walkup apartment a lot closer to wherever you now call home.

The thing that bugs me the most about the whole Social Security and pension problem, as legislated by Congress, is that Senators and Representatives have their own fully-funded, inflation-indexed pension plan, backed by the printing press. Those guys know something. They are smart enough not to get involved in Social Security. You Social Security recipients out there can't control your destiny like they can. You people with private pension funds can't index your pension payments to inflation. It is evil for Congress to legislate a program and then exempt itself from it. If Congressmen had to face the full consequences of an inadequate retirement in some small roomette on South Collins Avenue in Miami Beach and rock away their lives in genteel poverty, maybe they would be a little more careful about the kinds of laws they create and the kind of inflation they dump on our society.

The Death of the Corporation

The third arena of the Liquidation of America is the American public corporation.

A corporation is a legal entity owned by people called "stockholders," whose ownership is represented by "stock," or "shares." Public corporations collectively have millions of stockholders who hope to get their share of the corporate profits as "dividends."

When a corporation makes a profit, it pays corporate income taxes and dividends out of those earnings. If it doesn't have profits, but continues to pay dividends and taxes, the money must be paid out of capital. There is no other source. If it continues to pay out taxes and dividends without sufficient earnings, the company is liquidating its capital. Of course, no well-run business would do anything so stupid. Right? Wrong! Many of America's great corporations are in quiet liquidation, just like American savers and pension plan owners.

Standard corporate accounting methods are based on the assumption that dollar values are constant, and that when you compare 1982 earnings against 1975 earnings, you are comparing apples and apples. These accounting methods do not take into account the erosion of the dollar through inflation.

Consequently, a significant number of American corporations, perhaps the majority of them, after recalculating to allow for inflation, are not producing sufficient earnings to cover their taxes and dividends.

If you want an explanation for why the Dow Jones Industrial Average hasn't gone anywhere since 1966, you don't have to look any farther. We have all read in the paper how "the stock market is undervalued," how "all the money is standing on the sidelines" ready to move into the market, and that we are looking at the "beginning of the next great market boom." We have been waiting sixteen years! The stock market peaked in 1966 and has never equaled those highs. The market is smarter than all of us, and is probably priced about where it should be at any given time. It is perhaps a little high, if anything, because for years, corporations have been engaging in a form of corporate cannibalism.

All during those years, because of our non-inflation-adjusted depreciation tax laws, corporations have not been able to set aside sufficient reserves to truly cover the cost of replacing or modernizing obsolete or worn out plants and equipment, when those replacement costs are climbing at a rate of about 25% a year. In effect, they are setting aside nickels where quarters are needed.

For those of you who don't spend a lot of time wading through the intricacies of corporate balance sheets, let me explain what is meant by "depreciation."

A piece of capital equipment, such as a piece of machinery or a building, is assumed to have a certain life span before it is worn out or obsolete. Each year the company is allowed to subtract from its pre-tax earnings as a deductible expense a certain percentage of the original cost of that equipment until it is fully "depreciated," and assumed to be worthless. The loss of value is a legitimate, deductible cost of doing business. Theoretically, the depreciation deduction from earnings should allow the corporation to save enough money in taxes to set aside the necessary capital to replace that plant or equipment. That works out well enough in a noninflationary world.

However, when inflation drives up the costs of replacement, and the depreciation allowance is not sufficient to generate enough tax savings to pay for replacement, in reality the earnings of that corporation have been overstated, because truly adequate depreciation allowances would have reduced profits. Taxes are then computed on these overstated profits and the government takes its tax bite out of those nonexistent earnings. But that's only the beginning of our liquidation story.

Most corporate tax accounting is on the "accrual" basis. This means that the corporation doesn't just report cash transactions; the earnings will also reflect purely inflationary increases in the market value of the inventory on the shelves. Falling sales could actually have given you an operating loss that was draining your cash and you would still show taxable earnings, if the inventory has increased in price due to inflation, despite the fact that even when that inventory is sold, the company will simply have to replace it at even higher prices.

The ultimate extension of this concept to its illogical conclusion was demonstrated to me when I lectured in Brazil. One store owner told me that she often doesn't open her shop because the value of the inventory on her shelves, with the impetus of 70% inflation, is going up too fast. She would just pay taxes on the profits if she sold it. Why sell it? She has no inventory tax.

A significant percentage of American corporate earnings represent "inventory profits" which do not reflect any real economic activity, and the government also takes its tax bite out of these alleged "profits." In effect, this is an inventory tax, not an income tax. It is also a confiscatory tax on capital.

The combination of inadequate depreciation, plus inflated

inventory profits, means many American corporations are not producing sufficient "real" earnings to cover their taxes and the dividends they are paying out to stockholders. If the corporation has no real inflation-adjusted earnings, it is paying taxes and dividends out of capital and surplus and is in the process of liquidation to the government and to its stockholders.

The Federal Accounting Standards Board (FASB) has proposed a double entry form of reporting which would require disclosure of the effect of inflation on earnings, but no one is satisfied with the procedures yet. It is so complex that it might be of little value for the average guy to try to figure out what XYZ Widget Company is really doing, earnings-wise. And taxes would still be computed according to present "generally accepted" accounting methods, so the tax bite would remain the same. At least they are thinking in the right direction, but that doesn't change the facts. Corporate earnings are still generally overstated and, in many instances, the real earnings are not sufficient to cover taxes and dividends. Because corporate officers generally receive bonuses and other extra compensation on the basis of reported earnings, don't expect a stampede from the boardrooms of America to change those accounting rules.

The stock market reflects the sum total of everything that is known about business or the world around us, and stock prices have declined dramatically in purchasing power since 1966. As I said in Chapter 2, the Dow would have to go to over $3600 (in 1982 dollars, and they're not so hot) to get even with the 1966 Dow in purchasing power. This is why long-term investors ought to stay out of the stock market. It's now strictly for speculators, looking for special situations and rallies. The buy-and-hold, widows-and-orphans stock era ended in 1966. It's a different world, now. In the next few years, I expect the market to go essentially sideways, after adjusting for inflation, giving the buy-and-hold investor an after-tax return less than the rate of inflation.

Going Broke With Your Broker

I spent several years as a stock broker. One of the reasons I got out of the business was the difficult conflict of interest in which I found myself. I was stuck between my family's income needs and the customers' best interests.

Stock brokers are generally paid on commission, based on sales. They are not rewarded according to the quality of their advice or the profits made by the customer. This can create certain obvious abuses, such as the practice called "churning," where the broker artificially stimulates a lot of in-and-out trading to generate commissions. This is relatively rare in the industry because it is so obvious and easy to trace. But there is a much more subtle kind of abuse which, because of its seductive nature, is well nigh irresistible.

The market goes through bull and bear phases. There are times when every broker knows deep down in his gut that the market is in a general retreat which could last for months, and that his chance of beating the odds for his customers by finding a stock which will go contrary to the trend is, at best, dubious. And yet, if he does not buy and sell for his clients, there is no meat on the table. There is an immense temptation to persuade oneself that a bear market is going to turn around tomorrow, or that you have found the one hot stock that will buck the trend. This is not an overt decision made by a broker, and not all of them give into it, but this temptation rises naturally from the financial pressures of the situation.

It could be argued by brokers that they and their customers can make money by going short in bear markets, but that is speculation, pure and simple, having nothing to do with investment, and I don't think there is one investor out of a hundred who is emotionally equipped to trade from the short side.

If broker compensation were based on the percentage of increase of the portfolio of their clients, over and above the rate of inflation, I would be willing to bet there would be a lot of different investment decisions made, and far fewer brokers in the business.

This in no way implies that brokers are bad guys, any more dishonest or insincere than any other class of people. I think, however, that it goes against human nature to routinely expect someone to act contrary to his own financial interests to serve your best interests. This is just one more factor that makes it difficult to beat inflation by investing in stocks.

The Mopping-Up Operation

Just as corporate capital is being liquidated, so is much of the capital of the widows and orphans who bought AT&T, IBM, General Motors, and U.S. Steel for the long haul.

Even those stocks which seem to have shown price advances have often produced significant real capital losses to investors, while producing taxable profits. A common phenomenon among my clients is the person with a portfolio of common stocks he has held for years and a large paper profit. He has a net loss of purchasing power after adjusting for inflation, a desire to sell out and switch into sound inflation hedges, and a huge potential capital gains tax that freezes him into immobility. The net effect is confiscation of capital by government. Even if your stock went up enough that you broke even with inflation, after you have paid the capital gains tax when the stock is sold, the odds are you end up having lost the game. Then, of course, you shouldn't forget the income tax you paid on the dividends you received.

The Nationalization of Corporate America

Not only are American corporations being liquidated by taxes, but it can be rationally argued that American corporations have been three-fourths nationalized.

Suppose the United States government suddenly announced that all American corporations were to immediately hand over to Uncle Sam 77% of their outstanding stock. Of course, that would cause a revolution. In my opinion, the exact same thing has already happened through the taxing process, but poor Boobus Americanus ins't aware that it has happened. When Uncle Sam and his bureaucratic or elected officers complain about "obscene corporate profits," it's got to be all for show, because the principal beneficiary of American corporate profits is government.

In 1979 American corporations earned approximately $243 billion in profits. Let's see who got them. (Many thanks to Irwin Schiff and his marvelous book, *The Biggest Con: How the Government Is Fleecing You,* for this concept.)

Total Profits	$243 billion
Less retained earnings (essential for growth, operating capital, R & D, etc.)	92 billion
Total available for distribution to stockholders	151 billion
Less corporate income taxes	96 billion
Benefits paid to stockholders (dividends)	55 billion
Less personal income taxes paid by stockholders on dividends	22 billion
Total net benefit to stockholders	$ 33 billion

To rearrange these figures a bit, it seems that out of the $151 billion available for distribution to the stockholders, the IRS grabbed $118 billion in personal and corporate taxes, or 78%, and inflation has eroded the value of the pittance that's left over for the stockholders. Who then grabs most of the profits of American industry? Uncle Sam, to the tune of 78% of those profits! He is, in effect, the beneficial owner of 78% of the company. He didn't invest in the business, he didn't do the work, and up until now, he hasn't taken any of the risk.

The risk was the privilege of the "minority shareholders," who end up with only 22% of the total benefit.

"But," I hear you say, "look at all the people who benefit from the expenditure of those tax monies. That money isn't just lost."

No one in his right mind would argue that no one benefits from the expenditure of tax monies. In fact, Congress keeps spending money because of the political clout of those who do benefit. The serious issue is that the formless entity that we call "Uncle Sam," which can mean Congress, the White House, or unelected bureaucrats, will be the ones who decide how the money is spent, rather than the company that produced the money, or the stockholders who risked their capital. And generally speaking, those with whom Uncle Sam shares the booty will be the most unproductive segments of our society. Finally, Uncle Sam will have taken a 40% administrative "bite" as the money has made the round trip to Washington and back to those favored constituents on whom it chooses to bestow its benefits.

Who takes the losses if a corporation goes bankrupt? Up until now, not Uncle Sam, but the Chrysler, Lockheed, Penn Central, New York, and Bunker Hunt bailouts may be a recognition of the reality that Uncle Sam has a bigger interest in them than anyone else, due to the aforementioned pension liabilities. The nationalization and liquidation of American industry may be coming out of the closet, revealing for all to see the dangers of the Disintegrating Eighties.

The irony is compounded when you realize that government has tied down corporations with a horrible multiplying web of hundreds of thousands of regulations, which restrict their activities and drain their operating capital and resources and consume management time, and they have to pay for their own chains through taxation. Not only is government venal, avaricious, and greedy, but it's also stupid. If you could find somebody who was willing to put up all the money and give you 78% of the profits, while doing all the work for you and assuming all the risk, wouldn't you treat him a little better? A good draft animal is entitled to at least an occasional pat. But Uncle Sam spews forth his anti-business rhetoric, which has turned high school students so much against corporations that, according to one recent study, those high school students hold the following opinions:

1. 67% see no need for profits.
2. 62% think the government should provide jobs.
3. 40% could not name one advantage of capitalism over communism.
4. 61% felt a worker should not produce all he can.
5. 50% felt the government contributes most to national prosperity.
6. 66% think the best way to improve our standard of living is not by workers producing more, but by giving workers more wages.

And to top it all off, in another similar survey, American high school and college students concluded that the average profitability of American industry was close to 50% of sales, as opposed to the real figure of 4%. Against that background, no wonder the public cheers when government confiscates the wealth of big business or the rich, or slaps a "windfall profits tax" on big oil, despite the fact that it is really a tax on consumers, the corporation being only the tax collector.

Capital Theft

Looking at the liquidation of America from another angle, I submit that the real capital gains tax in this country is not just 25% as most people think, but is often well in excess of 200%. The average person who thinks he has a capital gain profit has often made nothing whatsoever. His Potomac partner ripped off the whole thing.

In order to understand this concept, you must remember that inflation is also a tax.

Let's say you bought some land two years ago for $100,000 and you sold it today for $130,000. The capital gains tax on the $30,000 "profit" would be approximately $7,500, depending on your tax bracket, theoretically, leaving you with $22,500 in after-tax profits.

However, the true profit on that transaction was not $30,000. Look again. Two years of land price inflation around 15%, about the same rate of increase as all costs throughout society, accounted for the whole $30,000 profit. If the whole nominal gain was general inflation, then you had no true profit. Your capital gains tax of $7,500 means that the tax rate on your nonexistent gain was not 25%, but was infinite. It was a confiscatory liquidation of your capital.

A Moral Issue

The Liquidation of America offends me from several points of view. First, I consider it a clear-cut moral issue. It is the unobserved, surreptitious theft of my purchasing power and, as not one American in 10,000 is aware of the process, it is dishonest and sneaky.

I also violently object that I cannot effectively pass on to my children the sound principles of thrift and savings that I was taught as a child as part of my Mormon heritage. I know that if I teach them what I was taught and they save their money in the bank, they will be liquidated by the great inflation of the 1980s. I find this immensely offensive and, in fact, when I think about it my bile boils. I have to teach my children to be speculators, to find some way to keep their capital growing, to be borrowers for investment, rather than prudent savers, and this runs so counter to what I believe should be sound principles in a sane world that it is like living in a universe gone crazy, playing a game while trying to understand the rules which bear no relationship to normal reality, while someone changes them without telling me. In that direction lies madness.

It also means that in its efforts to save itself and the system, the government will do some things that you won't like, if you have been one of these traditional savers. In a full-scale disintermediation panic, the government will not hesitate to freeze your money. It will not hesitate to shut the bank doors and ration your money back to you at the rate it wants, not the rate you want. In effect, the government will act like the body does when it is in danger of freezing. It will extract the blood from the extremities, and government considers itself and the banking system the vital organs, and it will act in a self-preserving way to try to save the fabric of society. In fact, it will do anything it can to save the currency, except stop the inflation process. There is nothing a politician hates more than rising prices—except falling prices when they affect the income of his constituents.

Just remember, when you sit down to do your income taxes you are paying capital gains taxes on investments where there was no real profit, and your capital is being liquidated.

You will be paying income tax on dividends and interest that represent no real profits, and your capital is being liquidated.

The purchasing power of your principal in the bank, the credit union, or the savings and loan is being siphoned off by a myriad of taxes, including the most pernicious—the inflation tax, and you are being liquidated.

And when you get all upset about the "obscene profits" of American corporations, I suggest that you weep for them, and by extension, for yourself, because many of those companies that you resent for their alleged "profit-gouging" are not making sufficient money to maintain their life. They are being mugged. They are slowly being bled to death by inflation and taxes. Whenever you see the government "shifting the tax burden" from "consumers" to "big business," you should view this crooked farce for what it truly is: a dishonest, concealed way for government to extract capital from the consumer, while making corporations their tax collector, which assures they will get blamed and the real criminals go scot-free.

CHAPTER 4

When You Have a Hammer
in Your Hand,
Everything Looks Like a Nail

The Legend of the Watchbird—1999 A.D.

Man has finally achieved perfect freedom from violence. He has invented the watchbird—a system of intelligent, flying robots that blanket the Earth, programmed to detect violence before it occurs, and strike down the violent one before he can do harm. And they can transmit their experiences to each other, learn, and make increasingly sophisticated judgments.

Their first action prevents a robbery and shooting in a grocery store. Their second prevents a killing by a hired assassin, to the cheers of a grateful world. The third, however, strikes down a prison executioner and prevents the death of a murderer. Then the watchbird network decides animals should not be killed, and destroys a slaughterhouse worker to save a hog. Soon the victims include a surgeon about to make an incision, an old man about to swat a fly, a fisherman reeling in his catch, a farmer reaping his wheat (plants are living things). Within weeks, the world is starving because the watchbird will not allow food to be harvested, as the ever-industrious watchbird expands its definition of violence and performs its new self-appointed tasks.

When man recognizes what he has made, he tries to deactivate his creation. The watchbird concludes, however, that he himself is also a living thing, and he strikes down his creators. So a stronger and more violent robot, the hawk, must be created to destroy the watchbird. But, in their haste to eliminate the watchbird, scientists have programmed the hawk to kill indiscriminately also, and it, too, can only be destroyed by a more powerful machine. . . .*

Alexis de Tocqueville, the great French observer of American life, who traveled and wrote in America in the 1800s, had awesome insight into the character, personality, and future of America. He could have written today rather than in the last century. Perhaps none of his observations of our future is more pertinent than his vision of our overregulated present and our omnipresent government, which

> . . . everyday renders the exercise of the free agency of man less useful and less frequent; it circumscribes the will within a narrower range and gradually robs a man of all the uses of himself. The principle of equality has prepared man for these things; it has predisposed men to endure them and often to look on them as benefits.
>
> After having thus successfully taken each member of the community in its powerful grasp and fashioned him at will, the supreme power then extends its arm over the whole community. It covers the surface of society with a network of small complicated rules, minute and uniform, through which the most original mind and the most energetic characters cannot penetrate, to rise above the crowd. The

---

*Adapted from "Watchbird," a short story by Robert Sheckley, copyright © 1953 by Galaxy Publishing Corporation.

will of man is not shattered, but softened, bent, and guided; men are seldom forced by it to act, but they are constantly restrained from acting. Such a power does not destroy, but it prevents existence; it does not tyrannize, but it compresses, enervates, extinguishes, and stupifies a people, until each nation is reduced to nothing better than a flock of timid and industrious animals of which the government is the shepherd.

Horror Stories

This is not essentially a book about the evils of government. It's a book about money and how to survive the Inflationary Eighties. I'm diving into the subject of galloping government power only to make the economic point that our structure of freedom has given us unprecedented wealth and opportunity, and that if the American free enterprise system and the incredible climate of freedom on which this nation was based is compromised by unconstitutional regulatory chains, none of my financial advice will do you any good. Your profits will bring you no pleasure.

The cancerous growth of the power of governmental regulatory agencies, often freed from Constitutional restrictions, is the most direct assault on freedom. The following points may blow your mind:

1. For every law passed by elected bodies in the United States, there are now eleven regulations passed by unelected bureaucrats, which are binding upon you and have the force of law, often with criminal penalties, including jail and fines.

2. If regulatory agencies bring a legal action and are defeated in the courts, they often repeat the process in another jurisdiction until you are bankrupt. Most defendants knuckle under to avoid a hassle or avoid bankruptcy. We'll knuckle under to the IRS if the money involved is smaller than the legal fees it would take to fight it. Government often wins by default, simply because it can throw its battalions of attorneys

at you. Constitutional guarantees don't apply. The Supreme Court has ruled 8-0 that you are not entitled to jury trials in "administrative proceedings."

Let's say the FDA claims that your health-food store is in violation of the labeling laws, because on one shelf you sell a book advocating vitamin C for the common cold, while there are vitamins for sale on the other side of the store. This constitutes "misbranding" of the product by "claiming a cure" for it, which, by their rules, makes a drug. They can then arrest you and your clerk and confiscate the vitamins and burn the books, under current regulations. This has actually happened. It even happened once when the vitamins were on the third floor of a department store, and the bookstore was in the basement. And you may be bankrupted by the cost of the legal battle, even if you should win, because you can't sue for damages. Most Mom-and-Pop health-food store owners don't have the resources to fight, so freedom of speech and freedom of the press are trampled on.

If the IRS comes after you, as they did Harry Margolis, you lose, even if you win. Harry Margolis is a San Francisco tax attorney who utilized what he felt were legitimate loopholes in the IRS code. He set up offshore tax havens in the Cayman Islands for his clients. The IRS knew he would win in the courts, which he did, but the IRS brought charges against him simply as a lesson to any enterprising attorney or accountant who gives his clients the benefit of the doubt in the gray areas in the IRS code. The IRS knew they would win, even in defeat. Harry Margolis has been dealt a severe financial blow, and I'm sure the lesson is not lost, as every tax consultant in America was watching.

Just to get your blood boiling, I'd like to give you some personal horror stories which I believe are typical of the bureaucratic mentality—not just nit-picking isolated instances. Just because I name some agencies and not others does not mean the other agencies are okay. I just haven't tangled with the others. This bureaucratic expansion-of-power mentality is as natural as breathing to all regulatory bodies, from the Federal government right down to the smallest town zoning commission. Obviously, the bigger the entity, and the farther it is removed from Main Street, the more impersonal and dangerous it is to personal freedom. These true horror stories can set the scene for what will follow.

WATCHBIRD ENCOUNTER #1. Back in 1974, before I founded my newsletter, I was a distributor of Neo-Life nutritional products. One day I got a call from Neo-Life informing me that my check to them in payment for merchandise had bounced. I immediately called my bank to find out what had happened, as there was more than enough money to cover my check. I was informed that the Internal Revenue Service had levied $12,000 from my account to pay for an alleged tax deficiency. The bank gave me the name of the IRS agent and I gave him a call. I asked him why? He said, "You owe us taxes for two years ago." I said, "How much?" He said, "We don't know exactly how much. We're still determining that." I then said, "How did you know how much to levy from my account?" His answer: "We just made sure we took enough." "Why didn't you give me a call? This could have been settled without taking money out of my account. I have checks bouncing all over America." "Because if you had had prior notification, you might have taken your money out of the bank and we could not secure our interest."

I finally got together with the agent, and it was determined that due to a miscalculation in my return, I owed $35. It took two weeks to get the lien lifted so that I had access to my funds. In the meantime, my credit with my suppliers, my bank, and the department stores where we had sent checks for payments on account was in tatters. My nervous suppliers put me on a cash basis, which meant driving forty miles with certified checks every time I wanted to buy products for sale to my customers.

The IRS didn't give a damn how much inconvenience it caused me. Their internally generated regulations permitted them to act as they did, and that is precisely how they acted.

WATCHBIRD ENCOUNTER #2. In 1972, I began a chain of weight reduction centers. I had developed an approach to weight loss, combining diet along with food supplements, exercise, and behavior modification, that was helping people to lose weight in a rather unique way. I had reduced my weight from 240 pounds down to 175 pounds using these techniques, and I wanted to share them. We were advertising for people to come to public meetings which described the method and system, and we gave everyone a moneyback guarantee. If the program didn't work for them, they could get a refund of all monies paid. I was operating out of a headquarters in my home. We only had three franchised centers and it was really a very young "Mickey Mouse" back-pocket operation. But it was run conscientiously and honestly, and hundreds of people had lost tons of weight.

One day an employee of the Federal Trade Commission knocked on my door and announced, "We have been doing a routine surveillance of advertising and we've come across your ads, and we want to investigate them to see whether or not you have violated Federal law." "Has anyone complained?" "No. This is just routine."

Believing my skirts to be clean, I stupidly gave him carte blanche to examine what we were doing, look at our records, talk to our clients, examine our sales materials, attend our meetings, etc. At the time it was only a minor nuisance. After all, what do we have to fear from our Uncle Sam if our hearts are pure?

I soon found out. Two weeks later, he came back to my office and announced that I was dealing fraudulently with my customers and that I had to do "corrective advertising" telling the world about my "fraud," make significant changes and additions to my present ads, and sign a "consent decree."

I was stunned. There had been no complaints of any kind to the Federal Trade Commission, the Better Business Bureau, or anybody else. We had conducted our business honorably

78

and had bent over backwards to make sure that anyone who was not satisfied received a refund, even if they had not technically met the requirements. Before anyone could begin the program, they had to read and sign a statement describing what the program could and could not do for them, and we even had them listen to a twenty-minute tape and acknowledge in writing that they had heard and understood. Then, if they did not receive the promised result in weight loss, we would usually give them their money back, even if we had reason to believe they had been cheating on the diet. What more could you ask of an honest businessman?

Well, it seems that according to this man, the advertising was fraudulent if it didn't announce to everyone that there were qualifications to the guarantee and didn't print the entire guarantee in full in the ad. It was rather lengthy, and it would have increased my advertising space and cost by approximately 40%. It seems, also, that I would be required to announce that everyone who came into the program would have to buy a certain line of supplements. It seemed that the ad would have to carry a very large disclaimer that I was not an M.D., and that the diet had "significant health dangers for the average person," despite the fact that we had never had a health problem with anyone who had come through our clinic under our supervision, and despite the fact that I had good medical consulting help, and required a physical and a medical release from the private physician of the client.

When I asked him what a "consent decree" was, the answer boiled down to a document that I would sign, which would say, in effect, "I haven't done anything wrong and I promise not to do it anymore." This would then be published, along with all the government allegations, in such a way that anyone who might have an axe to grind would come out of the woodwork to harass me. Then after my reputation had been thoroughly damaged, the SEC could, at their discretion, renege on their agreement to no longer pursue the case. But I was assured by this bright young man that "obviously the

FTC would never do anything like that," and I wish you could hear the sarcasm in my voice as I dictate that line.

I was given a week to give him an answer, and I did a lot of thinking during that time. At the end of the week, I got on the phone and called my friend from the government and informed him that I was not going to sign his consent decree. I hadn't done anything wrong, and I was not going to allow the world to think that I believed I had. I informed him that all he was interested in was a scalp to hang from his belt, and I was not going to provide it. I then said to him, "I have no reason to feel guilty. No one has complained of any wrongdoing on my part. No one has been hurt by my program. I am an honorable businessman. I will not sign your consent decree, but I have decided that I'm going to eliminate my money-back guarantee because it has too high a probability of causing me hassles from the likes of you. Therefore, no one can ever get their money back if the program doesn't work for them. You, sir, have just won another victory for the consumer." And with that, I hung up.

In a matter of seconds the phone rang again, and the same guy informed me, "We can send waves of attorneys against you. We know your financial situation and you cannot afford a protracted legal fight. I suggest that you reconsider your decision." I chewed that over for a minute and informed him, "If you think that scares me, you're crazy. I lost everything I had once, and I not only found it wasn't the end of the world, but it was a time of great character growth for myself and my family. I have access to the media. I do radio and television talk shows, and I will fight you from every platform I can find. I will expose you to any audience that will listen. I want the world to know what kind of a tyrant Uncle Sam and his minions can be. If you think that going broke frightens me, it doesn't. Being broke isn't the end of the world. I was smart enough to come back from that once, and I can do it again. My conscience is clear. Bug off!"

That night I slept like a baby.

All was quiet for about six months w...
a letter from the Commissioner of the Federa...

I've lost the letter, so I can't quote it exa...
tell you what the essence was.

"Mr. Ruff, we have examined your case...
mined to take no action at this time. That doe... ...at
you have been exonerated from the charges aga... ...ou, and
we will be watching very closely to see whether or not there
are other violations of Federal law. Sincerely . . ."

Sincerely, indeed! These guys didn't have a leg to stand on
and they knew it. It was only after a week or so had passed
that I realized what a strain I had been under, and my
imagination began to run wild as I thought how many small
businessmen with limited resources who have not had the
testing in life that I have, have quietly caved in to a dictatorial
government exceeding its statutory authority, just to avoid the
hassle and the cost.

WATCHBIRD ENCOUNTER #3. Shortly after the
founding of my newsletter, *The Ruff Times*, we got a call
from the Securities and Exchange Commission about registering
my newsletter under the Investment Advisor's Act of 1948. It
seems that when this law was originally passed, it was
intended to regulate those who manage people's money so
that no abuses could occur, such as investment advisors
taking a position in a security or an investment and then
touting it, causing their clients to jump in and buy, thus
running up the market and giving quick profits to the advisors.

This had been expanded by creeping arbitrary regulation in
recent years to cover all investment advisors, including those
who don't manage anyone's money, and the newsletter industry had capitulated.

After consultation with my attorneys and a thorough exam-
ination of the law, we concluded that we could avoid registering
and function reasonably well if we simply did not discuss
specific securities in detail, nor recommend them, and, of
course, we had no intention of personally managing anyone's

s. *The Ruff Times* was structured in such a way as to leave us outside their regulation.

As I'm sure you have guessed by now, if you've read anything I've ever written, I have an almost anarchistic loathing of government, a healthy attitude shared by Thomas Jefferson and a lot of great Americans who truly perceived that government is a singularly dangerous beast, a necessary evil that had to be bound, and the Constitution was the chain that they used to bind it.

I paid a brief visit to the local SEC offices in San Francisco. It was concluded that we were in a gray area and they preferred that I make some minor changes in my newsletter to stay outside their area of regulation. We left with an uneasy truce, and that's the way it stands as this is written.

The Constitution guarantees freedom of the press, freedom of speech, and freedom of expression. Right? Apparently not. Let me tell you what you cannot do if you are a Registered Investment Advisor.

1. You cannot spend your money as you see fit. You are required to escrow 100% of the subscription funds as received, and only release them to yourself proportionately with each issue of your newsletter—in my case, one twenty-fourth of the money at a time. This ignores the fact that I spend as much money in marketing and direct-mail costs obtaining a new subscriber as he pays me in the first year, all before I even get the subscriber. My capital requirements would increase by the total amount of one year's new subscription income—in my case, many millions of dollars. We could not grow. The sheer complexity of the computer program to account for hundreds of new subscriptions and renewals each week is mind-boggling. The regulation is impossible. Most old-timer newsletters are exempt from this requirement under grandfather clauses.

2. I could not make personal investments without first notifying my subscribers I was going to do so. This totally inhibits my personal ability to act quickly in fast-moving markets.

3. I would have to disclose the most minor details of my financial condition and those of members of my family, and executives of my company, even including our warehouse supervisor, in a way that would rape our personal privacy.

4. Because "generally accepted accounting methods" provide for the setting aside of reserves on paper for fulfillment of future issues of the subscription when money is received, it gives you an artificial paper loss, which is reported for tax and accounting purposes—an excellent tax shelter. Without lengthy explanations or relatively sophisticated understanding on the part of the reader, it would look like a newsletter operator is going broke when he is not. The SEC regulation requires that if you are in a "net deficit position," you must disclose this information to your subscribers. It would take almost a whole newsletter issue to explain why, despite the fact that I look like a loser, their favorite financial advisor is not going broke. That's not the world's greatest P.R. A lot of older newsletters are functioning under grandfather clauses in this area too, where the requirements are not as onerous, but no such amnesty has been offered me, in the event that I register.

5. I would not be allowed to use testimonials. To sell my newsletter, I have used testimonials from George Bush, William Simon, Howard Jarvis, Senator Orrin Hatch, etc. If I register, that's no longer permitted. The same standards of advertising that apply to the announcement of a new stock issue are assumed to be appropriate and adequate for a publication which is trying to sell its services.

6. I would be required to pass the appropriate examinations

and register as a securities advisor (easy enough for me), even though I had no intention of giving specific recommendations in stocks, and so would my partner who was President of the company (I am Chairman of the Board) and all of our department heads, including even our warehouse manager (not so easy for them). After doing that, we would all have to pass similar tests to register in the twenty-nine states which require such registration, which would necessitate an incredible amount of travel and an awful lot of testing, despite the fact that most of the preparation for that testing would be totally inappropriate for what I was attempting to do with *The Ruff Times*, and useless to most of our staff.

I had two choices. One was to knuckle down and register, accept the restrictions and raise the capital, and be free to write about individual securities, or I could refuse to register, and avoid their regulatory authority by not referring to specific securities, which would in effect be an inhibition of my freedom of speech. I chose the latter course as having the least loss of freedom, and the only practical one for us. Fortunately there were enough things to talk about in real estate, gold and silver, etc., to be able to help people beat inflation without having to talk about stocks and bonds, but my rights have been trampled on.

The chilling effect on what I can write or not write, and the extra expense involved in having our attorneys examine every issue to see whether or not I might inadvertently wander into the SEC regulatory grasp, is as flagrant a violation of the freedom of speech First Amendment guarantees of the Constitution as could possibly be conceived. What about those financial requirements? The SEC's argument is that if a newsletter writer goes broke, subscribers might not get a proportionate refund of their issues unless the money is escrowed. Why is that not important for *Field and Stream, The Wall Street Journal, Forbes* magazine (which has columnists who give specific advice), and *Jack and Jill,* for that matter? The financial requirement has nothing to do with securities regulation. It is simply an unconstitutional extension of statutory authority, as the Constitution guarantees that there will be "no laws abridging the freedom of the press." If a newsletter published every week is not the press, I don't know what is. The regulations make an interesting weasel-worded distinction between such publications as *Forbes,* which take advertising and sell on the newsstand (the press), and publications like mine (not the press?).

The net effect? I have not registered and do not intend to. I intend to stay outside their regulatory grasp, that being the lesser of the two evils. I will also work for legislation reaffirming our Constitutional rights and exempting publications such as mine from any regulation, as long·as they are not managing people's funds.

I'll fight 'em on the beaches. I'll fight 'em in the forests. I'll fight 'em in the streets. But I will not yield to this kind of tyranny.

WATCHBIRD ENCOUNTER #4. In January, 1979, I received a fascinating letter from Mr. Robert H. Hartline, Supervisory Agent of the Eleventh District of the Federal Home Loan Bank Board, as follows:

Dear Mr. Ruff:

We understand that during a December 24, 1978 telecast of the program, *Ruff Hou$e,* you made a statement to the effect that people should not put their savings into Savings and Loan Associations.

We request that you provide us with a copy of the text of that statement and any explanation of the reason for such a statement, so that we may determine the propriety of the statement and whether it complies with applicable laws.

Your early response will be appreciated.

Sincerely,

I found it frightening that a government agency would consider it had the right to "determine the propriety" of something I said.

In the show under question, I read a letter from a viewer wanting to know whether he should put his money in a Federally insured bank or savings and loan. My answer was:

No. I wouldn't put it in a bank or savings and loan right now. Your rate of return on those investments will be less than the rate of inflation. That, plus the fact that the "profit" is taxed, makes you a loser. Second, we're moving into a recession, and possibly into a depression, and our banking system and our savings and loan system are moving into this in considerably weaker condition than when we went into the recession in 1974–75. I happen to believe that we will see headlines in the not too distant future telling us that there are some very serious things wrong with our banking system, as we did in 1975. If you want to sleep well, no, I would not put money there.

We're going to see some headlines that will shake our confidence. The Federal Deposit Insurance Corporation only has enough money to insure about 1.3 percent of all bank deposits. That is also true of the Federal Savings and Loan Insurance Corporation. I don't think that is adequate to deal with serious runs on the banks, which I think are possible in the next year or two. So in the interest of sleeping well, I'd rather be out of the banking system.

A little research by my attorney produced the fact that Mr. Hartline's objection was based on a law passed February 3, 1938, which says:

Whoever willfully and knowingly makes, circulates, or transmits to another or others any statement or rumor, written, printed or by word of mouth, which is untrue in fact or is directly, or by inference, derogatory to the financial condition, or affects the solvency or financial standing of the Federal Savings and Loan Insurance Corporation, shall be fined not more than $1,000, or imprisoned not more than one year, or both.

This amazing law allows an official policy of concealment of the true condition of a bank or the banking system, and allows people to blithely make commercial deposits, buy bank stocks, and purchase CDs in troubled or even insolvent banks, while the government works secretly behind the scenes to bail them out. That's fine as long as the whole system is basically stable, and only an occasional mismanaged bank gets in trouble. In that case you go to your bank one day and see that it has another name over the door, having been secretly acquired by another bank. But if the whole system should come under great strain, then the FDIC and the FSLIC could have a monstrous liability, as they would have been partners to a conspiracy to conceal material acts important to prospective investors and depositors. This law would prevent anyone from warning depositors and investors. As I indicated in *How to Prosper During the Coming Bad Years*, it is the government's policy to pay all claims on all deposits, even over-and-above the insured amounts, to avoid lawsuits over losses resulting from your naive investment in stock or CDs issued by an insolvent bank whose condition was concealed by the FDIC.

The issue raised by Mr. Hartline's letter is the government's power to intimidate my free speech. There are two basic principles in conflict. One is my First Amendment right and need to warn people of financial dangers for their own individual decision making. The other is the government's desire to have privacy while it maneuvers behind the scenes. This assumes that statements such as mine could cause a banking panic, which, if true, puts me in an interesting dilemma. Do I speak the truth in time to allow some people to get their money out of the system? Or do I swallow my tongue, hoping somehow the system will survive and everyone will be all right? You may not agree with my choice, but I hope you agree I have a genuine moral dilemma.

Free speech might have its hazards and, in some cases, might prove embarrassing in the short run, but in the long haul, free speech is indispensable to our system. This fundamental human right was intended to prevail over momentary governmental expediency. Without it, the system is vulnerable to bureaucratic tyranny. And that's precisely what I walked into.

If the banking system is sound, my statements won't hurt it. If it is so precarious it fears statements from an obscure newsletter writer and fringe-time talk-show host, then it is in sorry shape indeed, and the sooner we found out, the better. In that case, collapse would be inevitable anyway.

As a practical matter, the government is not going to let the banking system "fail" anyway, in the classic meaning of the word. If we have runs on the banks due to a collapsing dollar, a liquidity squeeze with lots of bankruptcies, the Arabs withdrawing their short-term deposits, etc., the government will be loading up C-141s with mountains of paper money and flying off to cover the banks until the run has run out of steam. This explosion of paper money could convert us quickly from a credit economy into a printing press economy, but that's another subject.

At my next opportunity, when we were taping a *Ruff Hou$e* show, I went on the air and told my audience what had happened. I read the transcript of the previous show and I read Mr. Hartline's letter. I then looked sincerely into the camera and said, "Mr. Hartline, I'm not going to send you a transcript of that show. If you want it you'll have to subpoena it. However [dramatic pause], if anyone else would like a transcript of that show, simply write to me . . ."

I never heard anything from Mr. Hartline again. He had no right to determine "the propriety" of my statements. If he chose to bring charges against me, I was ready to fight, raising the Constitutional issue of freedom of the press.

The last I heard about the incident was some months later when one of my associates attended a party in Washington at which the head of the Federal Home Loan Bank Board was present. When my friend asked, "Have you ever heard of Howard Ruff?" his answer was, "I don't want to ever hear that name again." It seems Mr. Hartline had been bombarded with letters from my viewers, and virtue had triumphed.

Most people who are challenged by a government agency aren't so lucky as to be able to rally public opinion and embarrass someone on the tube. I obviously have weapons at my disposal that most people don't have. I still find the incident chilling.

The above four incidents have led me to ask this question of most audiences I address: "How many of you in this audience love your country, but fear and distrust your government?" Almost every hand goes up. The people I speak to are middle-class America—the backbone of this country. These are the people who marched off to war in Europe, Okinawa, Korea, and Viet Nam. These are the people who pay the taxes, support candidates, save their money, love their families, give to all the diseases, and personify all the values that have built this country. And yet, they fear and distrust their government. That is an incredible evolution of attitude from my days as a child when we all saluted the flag before the first class of the day, had a brief prayer, and venerated our President as our leader. The disintegration in the attitude of Americans toward their government is unparalleled in our times, and, in fact, corresponds to the growth of illegal government power in our lives.

Thomas Jefferson said, "I have sworn . . . eternal hostility against every form of tyranny over the mind of man." And if that tyranny comes from our own government, we owe it to the Republic to expose it and root it out. As long as government remains our servant, it is a tolerable and necessary evil. When it tries to become our master, we must fight back.

In a Democratic Republic such as ours, government is supposed to be an extension of the will of the people, but now it has taken on a life of its own. Whenever elected government, as personified by your city council, your state legislature, or the Senate, is still responsive to the will of the people as it perceives it, it has adopted the "Robin Hood Syndrome." The majority of people in this country have perceived themselves as Paul, benefiting from having robbed Peter, and they think Peter is endlessly rich.

Violating the "Separation of Powers" Doctrine

If you were to isolate the biggest single threat to our system posed by regulatory government, it is that it violates the Constitutional principle of separation of Executive, Legislative, and Judicial powers, in that it can conceive a regulation, and sneak it through the Federal Register (Legislative), charge you with a violation (Executive), then act as judge, jury, and executioner (Judicial). The accused have little or no recourse, as the courts have generally upheld the regulatory power of agencies launched by Congress.

When all is said and done, regulatory government is the arch-enemy of free enterprise, and free enterprise is the goose that has been laying golden eggs. When you abuse the goose that lays the golden eggs, she stops laying. When she dies, you can only feast on goose for a little while. Then you have neither eggs nor goose. Not only is free enterprise at stake, free anything is at stake.

The usual argument for regulatory government is that it is protecting us for our own good. I'm convinced the good which it accomplishes is outweighed several times over by the costs incurred and the evils which it does. Some great philosopher once said, "If I knew that a man was coming to my house with the express purpose of doing me good, I would lock all my doors and arm myself against him."

The following piece of whimsy, constructed in a weak moment, might illustrate a point:

NORTH PLATTE, NEBRASKA (API) JULY 26, 1858. The Federal Trade Commission and Department of Transportation, together with the Department of Commerce, have just recalled all stagecoaches of the Wells Fargo Company and the Bison model of the soft-top vehicles manufactured by the Conestoga Wagon Company of Independence, Missouri.

The noted consumer advocate, Jim Bridger, pointed out that motion pictures taken of an Oregon-bound wagon train being chased by Indians, showed that at high speeds, the wheels tend to turn backwards, creating a safety hazard.

It is anticipated that westward migration will be delayed up to two years, and some families will be forced to bivouac along the Oregon Trail.

Washington has assured the grateful travelers that food relief shipments, food stamps, and Federal troops will be provided. They were also assured that they would be on their way within two years.

Here are the twentieth century's three greatest lies in ascending order of immensity: (1) My wife doesn't understand me, (2) my check is in the mail, and (3) I'm from the government and I'm here to help you!

Why have we allowed government to gain such power over us? We are seeing the fulfillment of the prophecy quoted in the introduction of this book in which Professor Alexander Tytler pointed out that the later stages of the decline of a democracy are apathy and dependence.

We can blame most of it on an unholy, three-cornered

alliance. First, there is the public, who demands protection from the vicissitudes of life. That's you. Then there are our Congressmen and Senators who want to have their names on a piece of important legislation, and the real plum is to sponsor a new agency. That is the best way to become immortal, because your creation will never die. Last, there are the government bureaucracies whose very existence, livelihood, and future hopes are dependent upon the creation, extension, and perpetuation of more programs.

Perhaps the best example of this is the Department of Education, created by President Carter. It is instructive to note that at the Democratic National Convention where Mr. Carter was nominated for a second term, 60% of the delegates were on some public payroll, and 40% of them came from the various teachers' unions, and they voted virtually unanimously for Jimmy Carter. Their prize was a new cabinet level agency, the Department of Education, dedicated to the building of an educational empire—a perfect example of the Unholy Alliance at work.

Here is the evolution of a new agency:

1. An evil is perceived. The wheels turn backwards on movie stagecoaches. It is decided the evil can be corrected with broad, sweeping new legislation. Then an agency is set up to oversee the correct application of the "remedy." The coaches are recalled.

2. The agency is given a broad mandate, with power to issue regulations with the force of law and with appropriate penalties to fill in the details that Congress couldn't be bothered with. This is an assumption of legislative powers.

3. The agency is given power to ferret out violations of its regulations, bring charges and prosecute the violators (the executive function), then sit as judge and jury, determining guilt or innocence (the judicial function). It

then pronounces appropriate sentence. Strangely enough, the agency rarely loses a case!

4. Agency personnel are immune to personal liability, and you receive no damages, legal fees, or expenses, even if you win. And the pioneers sit by the Platte River for two years.

This merging of the Executive, Legislative, and Judicial functions is the guts of what the Founding Fathers were trying to prevent when they drew up the Constitution, as it was the essence of King George's tyranny. For all practical purposes, checks and balances are dead in regulatory government.

This year Congress will introduce about 25,000 pieces of proposed legislation. This results in approximately 200 pages of the Congressional Record daily, at about $286 per page. Out of these 25,000, perhaps 400 will eventually be enacted into law. In short, with 535 people on both sides of Capitol Hill working full-time, less than one bill per Congressional office gets signed into law. (Thank goodness it wasn't two bills per office!) And very little of the voluminous Congressional Record involves actual laws that affect your life.

However, every day another book equally as large as the Congressional Record arrives at each Congressman's and Senator's office—The Federal Register. Unlike the Congressional Record, the Register means business. Nearly all of the fine print will become law, and it is all fine print—regulations proposed by government agencies, and a few Presidential Executive Orders. Every day of the work week, fifty-two weeks a year, the Register is published—about 60,000 pages a year. Very few of these laws are challenged by Congress. Most of them are immediately applied. Congress only gets 1.6% of its proposed legislation into law. Almost *all* of the regulations issued in the Register become law, complete with civil and/or criminal penalties. We now have a body of laws and regulations that has reached the point where increasingly often it cannot be understood or obeyed. It is too complex. It is too huge. It is possible for you, if you are a small businessman or professional man, to inadvertently violate the law twenty times a day and never know it. But you could be held liable for fines or imprisonment, or be required to publish corrective advertising confessing your "sins" before the world, or be subject to any number of penalties for laws innocently violated.

We found out during Prohibition that when laws are not respected, law and order breaks down. Our nation is built on a basic voluntary respect for its institutions and for reasonable laws, based on our conviction that these laws have been enacted by our elected representatives who are responsible to us. That is less and less true every day. As Honoré de Balzac said, "Bureaucracy is a giant mechanism operated by pygmies."

Why has the growth of government power defied the best efforts of our last five sincere Presidents to limit it? It's the good old American Profit Incentive. Government pay scales and GS ratings are based, to some extent, on the number of employees and the size of the budget being supervised by the individual being rated. Consequently, there is a built-in financial incentive to create a multiplicity of regulations that need to be supervised, and that require more enforcement, legal, administrative, and clerical staff.

This idiotic system hurts us in two ways.

1. It increases the costs of government so that the tax burden confiscates the money that might have been spent productively in the free economy to create real jobs.
2. It adds to the budget deficit, so more money has to be created by government to pay its bills. This is inflation.

We don't lose our freedom all at once. A book by Rene Baxter recalls the story of Gulliver, who was shipwrecked

94

and washed ashore unconscious. When he woke up he was tied down, not by a thick rope or chain, but by thousands of threads, none of which individually was strong enough to imprison him, but collectively were able to restrict his freedom, and he found himself in bondage to a race of pygmies.

We are rapidly drawing closer to the point where our bondage to the pygmies who run our bureaucracy will be total. If we can no longer control those who are supposed to be serving us, then we have lost something far more precious than money. We've lost freedom.

Freedom made us the most powerful, productive, and influential nation on earth. As freedom is lost, we will find ourselves increasingly beset with the same kind of troubles that plague communist countries, and which are solved only by repression, generally at the demand of "the people." Controls never atrophy. They only proliferate. Unfortunately, rather than recognizing regulation as one of the root causes of our stagnant economy and freeing us of our shackles, most of those people who make our public policy have decided the best thing for us is "a little hair of the dog that bit us." More controls! More regulations! More misguided attempts to legislate out of our lives every problem that a bureaucrat can dream up to expand his influence within the bureaucracy!

The Secret Cost of Government

Government is forcing up prices with regulation. A recent report by Sanford Goodkin, one of the nation's most respected and oft-quoted real estate consultants, indicates that approximately 20% of the cost of a new home is due to the costs of government regulation. In California, you can almost double that figure.

Regulation distorts the decisions of businesses which are often forced to relinquish a perfectly intelligent, well-conceived business plan because it runs afoul of some government

95

regulation. The costs of regulating are in the tens of billions of dollars a year and passed on in the cost of everything you buy.

J. R. Johnson, President of Royal Industries, wrote a marvelous financial analysis of the cost of government three years ago:

It took 142 years—1789 to 1931—for our Federal government to spend $100 billion. 31 years later, in 1962, our government managed to spend $100 billion in one year! It took only nine more years to get to the $200 billion per year level, and three years later, in 1975, we went over the $300 billion mark. Now it's getting easy! This year the Federal government will spend over $400 billion. That's a billion plus per day. [Now, it's over $650 billion. HJR]

What is a billion? It's a lot. One billion seconds ago the first atomic bomb had not been exploded. One billion minutes ago Christ was still on earth. One billion years ago men were still living in caves, yet one billion dollars ago, in terms of our Federal government spending, was yesterday.

The labor force employed in private industry grew about 36 percent in the years from 1955 through 1973. In that same period, the government labor force—Federal, state, and local—grew about 90 percent, or a rate two and one-half times that of the private sector.

In 1953 the average family in the U.S. had an income of $5000 and paid 12 percent of that in Federal, state and local taxes. In 1974, the family income had increased handsomely to $13,000, however, 23 percent of that income went for taxes.

We can give thanks to those who wrote our Constitution. They provided for our government of checks and balances. The more checks the government writes, the worse the balance becomes.

Mr. Johnson goes on to say:

Government regulation, by its very nature, causes all kinds of reports to be submitted to the regulators. Recently someone counted 15,000 types of Federal forms. Businesses file more than 114,000,000 forms every year. Twenty-five years ago the Hoover Commission reported that a million reports a year were filed reporting there was nothing to report. A major oil company stated last summer that 636 miles of computer tape are required simply to store the information required by the Federal Energy Administration alone. General Motors recently stated that in 1974 they spent 1.3 billion dollars on compliance with government regulations. [They use 23,000 persons simply to fill out government forms. HJR] The Federal Office of Management and Budget was asked recently to calculate what consumers pay for the regulations imposed by the government. They replied that while impossible to calculate precisely, the annual cost "might" be as high as $2000 per family, or a total cost of $130 billion per year—an amount roughly equal to all personal income taxes.*

One new weapon given the agencies to help them to expand their intimidating power is an 8–0 ruling by the Supreme Court that the Seventh Amendment guaranteeing jury trials does not apply when you are under attack by a government regulatory agency. They held, in a case with OSHA (Occupational Safety and Health Administration), that the defendant was not entitled to a jury trial, and that the Seventh Amendment right was not absolute.

This is utterly incredible. Our forefathers recognized that we had a right to a trial by a jury of our peers.

*Taken from a speech given before a Chicago automotive group in 1978. Reprinted by permission of J. R. Johnson.

Remember, if you are a businessman attacked by OSHA or the FTC, or a seller of vitamins under assault by the FDA, or any other target of bureaucratic meddling, the penalties can be as severe as a criminal offense. And you will be tried by the agency that is accusing you. That is bad enough, but now you cannot have a jury trial if the agency doesn't want you to. It is not possible to overstate the seriousness of this Constitutional threat.

I have five principles of government.

Ruff's Principle Number 1:	Government is not compassionate or wise. Government is impersonal and stupid.
Ruff's Principle Number 2:	When government solves a problem, it invariably creates two problems of equal or greater dimensions.
Ruff's Principle Number 3:	The true function of government is to make small problems worse.
Ruff's Principle Number 4:	It is the tendency of all governments to increase their power at the expense of the freedom of its citizens.
Ruff's Principle Number 5:	True patriotism requires resistance to that expansion of power, within the spirit and letter of the Constitution.

Let's look at a few of the worst of the Watchbirds.

The Food and Drug Watchbird (FDA)

The FDA kills people. Many drug discoveries sink quietly into oblivion because the bureaucratic and legal costs of nursing a new drug application through the FDA are so high, and it takes so long, that it becomes uneconomical to continue to develop, license, and market a drug that might save only 5,000 or 10,000 lives. The market is too small for sales to support the artificial costs of government regulation. Many of these drugs are in common usage in other civilized countries, saving lives every day.

Because of the FDA, you probably pay 50% more for drugs and vitamins and are denied the use of effective remedies. Your freedom of choice is impaired, and if you seek unapproved drugs in other countries where they are legal, and bring them home, you can be jailed for smuggling.

I've watched the vitamin and health food industry locked in a death struggle with the FDA, with the industry screaming about the preservation of everyone's freedom to be able to take the vitamin of their choice. Then I see the same people screaming for the FDA to regulate or ban food additives. On the one hand, they claim freedom is at stake; on the other, they want stricter regulation of the "bad guy."

This is a microcosm of society. "Give me freedom, but there ought to be a law to put that bad guy in his place." We can't have it both ways. As Pogo says, "We have seen the enemy and he is us."

The vitamin industry didn't realize that when you hand the government a sword and they finally vanquish the enemy you sic them on, they never put down the sword. They look for new worlds to conquer. They are likely to turn and use it against you, and the FDA has brought the entire vitamin and natural health industry under siege. The history of regulatory government is the history of bureaucrats looking around for new worlds to conquer, with each step in the assault on freedom appearing to be the natural consequence of the last step. When you have a hammer in your hand, everything looks like a nail.

One of the most dangerous aspects of FDA regulation is that many of the regulations are passed in areas that are essentially scientific issues still under dispute.

For example, the whole vitamin and protein supplement controversy is based on the opinion of mainstream nutritionists. They say supplements are useless. However, a very talented and respected minority vigorously disagrees, and says they are essential to health in a highly stressed modern society, and that everyone should be using them. This includes such men as Dr. Roger Williams, a Nobel Prize winner at the University of Texas; Dr. Linus Pauling; and many others of impeccable credentials.

The FDA starts with a predetermined conclusion, holds hearings, generally listening only to friendly, mainstream, orthodox witnesses, and sets up regulations governing potencies, Recommended Daily Allowances, and legal dosages. The current orthodox majority opinion is now frozen into law, and it becomes "consumer fraud" to advocate unpopular views or the minority position. It becomes illegal to compete in the free marketplace with products and ideas which do not adhere to a government-approved conclusion. It can even become dangerous to continue research to demonstrate otherwise, as you come up against the power of the government propaganda mills. Bureaucrats never back down. They never make a mistake, and as a result, scientific progress screeches to a halt, frozen into concrete, based on the current consensus.

Just look at the long list of advancements in science and medicine which resulted in the ridicule and heartbreak of the great pioneers: the electrocardiograph, the electroencephalograph, Dr. Lister and his germ theory of disease, and the polyunsaturated fat approach to the reduction of the risk of heart disease, not to mention Galileo.

Today, Lister would not only have to fight the AMA, but the AMA would have behind it the regulatory power of government, which would jail and fine him for promoting his unpopular views. We would probably still have new mothers dying of childbed fever, as doctors go from the autopsy room to deliver babies without washing their hands.

Sir Alexander Fleming, the discoverer of penicillin, would

never even have reached the human experimentation stage under present FDA rules, as penicillin causes severe side effects in rats and dogs.

Dr. Michael DeBakey, the heart transplant pioneer, said in a recent interview in Salt Lake City that, under current regulations, his pioneering surgery would have been impossible.

In the application of my second law of government, "When the government solves a problem it creates two or more problems of equal or greater dimensions," I am convinced that the problems created by the FDA in their attempt to solve problems can be lethal.

The Environmental Protection Watchbird (EPA)

The FDA is not the only agency that kills people. When it gets together with another agency, the EPA, the results would equal the most exciting fantasies of the Hillside Strangler or Jack the Ripper.

The EPA gave us a perfect example of mindless government at work when we had a series of grain elevator explosions in late 1977. These chain explosions completely destroyed four huge grain elevator storage complexes. Grain dust is up to fifteen times more explosive than coal dust, and an explosion is easily set off when the humidity drops below 35% or 40%. The obvious answer is to vent the accumulated dust out of the silos. However, EPA rules prevent this, as it would pollute the atmosphere. Well, okay, let's use humidifiers to raise the humidity level above the flash points. Oops! This is forbidden by the FDA, which says that the increased moisture would adulterate the grain. So the dust accumulates and, as a result, more than fifty people have died and millions of bushels of grain are gone, all because of mindless government that acts like an octopus with no central nervous system to coordinate the tentacles.

The story is told of Moses arriving at the shores of the Red Sea. Pharaoh's army is behind him, nothing but water in front of him. He cries out, "Lord, what do we do now?" Nothing happens. Pharaoh's army is getting close enough to feel the hoofbeats in the ground. Finally, in desperation, Moses screams, "Tell us, Lord, what do we do? And please hurry!" And the voice of the Lord comes to him, saying, "Not so fast, Moses, we haven't completed our environmental impact study."

The EPA will protect the air and water by raising the cost of your new house or apartment in that nice new development. Construction can be delayed for one to two years, while an "Environmental Impact Report" is approved. In the meantime, inflation increases the cost of construction 25% a year, taxes and interest pile up to be passed on to you, the buyer, and the house or apartment might end up being priced out of your reach by the time construction is complete, and your freedom and your pocketbook have taken another beating.

The Health and Human Services Watchbird

For sheer dumbheadedness, Health, Education and Welfare, or HEW (as it was known before it spawned its misbegotten offspring, the Department of Education), probably beats them all.

Some time back, HEW decided that Brigham Young University, a private institution owned and operated by the Mormon Church, was violating anti-discrimination laws when it required that off-campus housing for students be segregated by sex. All landlords in Provo, Utah, and surrounding communities who wish to house students attending the university have to agree that they will abide by certain regulations, otherwise they will not be certified for housing. These regulations are all pretty reasonable. Being a landlord in Provo, I have no problem with them.

Among these regulations is the rule that housing cannot be mixed by sexes. If you have an apartment building and want to house students, it is either for girls or for boys, not for girls and boys.

HEW decided that this was discriminatory and launched a suit against BYU. To their everlasting credit, BYU fought them tooth and nail and, with the resulting publicity, eventually worked out a "compromise" that saved face for HEW but actually was a total victory for the university. But hundreds of thousands of dollars of legal fees were expended. BYU is a religious institution that requires all of its students to sign an "honor code" agreement regarding personal behavior. Everyone who attends the university knows and understands that's a condition for attending, and voluntarily agrees to the terms. The university receives no public funding. It is subsidized by the Church of Jesus Christ of Latter-Day Saints, which pays approximately three-quarters of the actual cost of an education. The rest comes from tuition. They don't receive Federal grants, contracts, or subsidies of any kind.

HEW justified its actions toward the university by claiming that the university was publicly subsidized. When BYU violently disagreed, HEW argued that if any student attending the university received a government guaranteed loan, or was receiving GI bill benefits, that constituted "government subsidies for the university." That logic is similar to arguing that Safeway is government subsidized because it accepts food stamps, and Social Security recipients cash their checks there. BYU finally won the fight, mostly because HEW lost their nerve as a result of a lot of embarrassing publicity, but at great cost to all concerned.

In a somewhat similar alleged discrimination case at Grove City College in Pennsylvania, the judge hearing the action made an incredible statement, revealing the extent to which the deck is stacked. Judge Feldman wrote that, under the law, he had no power to find any HEW regulation illegal, since

... there is very clearly given to the director [of OCR— The Office of Civil Rights] a total and unbridled discretion to require any certificate of compliance that he may desire, reasonable or unreasonable. There are no guidelines.

In early 1976, a widely publicized incident boggled my mind.

Scottsdale, Arizona, school officials wrote to the Equal Opportunities section of HEW asking clarification of Title IX, the anti-sex-discrimination provision of the Education Amendments of 1972. "Were father-son banquets forbidden?" the officials asked.

The request landed on the desk of Helen Walsh, Title IX coordinator for the region.

Ms. Walsh remembered how, when she was a child, her school in Massachusetts sponsored a father-son banquet featuring Bob Cousy and Tom Heinsohn, the Boston Celtics' superstars. Because she was a girl, she couldn't go, but she sneaked out and watched through a crack in the door.

Now, it was her chance to get even. "No, Scottsdale, Arizona, you can't have father-son events because they discriminate between the sexes" was her stance.

Recently she was asked to rule on whether or not a school could select an outstanding boy student, and an outstanding girl student.

Here is what Ms. Walsh said: "The answer, of course, is 'no.' You can pick two outstanding students, but they might be two boys or two girls.

"You couldn't say the valedictorian has to be a boy and the salutatorian a girl—they're just the two top scholars."

President Ford, seeing the perfect chance to act "Presidential," denounced the "dingle-brained bureaucrat" who produced the ruling, but that missed the point.

This was not just a "dingle-brained bureaucrat" acting irrationally. This decision was approved by her boss and cleared through HEW's General Counsel. It's a dingle-brained system that chooses to regulate every aspect of our lives. Ms. Walsh's actions were rational, according to the rules, and consistent with the highest traditions of bureaucratic thinking.

Another bizarre example occurred when a school district requested an HEW clarification on the legality of having an all-boys' chorus in an elementary school. They were informed that it would be illegal sex discrimination and they could lose their various grants and Federal subsidies.

The school had been totally unsuccessful at getting the boys to join the chorus and sing with the girls, but they decided that if they could first get the boys singing in an all-boys' chorus, sooner or later they could bring the choruses together for special events and it would result in a strong mixed chorus.

Despite the fact that their intentions were well within the spirit of the regulations, unfortunately, some letter-of-the-law Pharisee concluded it was not legal.

Dear Sir, You're Dead!

Regulatory stupidity is contagious, and the disease seems to work its way down the bureaucratic ladder to state and local authorities, as reported by the National Taxpayers' Union:

> Illinois bureaucrats sent out form letters to deceased welfare recipients, informing them their benefits have been cut off because they are dead. Thousands of copies of the letters have been mailed out, reading: "Your assistance benefits will be discontinued. Reason: It has been reported to our offices that you have expired."

Helen Schumacher of the Illinois Welfare Division says she is merely following HEW regulations which require notification of recipients who lose their benefits. The regulations, she says, make no exception for the dead: "We're required to notify deceased persons of the cessation of their benefits. Recipients who want to dispute the decision are allowed an appeal."

And now the ultimate sick joke.

A Los Angeles County probation officer, assigned to counsel young girls at a detention school, was arrested on charges that he had lured a delinquent fifteen-year-old girl inmate to his home, had got her drunk, and then had had sexual intercourse with her, while being photographed by a sixteen-year-old girl. Ordinarily, this might just be considered one of the strange things that happens even in the best of probation departments. However, the case prompted Department District Attorney Ralph Mayer, who is acting head of the District Attorney's Special Investigations Division, to question some of the practices at Las Palmas School, where the probation officer worked. Mayer said:

> Both men and women probation officers are assigned to oversee these girls in cottages, and it is my understanding that male probation officers are often designated to make sure that girls get showered and in bed by nine-thirty at night. Probation officers are assigned to this duty regardless of sex.

When he was informed of Mayer's criticism, a Probation Department spokesman said that Federal laws that prohibit sex discrimination (HEW) were the reason male officers were assigned to girl's wards and female officers to boy's wards.

The Federal Trade Commission Watchbird (FTC)

WASHINGTON, D.C.(API) FEBRUARY 1, 1981. If you noticed a different pattern in Santa Claus' visits to your children last year, you can blame it on Uncle Sam. During August and September last year, there were six weeks of secret hearings in Washington, regarding a Mr. S. Claus from Northern Alaska. It soon will be announced that Santa entered into a consent decree with the FTC. Without admitting guilt, he agreed that, beginning in 1981, he would no longer discriminate between "naughty" and "nice."

A spokesman from The Moral Majority commented, "This infamous decision has taken away one of the last weapons available to parents in maintaining authority over their children. This is but another example of government intrusion into our private lives."

The FTC perceives its role as the disloyal opposition to the capitalist free enterprise system. Its primary function seems to be to make it as difficult as possible for business. The people that staff this agency are the most notorious in Washington for their visceral distrust and hatred of business and profits. Most of them are as anti-corporation as Lenin. Their fundamental assumption is that all corporate executives are greedy bastards who will gouge, defraud, and endanger the American public whenever given the opportunity, and that only our stalwart guardians at the FTC prevent us from these disasters.

Sometime back, *Forbes* carried a fascinating article on a proposed used car window sticker emanating from the FTC, to be placed on each used car, which warranted that the used car dealer would be responsible for anything that went wrong with the car during the warranty period after you bought the car. The vice-president of the National Automobile Dealers Association says it will cost $200 or more to inspect a car well enough to fill out the sticker. The government says it's only $15, but you can't even get a mechanic to raise the hood for that. And that's just the pure inspection cost, not including the cost of repairs.

If the dealer marks something "not okay," you pay the cost of fixing it. If they mark something "okay," the dealer is required to pay the cost if it breaks down. And it doesn't matter whether you buy the car with a warranty or "as is." This means that when a dealer sells a car, he has no idea what his liability might be for eventual problems that were not apparent on inspection. If he had any sense at all, he will jack up the price $100 to $200 to protect himself. There ain't no free lunch. The FTC is not imposing this same requirement on individuals who sell a used car because, according to the FTC, "individuals are more honest than used car dealers."

The cost of creating a perfectly risk-free world is beyond the ability of any society to pay, although it doesn't seem to be beyond the ability of government to fantasize. Such proposals should be laughed into oblivion.

The FTC has also taken legal action against "deceptive" testimonials, such as celebrity endorsements on behalf of services or products that the hired talent doesn't personally use. Joe Namath can't sell panty hose and Pat Boone can't sell a certain acne preparation.

But now they've really gotten clever. They have decided to protect my children from being seduced by television into begging for fattening, tooth-rotting cereals. This one almost tempted me to be on their side, but truth and free market principles finally prevailed, at least down deep in my heart. I know I might offend some people who are interested in "consumer protection," but I am also interested in the consumer's pocketbook. It's an assumption of authority way beyond the statutory intent of the legislation that set up the FTC in the first place.

Apparently some of my kids have inherited my predisposition to sugar addiction and, in the case of one child, a persistent weight problem. To that child, sugar-loaded cereals are like alcohol to an alcoholic, or dope to a junkie.

My kids are like your kids on Saturday morning. They like to get up and watch their cartoons heroes, and because Saturday morning is the one time I can sometimes sleep in, when I do go downstairs they may have been watching those commercials for an hour or two.

Many of those cereals contain up to 40% sugar, and all of their advertising is directed at children. It's deceitful and immensely seductive.

When the FTC poses as my friend, however, I pull the wagons in a circle. Now they are protecting my children from the Cookie Monster. They have found the perfect issue. On their side will be every parent who worries as I do about my kids, but who does not understand the corrupt, sugar-coated nature of government regulation. Arrayed against them will be an unlovely self-interest group of cereal and toy manufacturers, network advertising executives, ad agencies, and a few lonely free-market voices. Those easy-to-hate corporate so-and-so's in the cereal industry, who don't care what they do to my kids' teeth, will be hiding behind the legitimate freedom issue. They are precisely the kind of predatory wolves I would just as soon not have on my side.

How do you resolve the dilemma? Well, I've got to come down on the side of freedom. It's my responsibility to regulate my kids' diet and their TV viewing habits, not the FTC's. It's my responsibility to instill in them sound principles of good nutrition and healthy eating so they will, of their own volition, decide to stay away from those things. It is my responsibility to get up early and sit with them when they watch those commercials, and tell them all of the sneaky, deceitful things that are built into those potent messages. It is my responsibility to encourage my wife to plan good healthful breakfasts that are so attractive they won't want that junk. And, unfortunately in this case, it's also my responsibility to defend the free marketplace of even unattractive ideas. I would support a district attorney who would go after those people in the courts for fraud, but not on the basis of our need to be protected from a potentially harmful product.

I detest tobacco and alcohol, but I defend the right of these people to expose their products to the marketplace of ideas. To complicate the issues still further, I concede that our children should be protected against certain things. I will fight to the death for a free press, but I'd like local laws with stiff penalties for allowing pornography and mind-altering chemicals, including alcohol, to get into the hands of children. My only real defense against pornography is parental training, and the creation in my home of such healthy attitudes toward sex that my kids don't have to go after illicit thrills in a quest for sexual knowledge. In other words, it is my responsibility and that of my wife to protect and educate my children against assaults on their minds and bodies. We live in a free marketplace of ideas and we must keep it that way. We should not abdicate our responsibilities to some government agency.

And heck, some people have decided that some things said on my TV shows are dangerous, and I don't want to arm government with a sword to use on my enemies on the tube, because they might use it against me. Every loss of freedom is preceded by a popular demand that the government "do something!"

I could go on and on with Alice in Wonderland stories of government dumbheadedness, but I think you've got the point. I'd like to reiterate that these are not just untypical examples of individual stupidity. These are the natural outgrowth of the regulatory mentality. These people are what I call the Controllocrats. These are the enemies of freedom. They just scratch away a little bit at a time and you can hardly even tell you're bleeding.

One of the reasons the regulatory agencies have been so difficult to control is that because of their sheer size and bureaucratic depth, trying to reverse the process, or even slow it, is like trying to push a string.

The President goes to the appropriate agency head and makes a pronouncement of policy. The agency head enthusiastically agrees and says, "You bet. We're going to cut that bureaucratic waste. We're going to simplify those regulations. We're 1,000% behind you Mr. President."

The agency then forms study groups, committees, and task forces, and as the enthusiasm works its way down through the organization, nobody can find the one guy who is truly responsible for anything. The responsibility is so diffused and diluted that it is not like a log jam where you can get the key log and everything breaks loose. There is no key log. There are only survivalists concerned with the preservation of their power and privilege. Those who are in charge of cutting the fat are part of the fat, and they are not about to wipe out their own jobs.

I'm not worried about inefficient feather-bedding bureaucrats who do nothing. All they do is spend your tax dollars. I'm worried about the dedicated public servants who get up every morning and go to work on time and conscientiously spend their day trying to figure out how to "do something."

Will Rogers said, "Be grateful you're not getting all the government you're paying for." That may sound funny but I take it very seriously.

I believe that the bureaucratic tiger is on a rampage and can only be caged by legislation. In Part III of this book I have some suggested legislative remedies that will clip the wings of the watchbirds.

As a parting shot, it would be appropriate to observe that the thing that makes these public servants so dangerous is that they believe they're acting in the public good. They take the title of "public servant" very seriously. They truly believe it is their responsibility to protect us from the vicissitudes of life. Rarely, if ever, does the concept of individual freedom even cross their minds.

I've known some "public servants" and found them to be really nice, well-educated, dedicated, ordinary people—the kind of guys you'd like to sit next to in church or let borrow your lawn mower. There is nothing overtly conspiratorial about this process of regulating. It is simply the natural outgrowth of a democracy which has grown fat and lazy and is willing to let decisions be made for it. It is the natural consequence of the Unholy Trinity of legislators who want to be perceived as "doing something," special interests that encompass almost everyone in America, and the bureaucrats themselves becoming entrenched as they make lifetime career decisions to protect themselves.

Reversing this process will be one of the great cat fights of the century as everyone on both sides of the front lines in that

111

battle believes that they are on the side of the angels. If we lose this battle, however, the edifice of this Democratic Republic will crumble as our freedom is further eroded. The Reagan administration and this conservative Congress must take a stand now. After 1984, it will be too late.

It would not be fair to close this chapter without raising the main question: Is there a place for regulatory government?

On the Federal level, almost none.

Most government agencies proceed on the assumption that they must protect the public from its own ignorance, bad judgment, or greed. I believe if someone is damaged by bad air from a steel plant, they can have recourse to the courts for damages. A few adverse judgments that cut into profits, and a company will clean up its act. If a drug company creates a drug that has serious side effects, this can be handled by legislation and the courts. I don't object to laws passed by elected lawmakers, subject to Constitutional review in the courts. That's the system designed by the Founding Fathers. It worked fine for 175 years. I believe, however, it is immensely foolish to give the unbridled power of the creation of regulations to unelected bureaucrats when you cannot "throw the rascals out" if you don't like what they're doing. It is an end run around the Constitution which was designed to make government fully accountable to the citizenry.

There is no question that some people benefit, that some lives are saved, and that bureaucrats can point with pride to some good that has been accomplished. It is the essence of my argument, however, that the net of the good is exceeded by the net of the bad, and that in the process of doing good through the coercive power of government, the unnoticed casualty is freedom. Unfortunately, freedom is not missed until it is gone. I feel passionately that we must first slow, then stop, and finally reverse the growth of power of the Controllocrats in the next few years. If we don't, the Inflationary Eighties will not be just another cyclical episode in a long and honorable history. It could be the end.

CHAPTER 5

Trouble on Oiled Waters

Way back in 1977, President Jimmy Carter launched his Moral Equivalent of War (MEOW) on energy. Energy lost! He decreed a series of government actions to "solve" the problem, which only guaranteed the even greater problems we subsequently experienced.

Shortly after that date, Dr. Vincent E. McKelvey, Director of the U.S. Geological Survey, was fired from that position. Two unrelated events? No way.

Dr. McKelvey was not fired for incompetence. About the time that Mr. Carter was announcing MEOW, Dr. McKelvey gave a speech in Boston observing that as much as 60,000 to 80,000 trillion cubic feet of gas may be lying under the Gulf Coast region, an almost incomprehensibly large number. This is 3,000 or 4,000 times the amount of natural gas the United States will consume this year. Even the bottom range of that estimate represents about ten times the energy value of all the oil and coal reserves in the United States.

In the same speech Dr. McKelvey also observed that a large amount of oil is still to be found in the United States.

At the time he was fired, official statements were issued that his firing had nothing to do with his Boston speech despite the fact that President Carter was trying to convince us we were about out of energy.

After hearing about this curious incident, I decided to invite Dr. McKelvey to be my guest on my television show, *Ruff Hou$e,* so we went looking for him. He was not easy to find. The last place we expected to find him was working for the U.S.G.S., the very organization which had discharged him from his position as director, but lo and behold, we found him working for them in obscurity in Switzerland. We invited him to come to California to tape an interview but he was most reluctant, to say the least. He said, "No." Then he said, "Yes." Then he said, "No." Finally he agreed to come but refused our offer to pay his expenses, saying his expenses would be paid by the government, and he would come only if he could spend a half hour with me prior to the show to agree on some ground rules.

When taping day arrived, I sat down to speak with him and found him to be a very frightened man. Nervous is not the right word. That would be an understatement. He is experienced in public speaking and television interviews so I'm sure that wasn't the problem. The sweat was pouring down his face and literally dripping off the end of his nose. He said, "I'll do this interview only if we do not discuss my firing or politics." "Why not?" I said. He responded, "I have been misquoted. I never disagreed with the administration. I have never said anything that would be in disagreement with present policy." I said, "If you had not been fired, you would not have been invited to be a guest on my show. Don't you want to go on the air and straighten out this 'misunderstanding' about your discharge? You should jump at a chance to clarify the misconceptions."

He finally agreed, but only if he could stop the interview at

114

any time, so I said okay, but I knew I would have to handle him with kid gloves.

He then handed me a copy of a speech which he had delivered subsequent to his firing, which used the same data as the Boston speech, but drew totally different conclusions, which were now very pessimistic about potential energy sources. He slightly changed the assumptions about population growth, and the rate of increase in the use of energy. He lowered his assumptions about higher future energy prices, which would discourage exploration and increase consumption. He thus arrived at a much more pessimistic estimate of how long those reserves would last. By making minute percentage changes in a consumption forecast, you can knock literally hundreds of years off the potential duration of energy sources. By stressing the financial difficulties and ignoring the potential stimulation of production from rising prices, he managed to shorten the period of relatively available energy usage, bringing the whole concept into consistency with the official line.

I can't prove it, but I believe that Dr. McKelvey was fired because his views were an obstacle in the way of creating the shortage psychology that was needed by the Carter Administration to get its energy legislation through Congress. Being just five or six years away from retirement, even without an overt threat, I think his payoff for changing his mind about the basic assumptions was to be able to quietly work out his retirement.

I feel sorry for Dr. McKelvey. He is not a bad man. He is just not a good back-alley political infighter, and he lost. He is a sound scientist, a good man ground under by the coercive power of a government determined to bulldoze any obstacle in the interest of a politically profitable "nonsolution" to the energy crisis.

There is now truly an energy crisis where there did not need to be one. Who is responsible for it? How did we get into it? How do we get out of it?

And last of all, how do we live with it until it is over?

The following thoughts are drawn from my testimony on the windfall profits tax bill before the Senate Finance Sub-committee on Energy and Foundations in February, 1980.

The energy crisis is not caused by shortages of energy in the ground at reasonable prices. Natural gas and oil supplies will outlive this civilization. The crisis is caused by controls and government interference in the marketplace. The oil companies didn't cause it, although they have often taken unfair advantage of it. The OPEC countries are not to blame, although they have gleefully capitalized on it. The energy sword was created in Washington and handed to the Arabs, and we should not be surprised that they are using it as a weapon to create the greatest transfer of wealth from one nation to another since the Conquistadors raped and looted the Aztecs and the Incas and transferred huge quantities of gold from the Western Hemisphere to Europe. A civilization of higher sophistication and values was financially devastated by a civilization in a lower stage of development, and history is now repeating itself. Never have so many been so vulnerable to so few.

If we do not solve the energy crisis, we face the same sad end as the Incas and the Aztecs, and for much the same reason—a monstrous, involuntary transfer of real wealth and power through a modern and sophisticated kind of plunder.

A Formula for Shortages

Dr. Milton Friedman has said, "We may not know how to end inflation, but we sure know how to create shortages; merely control the price of anything and it will soon be in short supply."

The evidence of that is all around you. What shortage are we most worried about? What is the one product that we have to periodically wait in long lines to get? That's right. Gasoline!

116

What products have dramatically risen in price as a result of shortages? That's right. Gas and oil!

What have been the most price-controlled commodities in the world? Right again. Gas and oil!

If we do not solve the energy crisis, the American Dream is over. At stake is the capitalist free enterprise system, and the corollary to that system is personal freedom.

It is not just a question of whether you can take your motor homes on long vacations, or ski behind your powerboats. Our food chain begins in the sands of Saudi Arabia. We pour 11 calories of energy into the ground for every calorie of food we produce, in the form of fertilizers, pesticides, and fungicides made from oil and natural gas. It is the energy used to power the tractors and the cultivators and the harvesters and the trucks that haul food to market. It is the energy required to ship that food all over the world, because American food production is the glue that holds civilization together. We export fully 40% of what we grow.

If we don't produce and export grain from the impossibly productive American cornucopia, much of the rest of the world faces famine and death. Famine produces mass migrations, war, and political upheavals, particularly in the lesser-developed countries that produce the minerals and raw materials that we require for our sophisticated civilization. The alternative is a descent into barbarism for much of the world.

It doesn't have to be this way, because there are natural methods of farming which are successfully being used to grow corn and wheat on a large scale in parts of Texas, Montana, and Iowa, which do not use these unimaginably huge quantities of petroleum and gas-based chemicals. Farm energy consumption can drop by as much as 30% while producing more nutritious, safer food. We could do without OPEC and still grow as much food if we had to, but not without a transition period of two or three years to recondition our exhausted soil, which is like an aging horse who can only pull a wagon if he is flogged into activity. We are flogging that land with ever-increasing amounts of petroleum-based products watching the production per acre gradually slip as the horse ages even faster because of the mistreatment.

At the moment, however, the entire farming economy is based on hydrocarbons, and we are dependent upon unstable, medieval monarchs, and religious fanatics to provide them. Doesn't it make you feel good to know that a Khomeini, or a Qaddafi, can determine whether or not there is bread in your Safeway store? And yet that is precisely the kind of dependence we have created, by legislation and regulation, almost as if we were following a death wish.

Why do we have energy shortages?

Is there a potential for becoming energy independent, not only for this generation but for our children and our grandchildren? How can we protect ourselves from the consequences of the stupid political policies that have brought us this crisis?

What should we change?

How can you structure your life so that it is not messed up by critical shortages of this vital commodity?

Now You See It, Now You Don't

There are almost infinite sources of traditional energy available to us within the borders of our own country.

Ever since the first oil well was drilled in Pennsylvania in 1859, the energy doomsayers have claimed that we are about to run out of oil. Although the doomsayers are still saying the same thing, the amount of oil they are saying we have left has been growing with each new generation of doomsayers. Year after year we have used more petroleum, and yet our proven reserves have expanded. We continue to discover more oil than we consume, with the exception of a few recent years when exploration was suppressed by government price controls.

Economics writer Jude Wanniski said:

> If you took all the liquid petroleum produced from all over the wells on earth since the very first one, and poured it into a lake the size of Chicago, roughly 227 square miles, that 330 billion barrels the earth has yielded so far would fill the lake to a depth of only 300 feet. The estimated petroleum, worldwide, that could be recovered at current prices and technology, would fill the lake to the depth of 2,300 feet.

Only about 2% of the continental shelf has been opened up for leasing by the U.S. government. A study made by our old friend Dr. McKelvey for the U.S. Geological Survey in 1968 estimated that there is a total of 1,576 billion barrels remaining in the continental shelf area. The National Petroleum Council estimates that there are about 3 million square miles of potentially favorable geological formations. Production is currently underway in less than 2% of the total area that might be promising.

One very conservative report from the United States Institute of Training and Research says that oil and gas from conventional sources will last until about the years 2020 to 2030, at least. The consensus of the report is that increased prices will make it economical to tap new sources, and additional petroleum and gas sources will probably be available, although at substantially higher cost, during periods of transition to usable renewable energy sources (even if the transition period should last 100 years or more). According to them, most of the world, offshore and onshore, has never been systematically explored. The report states the oil industry will be able to get more and more oil and gas out of the ground through technological advancement. Also, as prices increase, small fields with hard-to-get deposits that are not now economical may become more worthwhile. Lastly, more oil will be produced from so-called unconventional sources.

In other words, there is enough to last us at least the next 100 years, which should be plenty of time to make the necessary transition.

Certain things will have to change, however, before the transition can be made. More about that later.

Dr. Chalmer Kirkbride, who was the engineering consultant to the Institute of Gas Technology in Chicago, says:

> There is a deposit of 600 trillion cubic feet of gas in the Rocky Mountains that cannot be produced by primary production methods for a variety of reasons. There are systems and methods, however, that could make it profitable and, hence, available to the consumer, but the price ceiling (at the time of his report) of $1.42 per cubic foot at the wellhead for natural gas being sold in interstate commerce, is less than the probable cost of producing the gas.

Price, as any economist should know, if he has not forgotten it, is the means by which supply and demand are brought into balance. If the price is too low, then there will be insufficient supply and increased demand, causing shortages. What is more important, if the price is too low, there is no incentive to come up with alternative energy sources because the present available energy is still cheaper for the consumer than the alternatives. The gap is too great.

For example, many middle-class Americans could afford to build solar collectors for their rooftops to heat hot water and assist in heating their homes. The problem is that with natural gas and heating oil being kept so artificially cheap (even in excess of $1. a gallon for heating oil), the gap between the cost of traditional fuel and the cost of the solar collectors is so great that there is no economic incentive to install a solar heating system. Corporate financial and marketing divisions understand this, so the big, efficient corporate organizations don't unleash their creative engineering talent and mass production facilities on the problem. They are waiting for higher conventional energy prices to narrow the cost gap to create demand and lower sales resistance, and I don't blame them. When you try to get the country to depend on solar energy, you are asking us to fly in the face of our own financial self-interest, which is like trying to motivate a dog by pushing on his leash. You cannot get people to act contrary to their own economic advantage except by coercion, and coercion, hopefully, will never totally become the American way.

Mopping Up

President Carter commissioned a study by the Energy Research and Development Administration (ERDA) in the early days of his administration to determine the availability of natural gas at various prices. It was called the MOPPS Report, which stands for Market Oriented Program and Planning Study. ERDA came back with a report which predicted that if the price of natural gas was allowed to rise to $3.25 per thousand cubic feet, there would be double the reserves that we would have at the then proposed ceiling price of $1.75. The report was embarrassingly optimistic and arrived at the time Carter was launching MEOW to solve our energy problems, so MOPPS was sent back to the drawing board. The Department of Energy required the U.S. Government Printing Office to destroy all of the offending reports. The GPO did so in the following letter to its depository librarians:

ATTENTION: DEPOSITORY LIBRARIANS

The Department of Energy has advised this office that the publication Market Oriented Programs Planning Study (MOPPS), Integrated Summary Vol. I, Final Report, December 1977, should be removed from your shelves and destroyed. The publication was shipped on S/L 10,558 (2nd. shipment of February 7, 1978), under item number 429-P (El. 18.0011/1D). We are advised the document contains erroneous information that is being revised. Your assistance is appreciated.

J. D. Livsey
Director, Library and Statutory
Distribution Service (SL)

ERDA came back with another estimate which was still much too good, so they were asked to try a third time. The third time around they managed to create a mild crisis, but even at that they found fifty-five years worth of natural gas at reasonable prices. MOPPS's Executive Director, Harry Johnson, said that he believes the higher estimate was the correct one. Phillip Wyatt, MOPPS's Chairman, said, "The original estimate might have been a pretty good guess."

The Wall Street Journal estimated that the total deregulation of natural gas would bring in so much supply that it would force down the price of its near substitute, number 2 heating oil, which at that time sold at the price equivalent of $4. per thousand cubic feet (mcf) of gas. Total deregulation of natural gas prices could break the OPEC cartel, because it would sharply reduce the need for new oil and cut our imports. You see, fuel oil and natural gas are to a great extent interchangeable in American industry. A ready, dependable, price-stable supply of natural gas, even at higher prices than now, would reduce the consumption of petroleum in this country by significant amounts.

There are incredible amounts of natural gas available to us. For example, there are frontier areas that are suitable but a long way from pipelines where the long-term investment cannot be justified by the artificially low prices. At higher prices the pipeline investment would make sense. It has been estimated that on the Texas Gulf Coast there are 105,000 trillion cubic feet of gas 8,000 feet down. Even if U.S. consumption doubled, we could provide for our nation's needs for 200 years with 10% of the gas from this source alone.

For some years the government subsidized the import of liquified natural gas at $3.25 per thousand cubic feet from Indonesia and Algeria, while at the same time controlling the price of natural gas in this country at a fraction of that price.

Bill Brown, Director of Technology at the Hudson Institute, a think tank not noted for its conservative views, says that although he does not recommend it as far as fossil fuel reserves are concerned "there is no doubt in my mind that if we wanted to, we could continue to use energy at the present rate and even increase consumption and export oil in the future."

There is enough energy to last us about 600 years at the present annual consumption, if we use the recoverable shale oil. And if low-grade oil is included, there is ten times as much. The question is not "Are natural gas and oil available?" The only legitimate question is "At what price?"

The Carter Administration initiated a phased deregulation of natural gas and oil prices, which is obviously a step in the right direction, and President Reagan deregulated oil, but shied away from a prior plan to move up the total deregulation of natural gas from 1984 to August 1981, because the price of gasoline jumped ten cents at the pump within two weeks of oil deregulation. They ran for cover when the political flak began to fly.

How can we unlock our oil and natural gas resources? The only way to do it is to hang in there with oil deregulation and take all controls off natural gas, despite the short-term political consequences. Do it instantly! All at once! With no windfall profits tax! The phased-out natural gas deregulation we are going through now simply increases the incentive to hold back for the next level of allowable price increase. In addition to that, the deregulation plan as administered by the Department of Energy is so incredibly complex that there is now before the DOE a three-year backlog of cases from natural gas producers waiting for interpretation of the regulations. It will be a long time after the deregulation should have taken effect before the interpretation can be provided so they can take the necessary steps. I find it very difficult to obey laws I don't understand. When I know I might get in trouble by launching out into the dark, I tend to do nothing. And that is to some extent what the energy industry is doing. Instant total deregulation is necessary. Even the partial deregulation we have had to date has had a dramatic positive effect on new drilling and exploration in North America. Not enough yet, but enough to tell us we should hold our noses and jump into the deregulated pool. The water is apparently fine.

As I said before, in a free market, price brings supply and demand into balance. Price controls limit the supply. If we want conservation, we will have to allow the price to rise to the point where conservation becomes a matter of personal economic survival. The recent rise in gasoline prices to the $1.25 level has resulted in economizing. In fact, for the years 1979 and 1980, our consumption of oil and gas in this country dropped by 10%. Further price increases will result in further economies.

Three years ago I spent three weeks traveling in Europe by car. Gasoline was $2. a gallon, even then. So the Europeans adjusted. They drive small cars and there are zillions of mopeds on the streets (at 100 miles per gallon). The German economy has demonstrated that $2. a gallon gasoline is not necessarily a disaster. Because of the economics encouraged by high prices, they use 40% of the energy per capita that we do, and their standard of living is every bit as good as ours.

If we want economy, new supplies of gas and oil, and new alternate energy technologies, the price of existing energy sources will have to rise to the point where these objectives become economically feasible and economically desirable. Economic incentive is the key. Or, you can keep on pushing a string, asking people to use sources that cost more than those they can use without having to change their life-styles or make new capital investments. Fat chance!

If you really want cheaper fuel, deregulation will eventually give it to you, because it will cause a glut which will drive prices down. When the price rises, you will see oil and gas drilling rigs multiply like hamsters. The price will rise abruptly for a short while, then come back down in a year or two as new supplies flood the market.

Unfortunately, it is politically difficult to allow prices to rise, even temporarily, particularly in the cold, big cities in the Northeast where heating oil costs are a gut political issue. You can blame the political power bases of those cities for the price controls that have created this problem. Although President Reagan wants total deregulation, and did deregulate oil, the big city screams of anguish have sent him running for cover on the gas issue. If he takes the correct but politically dangerous deregulation route, eventually rising prices will produce new supplies and make economically feasible the development of alternate energy resources. When some major company realizes that they can give you an economic argument and sales pitch for long-term savings in order to sell you solar collectors, they'll jump into that market. Soon new technologies and mass production will bring the cost of those solar collectors down, reducing pressure on traditional energy sources, just at the time the supply of orthodox energy is increasing. The bottom would fall out of the price of traditional energy sources and no longer would OPEC have us by our economic throat. No longer would we have to distort our foreign policy for fear of losing whatever oil they choose to send us.

The "Windfall Profits" Tax

In a classic case of economic stupidity, Mr. Carter launched his phased deregulation program, and then canceled its positive effects by coupling it with the vicious windfall profits tax proposal. The windfall profits tax is one of the most deceitful, and dangerous pieces of legislation ever imposed upon the American people. It's like dangling a deregulation carrot in front of a horse, then making him throw up as soon as he has eaten it.

Future Econ. 101 students will study the windfall profits tax as the quintessential example of concealed taxation—getting at your pocketbook while you cheer for the pickpocket.

I recently was asked to speak to 400 high school juniors at Downey High School in Modesto, where two of my daughters went to school. I was given forty-five minutes to explain to them the functions of the free market, free enterprise system. I started with a multiple choice quiz and asked them the following questions.

"Gasoline today costs about $1.25 gallon. The amount of profit per gallon earned by the oil company is (1) 7.5 cents, (2) 30 cents, or (3) 57.5 cents." Approximately 12% of the students said 7.5 cents. Twenty-five percent thought all choices too low. The rest of the answers were distributed between the other two choices.

They about fell out of their chairs when I told them that 7.5 cents was the proper figure and that government was taking in various taxes over 35 cents a gallon—five times the oil companies' profits.

I then asked them, "How many stockholders does Exxon have?" Their lowest estimate was 15. Their highest estimate was 1,500. When they found there were 680,000, it blew their minds. I then asked how many were in favor of the windfall profits tax, and nearly every hand in the room went up. I said, "All right, who will pay it?" The answer? "The oil companies." "Who owns the oil companies?" I asked. "The stockholders," another astute student responded. "Who are the stockholders?" "A lot of rich people," was the response. I blew their minds again when I told them Exxon's largest stockholder was the Teachers' Pension Fund in Chicago, and if the fund doesn't get dividends from its investments, which means the distribution of profits from the corporations whose stock they hold, the teachers could end up on welfare. And those teachers are hardly rich oil billionaires. That one Exxon stockholder out of the 680,000, the Chicago Teachers' Pension Fund, represents over 50,000 teachers. So who will pay the windfall profits tax? Fifty thousand moderate income teachers in Chicago, among others.

My next question was, "Where do corporations get the money to pay their taxes?" A look of dawning comprehension came across the faces of a few students and the answer came back, "They get it from their customers." "Do the oil companies have $250 billion to pay out in windfall profits taxes?" (because that is the amount that this legislation would extract from those companies). The answer? "They'll get it from their customers at the gas pumps." "So who pays the largest percentage of the windfall profits taxes?" This time I answered for them. "The poor black in Detroit who can only afford a gas-guzzling Buick. He'll pay more of it than I will, because I can afford an economical Mercedes diesel, and I'll burn less fuel."

The windfall profits tax is a proposal by the politically astute to impress the economically ignorant and extract money from them. The average person thinks that when you tax an oil company you are taxing greedy billionaires, but corporations don't pay taxes. Consumers pay taxes. Corporations collect taxes from consumers and pass them on. Stockholders also pay taxes. And the big oil companies, the focus of hatred and envy of millions of Americans, are owned by widows and orphans, pension funds, mutual funds, college endowment funds, and other Americans, rich and poor, directly and indirectly, many of whom are depending on those dividends for their retirement and whose investment profits have reduced the cost of welfare, taxes, and higher education for Americans.

In the first place, the windfall "profits" tax has nothing to do with profits. The taxes are based on a percentage of the gross selling price of each barrel of oil. It can run from 50% to 76% of everything an oil company takes in in excess of $16 a barrel for some classes of oil. I'm not going to bother to explain exactly how it works, because the formula is so complex, I barely understand it myself. But it is paid before it is even determined whether the oil company has any profits at all.

Theoretically, and it probably will happen somewhere, an oil company could bring in an oil field where the cost of production is higher than the net they can receive for the oil after the payment of the "windfall profits tax," and it would have no profits at all. It might very well refuse to develop the field. I know I would. The irony is, this tax could reduce corporate profits to the point where the normal corporate taxes would decline sharply. The windfall profits tax ends up coming out of the pockets of the stockholders, most of whom are not rich, and out of the pockets of the consumer at the gas pump, most of whom are not rich, and into the insatiable political machine where it can be used to buy votes. The pork barrel is being paid for from the oil barrel.

There is no question that the windfall profits tax concept is the last great taxing frontier open to the politicians. They were able to push this through Congress with the overwhelming approval of the American public, even in the face of a nationwide tax revolt, only because of the ignorance of the American public as to what was being done to them.

It is impossible to overstate the importance of the windfall profits tax, both in terms of what it will do to energy production and in terms of the precedent established for taxing the American public while pointing the finger at a corporate scapegoat. Two hundred fifty billion dollars or more will have been ripped off from the American economy, and either showered upon politically powerful constituents or put into government "trust funds" which can only be invested in U.S. government securities, making this an incredible new source of Federal borrowing, giving them a classic end run around the tax revolt.

Because of the windfall profits tax, many sources of oil and gas that would be economically feasible at present prices will never be found or extracted, because after computing the windfall profits tax, it is a money-losing proposition for the corporations.

Because of the windfall profits tax, the oil companies will never accumulate the hundreds of billions of dollars necessary for them to punch holes in the ground all over America to make us independent of OPEC.

Because of the windfall profits tax, our dependence on OPEC will increase, making us vulnerable to political blackmail, and because of the Soviet designs on the Middle East, the survival of Western civilization may well be at stake, because they can literally strangle us.

The windfall profits tax could not have passed unless there was widespread hatred of the oil companies and fear of "obscene profits." If we deregulated without a windfall profits tax and created a big bulge in oil companies' profits, that would not scare me one bit. Their earnings, when measured by return on investment, are right in the same range as the bulk of American industry. Corporate profits are not obscene. There is no such thing as obscene corporate profits. Profits are distributed to stockholders. They are saved, spent, and invested, and recycled into the economic system. Profits are at the root of the capitalist free enterprise system. A healthy profit structure represents a healthy economy. Those who say we have to protect the consumer from profit-making corporations are in effect saying that the free market doesn't work, that the free enterprise system is philosophically bankrupt. That is socialist and communist dogma. They don't understand that the disciplines of the marketplace drive the ripoff artists back into line. Whenever someone is making too much money, the word gets around, then others jump into that business, creating the kind of competition that drives prices right back down. The energy industry is the most competitive industry in the world, despite protestations to the contrary by Teddy Kennedy and others of that ilk. Over half of the oil in this country is being found by the small independent operators. Those hard-nosed mavericks laugh at the fears of the politicians that the oil and gas industry is noncompetitive. You give those guys the slightest look at a potential profit and they'll drill the holes and take risks, and they'll find enough energy to produce competitive price pressures that will drive the major oil companies right back into line.

The truest and most basic and fundamental of economic laws is that you cannot tax away incentive and increase production. You don't encourage an activity by fining it. You not only have to allow them to accumulate funds for investment in new oil and gas fields (and it will require substantially more than they are making in profits now), but they have to have enough to reward their stockholders for investing their capital, to be distributed as dividends.

I am opposed to the windfall profits tax in any way, shape, or form. I am prepared to accept any relatively minor price gouging evils in the meantime in order to avoid the infinitely greater evil of stripping away the incentive of the only people who have the resources, the capital, the knowledge, and the rigs to solve our energy problems. If we don't spend those hundreds of billions of dollars of capital, we are going back into the Stone Age. Where will the money come from if they can't accumulate the capital? From government? No? Already the government is trying to pour back that ''windfall'' money into subsidizing low price heating oil, which can only increase consumption.

We Owe It to Ourselves?

If we continue our dependence on OPEC, we will continue to increase our economic vulnerability. We used to say in regard to our national debt that we owe it to ourselves. That's no longer true. We now owe approximately 30% of our short-term treasury debt to Germany, Japan, Switzerland, and the Arabs. Approximately 20% of our long-term debt is owned by these same people. They have recycled their oil profits into short-term deposits in New York banks, which have loaned the money out long-term to such credit-worthy borrowers as Chile and Zaire, Jamaica, and Argentina, Brazil, and Panama. The banks are committing the classic error of "borrowing short and lending long" which has created vulnerability of epic proportions in the American banking system. Because the Fed will do whatever it has to do to save the banks, it is now the "lender of last resort" to the whole world.

To give you an idea of how vulnerable we are, in October, 1978, when the dollar was sinking into the Atlantic, Kuwait had $2 billion in CDs in Morgan Guaranty Bank in New York which came due. In the past, they had been "rolling over" their DCs when they came due. But this time, because the dollar was sinking so badly, they wanted out. They said, "We want our $2 billion, and we will want our other CDs as they come due." The banks scrambled around in New York for three days trying to find $2 billion. No luck! Eventually Mr. Solomon, the Assistant Secretary of the Treasury, brought this problem to the attention of the White House, and they made contact with the Germans, the Japanese, and the Arabs to decide what they should do about this problem. The entire banking system of the Western world could have come down in a domino-type collapse.

Carter was forced to launch his "Save the Dollar" program, which was an abrupt change of fiscal and foreign policy. It worked temporarily. But, at that crucial moment, our foreign policy, our economic policy, and our financial policy were (and still are) dictated by desert sheikhs who are socially and economically only a few generations removed from Middle Ages feudalism.

This transfer of wealth must stop, even if it means allowing the oil companies to have their "windfall profits." If we do not end this stupid, unconscionable, immoral, and immensely dangerous transfer of wealth to OPEC, this nation may not survive as a free Democratic Republic.

Swallowing a Camel

When we created the Department of Energy (DOE), we strained at a gnat and swallowed a camel. Hysteria about oil company profits motivated us to create a regulatory monster to keep oil companies from making too much money. The first year budget of DOE was $10 billion, which to me is a lot of money. To put that in perspective, it represents $500,000 for each DOE department employee, $50 for each and every member of the total U.S. population, $266,871 for each of the wells drilled in 1976, $38.35 for each of the feet drilled in 1976, and $3.59 for each barrel of domestic crude oil production in the country. It exceeded the total profits of the world's seven largest oil companies, and that was only the first year's budget. The Department of Energy is an enemy of the people and should be abolished. They have done nothing but create shortages and add to the cost of gas, without allowing that money to create the profit incentive for production of more oil, and they haven't produced one calorie of energy.

In my opinion, the key to solving the energy crisis is natural gas, because it is such an abundant source of energy. It can meet many of our needs for generations. Even with the most pessimistic forecasts, it will last at least 100 years, and maybe as long as 600 years. There is no refinery bottle neck because it doesn't need refining. It is ecologically pure. It burns clean. It doesn't cause acid rain, like coal. Natural gas will bridge the gap, but only if we allow prices to seek their own market level.

On the scale of demons, energy is running neck and neck with the inflation monster that is devouring us, because it can cause the machinery of the Western world to grind to a halt and create starvation on a worldwide scale. The answer lies in freedom—freedom of the marketplace, freedom to enjoy profits, freedom for those who produce to get rich, since they take such risks to provide such benefits.

When I testified on this subject before the Senate Subcommittee on Energy and Foundations, I was asked some interesting questions at the conclusion of my testimony.

Senator Gravell asked, "Why do you think the cold turkey approach is necessary, which many consider would be inflationary because prices would rise?"

My answer: The problem lies in the definition of inflation. If you define inflation as rising prices, which most people do, cold turkey price deregulation would be slightly inflationary. But inflation is not rising prices. Rising prices are a symptom of inflation. Things other than inflation can cause rising prices, like a disease in the corn belt or widespread hail in the wheat belt, or a war in the Middle East. That's a market aberration, and it's usually temporary. Inflation is always, at all times and in all places, a monetary phenomenon caused by an increase in the money supply. Rising prices are the result, not the cause. The underlying and fundamental cause of inflation is the monetary and fiscal policy of the government— the creation of Federal deficits, as well as the immense expansion of the money supply to accommodate consumers who also wish to "deficit spend," to expand their standard of living, without increasing their productivity or their real income. The money they borrow is created out of nothing by the Federal Reserve through the banks to be sure that there is money there for them to borrow. That money is put into circulation and, in effect, drives up prices. If we deregulate energy prices, there is no question that the "price inflation" rate, which I distinguish from true monetary inflation, would rise temporarily. It could add as much as a point and a half to the price inflation rate, but that is a small price to pay for the long-range benefits down the road.

I might use a drug addiction analogy, a subject with which I'm familiar, having known some people who were caught up in hard drugs. When a man has a $100 a day habit, there is no way to cure it except to go cold turkey. He has to be willing to be sick for a while in order to get well. For a junkie, being sick from withdrawals is like turning fifty, an experience I just had. It's really bad, unless you compare it to the alternative. The point and a half increase in the inflation rate for a couple of years is tolerable when you compare that to the alternative, which is a long-term, almost infinite increase in energy prices. I am willing to trade off that temporary point and a half increase in the general level of prices in order to create the abundance that would drive those prices back down.

Question from Senator Wallop: "How can we increase our production when the refining capacity of the country is limited?"

My answer: "Natural gas is the key, precisely because it doesn't have to be refined. If you deregulate and create market conditions in which potential users know the supply is dependable, many corporations that are now burning fuel oil would turn to natural gas. Gas is the bridge, the wedge. This would buy the time for oil-refining capacity to be increased sufficiently to adjust to the increased supply of crude oil."

The deregulation of oil, but not gas, means undependable natural gas supplies and more oil consumption. You can't break up OPEC by only deregulating oil. Gas is far more abundant. At twice current prices, it is still cheaper than OPEC oil.

Question from Senator Boren: "Why is it we cannot seem to adequately alert the consumer of the fact that he is being set up for the biggest rip-off in the history of this country, in terms of the government capturing the oil that he is being asked to pay and sacrifice for through higher prices."

My answer: "It is the nature of government that, when it

134

wishes to tax, it tries to conceal the nature of the tax. Corporate taxes are the most efficient form of concealed tax, and the windfall profits tax is the slickest of all. I am even more concerned about the broader implications of the anti-business rhetoric that we have been hearing from government. And the oil companies are not the only target."

For example, in the first quarter of 1979 when the previous quarter's corporate profit picture was reported showing big increases, it was called "a disaster," "unconscionable profits," by representatives of the White House. This has helped to create an anti-business climate which makes it very convenient and politically feasible to place higher taxes on a business or industry. The public, not understanding the nature of corporate taxation, thinks those taxes are just wonderful.

When the subject of energy shortage comes up, there's an automatic suspicion of conspiracy, based on the anti-corporate hysteria in this country. This anti-profit feeling disturbs me greatly.

The free enterprise system is a terrible system, until you compare it with any other. There is no perfect system known to man, short of the kingdom of God. That doesn't seem to be just around the corner, so we will just have to live with the one we have. Of course, the free enterprise system has its inequities, but it has created more wealth and prosperity for more people than any system in the history of the world. The whole system depends on two things. First, profits to be distributed to the stockholders and reinvested. And second, the creation of pools of capital.

The windfall profits tax is perhaps more dangerous as a precedent than the immediate negative effect. Inflation has eaten away at the purchasing power of the average American saver faster than he can earn interest on his savings and has created a disincentive to save, so the pools of capital that might have been available to develop energy sources, to build natural gas pipelines in Alaska, and to explore off the coast of

Newfoundland will not have been accumulated. This reduction in the savings rate means that the capital has to come from somewhere else, so it has to come out of profits.

If you don't allow profits to be accumulated, where is the capital going to come from? The government says, "We'll take it away from the corporations so we can control how that money will be invested in more energy." Don't hold your breath. That money will be given back to the "poor" consumer to subsidize his gas and heating bills, stimulating more energy consumption.

After my diatribe on the windfall profits tax, Senator Baucus, a big-spending liberal of the Teddy Kennedy camp, said, "Mr. Ruff, I take it you are opposed to the windfall profits tax?"—a question mind-boggling in its sheer idiocy after listening to me for an hour. I responded, "I believe on balance you might say that, sir." Senator Baucus then asked if I was opposed to it in its entirety, or if I just wanted the tax rate modified. And I answered, "I am opposed to it in its entirety on both philosophical and practical grounds."

If we don't solve our energy crisis, we are flirting with a depression that could last decades. We may be looking at the end of things as we know them. The die has been cast. There is no way to go cold turkey without withdrawal symptoms. We've gone too far down the road.

What Will Really Happen?

The end result of all of this is that we now have a windfall profits tax, we have a Department of Energy, natural gas is still regulated, and we will have worse and worse energy shortages. During the recessions, we could very well see temporary fuel gluts, as a swing of 5% in either supply or demand can create either glut or shortage. But the energy crisis will be back, eventually destroying the internal combustion automobile as a viable means of transportation for most of us. This means the virtual collapse of the automobile industry. Chrysler and AMC are only the first. Ford is rapidly becoming a basket case, having lost $1.5 billion 1980, and General Motors will soon follow showing big 1981 losses.

How will our crises develop in the future and how can you anticipate and adjust?

You will see periodic shortages at closer and closer intervals. Those shortages will create pressures for increased fuel prices, which will result in demands for the reimposition of energy price controls, which will create more shortages. Every time the shortage temporarily recedes, we will breathe a sigh of relief, but we will soon be back in the same old bucket of bolts. If you have your head screwed on straight, you will take the necessary steps to be able to live in a world crippled by undependable energy supplies. And the strategies for dealing with and preparing for this problem will be discussed in Chapter 17.

In the meantime, the energy crisis is irretrievably linked with inflation, the root cause of the problems through which this nation will go in the next several years. Without radical changes it virutally guarantees a terrible combination of price inflation and economic depression, and changes in your lifestyle so far reaching that your children and your grandchildren will hardly recognize the world in which you grew up. We will someday reminisce about the good old days of $2.-a-gallon gas, and you had better plan your life accordingly.

When I finished my Senate testimony, four out of the five Senators on that subcommittee congratulated me for my testimony and said they agreed with me. Then three of the four turned around and voted for the windfall profits tax, and their laudatory remarks about my testimony were stricken from the record. It was this graphic display of cynical politics that caused me to say "That tears it! I'm getting politically active," but that story will have to wait until you get to Part III.

Now, as a device to integrate and summarize all that I've covered in this chapter, I'd like to give you a surefire formula for a wingding of an energy crisis.

1. CONTROL THE PRICE OF DOMESTIC OIL AND NATURAL GAS in an inflationary environment. This will guarantee that energy company profits on domestic oil and gas will be squeezed by rising labor and material costs, so they'll stop exploring and drilling at home, and will meet their profit responsibility to their stockholders by developing high-priced sources abroad, rather than in the good old U.S.A. That's where the profit is. This will increase our dependence on foreign oil. It also assures that energy company managements will protect themselves from the resulting uncertain energy future by using their precious capital to diversify out of energy and into shopping centers, banking, department stores, etc.

2. DEREGULATE PRICES, but demand that the oil companies plow back most of new profits into exploration, and tax away the rest, leaving none of the rewards of that high-risk exploration to the stockholders. If I were an oil man, I'd say to heck with it. Government took no risks. It invested no money. What right does it have to take all the rewards?

3. BUS KIDS ALL OVER TOWN, using millions of gallons of gas to implement a dubious social experiment most everyone hates.

4. MAKE IT NEXT TO IMPOSSIBLE TO EXPAND THE USE OF COAL, by creating expensive environmental regulations. Due to controls, oil is so artificially cheap, compared to coal, that power plants will be forced by economics to continue to use oil. That ought to be good for a few million gallons a week.

5. IGNORE TECHNOLOGICAL DEVELOPMENTS,

such as hydrogen cars, the Merkl oil-recovery process, the Oglemobile, and solar broadcast electricity.

6. INSULT MEXICO by refusing their $2.80 mcf natural gas, then later, backtrack, crawfish, and crawl, until they condescend to sell us oil at OPEC prices, while keeping their cheap natural gas for themselves.

7. PASS STUPID LAWS that prevent us from swapping Alaskan heavy crude to Japan in return for their imported light crude, which would save everyone money. This assures the Alaska pipeline will operate at far less than capacity because there is only one refinery on the West Coast that can handle heavy crude (also because of environmental regulations), and all West Coast storage space is brimming over. Only the smaller tankers can get through the Panama Canal (which we have given away anyway, and is only safe as long as Torrijos rules Panama and keeps his word).

8. CREATE A WEB OF REGULATIONS, permits, lawsuits, and delays, preventing Sohio from using an existing natural gas pipeline from Long Beach to the Gulf Coast where the refineries are, until they give up in frustration when the costs mount until it becomes uneconomical.

Of course, no sane government would do all those stupid things!

Do not conclude that I love the oil companies. They often act like arrogant pirates. But their responsibility is to maximize profits for their stockholders. Their stockholders either get a return on their invested money, or they simply won't invest anymore. If we do not nurture and cherish the idea of profits, the nation is doomed as a free enterprise system. If we do not have sufficient faith in the system to realize that deregulation will produce competition that will ultimately keep profits at reasonable levels, without government sticking its fat nose into the situation, then we are saying we no longer trust the free enterprise system.

I own no oil company stock, and I wouldn't know an energy company executive if he bit me on the nose. I just believe in freedom, profits, and sound economics in a capitalist system. You can't spur a horse to greater effort by cutting his oats ration.

Addendum

In this discussion of the energy crisis, I hope I have made it clear that the answer to our immediate energy crisis is allowing rising prices in order to encourage production of an abundant supply of gas and oil, a simple and achievable solution. As prices rise, it will become financially feasible for alternate energy sources to come on stream, and it will also become possible to recover oil and gas that is too expensive for us to recover now and add to our reserves. When the term "reserves" is used, it means oil and gas that is known to be available with current technology, at current prices. If it's too expensive to recover profitably, it is not included in the reserves. A technological breakthrough, or a simple price increase, and, *Voilà!* More rèserves!

Let's explore briefly some interesting developments in the energy field, not that I have researched them so minutely that I can give them an unqualified endorsement, because that's not true, but because these are examples of the innovative thinking and technological breakthroughs that could eventually relieve the pressures on nonrenewable and increasingly expensive resources.

Gasohol

Gasohol, the glamour fuel of the eighties, is a blend of gasoline and ethanol, which is alcohol made from cellulose, generally from sugar beets, corn, and wheat. It is touted as a way to aid the farm economy and stretch fuel supplies. The argument is that grain is a renewable resource, while petroleum is not. Gasohol is said to deliver more power with less pinging. It is touted as one solution to our energy problems, to say nothing of being a good deal for the farmers.

I would like to see further research and development of this product but I have reservations which will have to be resolved before I can really become enthusiastic.

A study by researchers at Louisiana State University's Coastal Ecology Laboratory has suggested that a factory for distilling alcohol from cane sugar, grain, or other crops will almost always eat up more energy than it produces. The article, published in *Science* magazine, says that even in southern Louisiana, where alcohol plants would benefit by being able to burn a mixture of sugar cane waste and cheap natural gas as fuel, the energy produced would average only about two-tenths more than the energy expended. Anywhere else in the country, the energy yield would be negative. Another study, also published in *Science*, estimated that current distilling practices would require the energy equivalent of two or three gallons of gasoline, or some other petroleum fuel, to produce enough alcohol energy to replace one gallon of gasoline. There is also some evidence to the contrary, but at present it is an unresolved scientific dispute.

Alcohol has been widely used as a motor fuel in Brazil. They mix 20 to 25 percent ethanol with all gasoline sold there, and to promote the use of pure ethanol the government provides 3 year loans for cars running on 100 percent alcohol by reducing the applicable vehicle tax to a third of its usual level. They also set the price of the alcohol at 11.5 cruzeiros per liter as compared to regular gas at 22.6, and premium at 36 cruzeiros.

One of the reasons that ethanol is so expensive in the U.S. is that sugarcane which is so abundant in Brazil is prohibitively expensive in America. When corn is used instead of sugarcane the cost rises to something over $1.25 per gallon. To make ethanol competitive with gasoline on a volume basis tax subsidies are necessary. Without these subsidies alcohol fuel is roughly twice as expensive as gasoline. One study concludes that "if ethanol has only modest potential as an extender of gasoline supplies in North America, then it's potential as a pure fuel has to be regarded as negligible. Brazil's special situation of a large land area suitable for sugarcane production and a relatively small automobile population has given ethanol its leading position there. But comparable use of it as an automotive fuel seems unlikely to develop anywhere else."

My second reservation is that I believe we are headed into an adverse, highly variable weather cycle beginning sometime in the next few years, which could last for twenty to forty years. Many climatologists believe the Northern Hemisphere is getting colder and the growing season will get shorter. This could reduce our ability to grow grain in Canada and the northern United States. If we became dependent on corn alcohol to drive our cars, the weather could become a major factor in determining whether we can drive or not.

It has been estimated by Dr. Joseph B. Bidwell, Executive Director of General Motors Research Laboratories that diverting America's entire corn production to fuel alcohol production would only produce a "net energy yield of only about 6 percent of the gasoline used for just passenger cars."

Using nonedible agricultural by-products, such as corn stocks, wheat chaff, sugar beet residues, etc., could change the cost equation a bit. But we still may be up against the law of Conservation of Energy in the development of gasohol and its further expansion and use. It may be an answer, but not until a lot of questions have been answered. Let's hope the answers are positive.

Burning Water

It has been an age-old dream to be able to extract power from water. Theoretically, we know it is there in the form of hydrogen. Nuclear scientists are trying to develop energy from fusion of the hydrogen atom, but there are also some interesting developments in the use of hydrogen as a fuel to power standard automobiles.

One example which has come to my attention is the Billings Energy Corporation, a research and computer company in Utah, run by Roger Billings, who has been separating hydrogen from water with a device called an electrolyzer, which runs off your house's electricity. The hydrogen is then converted into a "metal hydride," which is basically hydrogen combined with metal particles in a heavy pressure tank, forming a powder. This is converted back into a gas when it is released to be burned in the automobile engine.

Billings' experimental cars run on either gasoline or hydrogen with a flick of a switch on the dash, but require heavy, bulky, pressurized hydrogen tanks in the trunk. The major disadvantages of the system are the cost of the electrolyzer, if you are going to provide your own fuel (around $5,000), and the fact that more fossil fuel energy is consumed in creating the electricity to hydrolyze the water than is produced in the form of hydrogen. Also, because of the weight and bulk of the tanks, the car's range is limited, but it still could be an important breakthrough.

The Inertial Storage Transmission

I interviewed Vincent E. Carman on *Ruff Hou$e* and he blew my mind. He has developed a tremendous energy-saving idea which made the cover of *Mechanics Illustrated*. They evaluated it and said, "It works."

Large amounts of kinetic energy are expended when you brake your car. Carman's hypothesis was that if you could somehow store that energy, you could use it to propel the car until the stored kinetic energy was dissipated. He developed a method of doing just that.

Except as an emergency backup, this car has no brakes. The key is a new type of transmission, an "energy accumulator." When you let up on the accelerator, the transmission brakes the car. You have to learn to use your accelerator as a brake, as well as to make the car go forward. The energy used in breaking is not lost, but is used to pump oil under increasing pressure into an accumulator tank. When the car is ready to start and you step on the accelerator, the pressurized oil drives the wheels. The engine automatically shuts off until the pressure in the accumulator tank is reduced to the point where there is not enough sufficient stored energy to continue to propel the car, at which time a small computer kicks a solenoid and restarts the engine which recharges the accumulator tank and then cuts out again. In stop-and-go driving in the city, which is about 55% of the driving in the USA, the engine is off 80% of the time, creating an eerie silence.

That has obvious implications for gas mileage. The cars they have converted get approximately double the normal gas mileage in city driving. There is relatively little advantage in freeway driving, where you are not doing much braking.

Acceleration, using the stored energy, is tremendous, in fact, much more so than a typical engine. If you let up on the accelerator too fast, it's as if someone threw out an anchor.

Carman estimates it takes $1,200 to $1,500 to convert an existing car, but if it's mass-produced and installed at the factory, the cost would be roughly $150 per automobile, over and above present cost. The fuel savings would make up for that in no time at all, given what fuel prices will be in the near future.

So far, I have described a relatively simple and straightforward invention. Now the plot thickens! The invention was submitted to the Energy Research and Development Administration (ERDA), which referred it to the National Bureau of Standards (NBS) for testing. NBS tested it and, out of several thousand energy inventions evaluated, determined that this is one of forty-five worthy of funding and continued development. Because ERDA, according to Carman, was emotionally and financially committed to a fly-wheel system, this report was buried. In fact, it darn near took an act of Congress, or at

144

least a lot of pressure from a Senator, to get the report released, and at last report there had been no funding. The only reason Mr. Carman isn't starving is because his wife has a job.

Oil Recovery

Perhaps the wildest and most controversial guest I ever had on *Ruff Hou$e* was George Merkl. We got more letters from the George Merkl interview and reruns than from any other three shows we ever did.

This man is a refugee from the Hungarian revolt who came to America and made his fortune. He could have retired many years ago, but he and his associates put up their own money to form an energy company to back the development of an inorganic "polymer" (a fancy name for a liquid chemical substance made out of silicon). When as little as one barrel of this polymer is diluted and injected into depleted "stripper" oil wells, they produce again. The principle sounds simple. The polymer separates the oil from the structure and actually "cracks" the oil to separate it from the natural gas. The resulting increase in pressure starts wells free-flowing that haven't produced in years. In many instances, they produce more oil than they did in their heyday. The polymer can also produce natural gas from shale formations.

After we ran the interview we got a lot of interesting letters from private citizens asking questions, as well as some comments from the Department of Energy. DOE claims they've tested Merkl's process under laboratory conditions, and it's worthless. Merkl claims that they've never really tested the product as it should be used, under his staff's direction and supervision. He says their tests are invalid. He also claims it's been tested just as it was another surfactant, and it is really something totally different.

He has not been asking for any government money and isn't really selling his product. He simply goes to independent operators who own stripper fields, negotiates a joint venture, and goes into business with them, sharing the profits. He provides the product and the technical people and they provide the oil field. They are using the product in stripper fields in Ohio, Kansas, and Texas, and they are signing joint venture agreements regularly. He is willing to take the risks along with the producers.

The implications of this discovery are immense if it turns out to be anything near what Mr. Merkl claims.

There are a million and a half capped stripper wells in the country less than 1,000 feet deep. The big oil companies are not interested because they own very few of these shallow fields. Amoco, in testing it for cleaning up northern French beaches polluted by their huge tanker wreck, reported it was no more effective than other decontaminants. The French government, however, found otherwise and bought several million dollars worth of Merkl's product.

If Merkl is right, these dead stripper wells can produce between 6 and 35 barrels a day when treated with the Merkl process. With a million and a half of them, there is a potential flow of 9 to 50 million barrels a day, which could make us energy independent from that source alone for the next thirty to sixty years. These wells are not even included in the reserve figures that come from the petroleum industry or from the government.

I have had conversations with three people who have gone into business with Merkl, and interviewed one on my TV show. One has had outstanding results, one said it didn't work, and in the third case the results were still pending. They have still had to learn a lot about how to use the product, including how much to inject and whether to inject it directly into the well or drill another hole into the field and inject it there. There are some other technical and mechanical problems that I, frankly, didn't understand.

All I know is that this kind of development should be encouraged, not pooh-poohed, and it should be welcomed with open arms and minds as a potential breakthrough, and thoroughly and conscientiously tested.

The energy crisis has left us no option; we cannot afford closed minds unless we want empty fuel tanks.

In summation, here are the things we must do.

1. We must remove all bureaucratic barriers from the development of alternate energy sources.
2. We must use tax credits to encourage production, exploration, innovation, invention, and creativity in the energy field.
3. We must be willing to allow financial rewards to the people who risk their money and their time so they can benefit from their efforts and dedication.

I have other legislative recommendations which will help to resolve our energy problems, but I'd like to reserve them for Part III, "Free the Eagle," as part of our total political and legislative program for saving America.

CHAPTER 6

Conspiracy

Do We Need a Conspiracy to Explain Why?

During the recent Presidential race, the Trilateral Commission connections of George Bush, Jimmy Carter, and numerous powerful insiders in government became an issue. There is now a substantial and growing minority who believe that all of the world's troubles are the result of a conscious, calculated conspiracy, controlled by insiders such as David Rockefeller, Baron de Rothschild, Zbigniew Brzezinski, etc., who have formed organizations to rule the world such as the Bilderbergers, the Council On Foreign Relations, and The Trilateral Commission.

The theory goes something like this: Their plan is to create a one-world communist dictatorship which the Insiders will control, that will rule the world. Jimmy Carter was a totally manipulated puppet, and these people control even the governments of the Soviet Union and People's Republic of China. Every action taken by this country is consciously manipulated for their benefit.

Some of the best people I know share all, or part, of this view. I don't have a dearer friend on earth than W. Cleon Skousen, who wrote *The Naked Capitalist*, one of the first big-selling books on this subject. Subscribers have probably sent me 150 copies of Gary Allen's book, *None Dare Call It Conspiracy*. This is the general theme of publications such as *Spotlight*. Also, a series of articles in *Penthouse* magazine (clipped out by loyal subscribers and sent to me anonymously) has explored Jimmy Carter's Trilateral Commission connections.

I have some views on this rather touchy subject, and it is time to grasp the nettle.

Ruff's Recap of the Conspiracy Theory

The word "conspire" is from Latin, meaning "to breathe together," or "to secretly work together for a common goal."

By that definition, there are many powerful conspiracies loose in the world. The International Bankers can and often do manipulate this country's policies to their benefit through their immense political influence and the sheer weight of their economic power. They control the economies of dozens of nations through huge loans. Through their creations, the International Monetary Fund and the World Bank, they have been able to extract public funds to be advanced to these debtor countries so they can pay the interest on their loans to the international bankers. These "conspirators" often act like "citizens of the world," rather than citizens of the countries in which they reside. They also represent the great investment and banking houses of Europe and the great multinational corporations, including the oil companies and some of the huge manufacturing octopuses from Japan, West Germany, France, etc. These people literally make public policy.

These were the people behind the Panama Canal giveaway,

and the Shah of Iran's visit to America which triggered the Iranian hostage crisis.

Panama

The Panama Canal giveaway is the most naked demonstration of their power. The real story is frightening.

Torrijos, Panama's leftist dictator, owed many millions of dollars to New York-based multinational banks, including Marine Midland. There was no way he could repay them unless he could get his hands on the Canal revenues.

Sol Linowitz, a Director of Marine Midland and member of the Trilateral Commission, was appointed by President Carter to be our chief negotiator. His appointment was for one day less than six months, thus avoiding the possibility of an embarrassing disclosure of his conflict of interest in a Senate confirmation hearing. The treaty negotiations were completed one day before Mr. Linowitz's term expired.

The net result?

Torrijos got his Canal and its revenues and strengthened his iron grip on his country.

The New York bankers got the assurance they wouldn't have to write off their loans.

They also got a deal with Torrijos creating a "free banking zone"—no taxes or inconvenient regulation—so they now have a place to operate their international businesses without public exposure. Bank buildings are going up all over the Canal Zone.

The American taxpayer lost the Canal revenues and got a big bill for the transition, plus a graphic demonstration of the immnese political clout of the international financial power structure. Despite the fact that they acted in their own self-interest, I have no doubt that they also felt it to be sound public policy. It's amazing how often our own self-interest and our views of policy tend to coincide. And that's not just true of David Rockefeller. Farmers, labor unions, etc., tend to draw the same conclusions.

I don't believe, however, they are in total control of the world, and I cannot yet make the leap in logic that others have made, which concludes they can manipulate the smallest details of public life. Nor am I yet persuaded, as some are, that they want all of us to be part of a one-world communist state.

These unelected leaders have attained their immense power, influence, and fortunes by exerting decisive influence on controlled capitalist economies. I can see no logical reason why they should want to change that. They form organizations, such as the Trilateral Commission, for international monetary manipulation to make international trade cheaper and easier to conduct and to make the world safe for international banking. I also believe they were behind the recognition of the People's Republic of China.

Another Trilateralist, Jimmy Carter's good buddy J. Paul Austin, the President of Atlanta-based Coca-Cola, the man who introduced him to David Rockefeller who subsequently appointed him to the Trilateral Commission, announced Coke's contract with the Chinese the day after Carter announced our recognition agreement. On Chicago television the same day, Coke cans printed in Chinese were shown. Now that's fast action!

David Rockefeller actually spent six weeks in China arranging for future banking relations, months before Kissinger (a former and present Rockefeller employee, but then Secretary of State) made his secret visit to China to prepare for Nixon's visit.

These men are the inflaters—the deficit spenders. If governments did not run deficits on the state, city, and Federal level, one of the multi-national bankers' greatest sources of safe profits would dry up, which is the interest they earn by purchasing debt securities issued by these political subdivisions to cover their deficits. If there weren't government bonds, municipal bonds, or local sewer district bonds, etc., these organizations would have no safe place to park their money when it is not employed in direct loans or mortgages. These bonds have provided tens of billions of dollars of profits annually for the bankers. It is in their interest to have "controlled" inflation and "controlled" deficits. Profit, power, and freedom to operate are what they strive for, along with the protection of their accumulated wealth and privilege through special tax advantages.

Fortunately, they are not yet all-powerful. No one ever wanted to be President of the United States more than Nelson Rockefeller and he never made it. Despite his Trilateral connections, Jimmy Carter still lost the election to Ronald Reagan. No matter how hard David Rockefeller tries, he ran still only the third or fourth or fifth biggest bank in America, and not very well, either.

These men can and probably will miscalculate. The banking system which they dominate is gravely threatened by the events in our future (see *How to Prosper During the Coming Bad Years*), and I don't believe they are assured of being able to patch up their leaking ship as we sail into the great inflationary depression. Some of the conspiracy scholars have concluded that these people are deliberately leading us into a depression. I am not persuaded. I think they are arrogantly convinced they can avoid it or control it within reasonable limits.

So how does this sum up? They wield far too much power. They act in their own self-interest and get their way more often than not. They don't just influence the monetary system, they are the monetary system. However, they are a long way from being totally in control, and I hope they always will be.

They are not a monolithic conspiracy. They aren't even agreed on their objectives, and they fight among themselves. The Rockefeller center of influence wants to cast off gold as the world's reserve money and has fought tooth and nail for this, because it allows them to benefit from inflation and funding of government deficits through government securities.

The Rothschild family, on the other hand, with its huge gold and diamond interests, wants to re-enthrone gold as the centerpiece of the world monetary system, and the struggle has been going on for years. The International Monetary Fund (IMF) is the principal tool of the Rockefeller-centered philosophy, and the Bank for International Settlements (BIS) in Switzerland is the principal focus of concentrated economic power of the Rothschild clan.

Conspiracies? Yes. They take the form of shifting alliances, with organizations that come and go in prestige and influence, such as the Council on Foreign Relations, the Bilderbergers, and now, the Trilateral Commission. The core players remain the same.

Those guys couldn't lose in the 1976 Presidential election. Jerry Ford was a Nelson Rockefeller man all the way, as was most of his administration. And Jimmy Carter was David's boy. The "conspirators" were working both sides of the street and I'll bet they literally did not care who won. Public policy would have been pretty much the same no matter who won.

But total and complete control and a one-world communist dictatorship? I am unconvinced.

My advice is still good whether or not such a conspiracy controls us. Public ignorance and the great cycles of history are going to produce certain financial results that would happen in any case. Even the Rockefellers are not as big as the great worldwide marketplace of money, commodities, and ideas. We will have a hyperinflation and a depression, whether or not there is a conspiracy. Just keep taking my basic advice and live your life positively. Perhaps those who believe they are ominipotent in manipulating the world's affairs will themselves drown in the flood of paper they are creating. Perhaps their own creation will be Frankenstein's monster, which will destroy them.

I am wary of all great concentrations of power, whether it

be big government, big manufacturing, big banking, big oil, or big labor. I am alarmed by their ability to dictate public policies, but I'm not about to attribute to them powers beyond those which I can demonstrate they have. In the meantime, I believe I can make forecasts with reasonable accuracy simply by studying the great cycles of history and the repetitive nature of man's folly. Even David Rockefeller must obey universal law, or like King Canute, he will find that if he tries to command the tide to bend to his will, he will get his feet wet.

One last concern! I am disturbed at the attitudes and actions of some of those who have wrapped themselves in the conspiracy issue like a Holy Cause, but who use the concept to grind other axes. For example, there are those who never use the words "banking conspiracy" without preceding them with "Jewish," or "Zionist," or both. For them, it is a cover for anti-Semitism or white supremacy. I detest that. There are others who use the opposition to the conspiracy as a cover for attacks on capitalism by painting the big capitalists as devils.

There are those who use it as a lure for attracting people to their cause, their newsletter, or whatever they have to sell.

Then there are those responsible, concerned, academically qualified citizens, such as Dr. W. Cleon Skousen and Dr. Antony Sutton, who have done a scholarly job of tracing the real connections and Byzantine twists of the interlocking relations of the world's true power structure. They perform a legitimate service.

The real story behind these people, their power, their objectives, and their accomplishments, will probably never see the full light of day. Some of what the conspiracy buffs attribute to them is simply the result of natural cycles, market forces, climate change, and the collective actions of millions of people. But much too much of the world's power is concentrated in a few hands. I don't know for sure what these people really want, but in the meantime, I will bet my investment money that the fundamentals of economics, the impersonal markets, and the cycles of history are bigger than any of us, or all of us put together, and I will invest and plan accordingly.

PART II

Survival
Strategies
For The
Disintegrating Eighties

Chapter 7

A Track to Run On

Part I was the bad news, the scary stuff. Next comes the guts of my strategies for winning in the Inflationary Eighties. In Part II we will deal with specific steps that you can take to avoid the failure of the money, and the liquidation of America.

In *How to Prosper During the Coming Bad Years*, I gave you basic beat-inflation strategies, using gold, silver, diamonds, and real estate. In my presentation of the material in Part II, I have generally assumed that you have grasped those basic concepts.

I have attempted to develop strategies for people from all levels of the economic stratum. I've deliberately kept it simple. There are a lot of sophisticated techniques that could have been included in this book, but it is not my objective to make you a great expert. I want to give you the basic principles behind the investment and survival strategy steps, and sufficient knowledge so that you can work intelligently with a broker, a financial advisor, a merchant, or a supplier without getting ripped off, either by his cupidity or your ignorance.

There is no guarantee that all of these strategies will work out with precisely the timing that I have indicated. I'm sure I'm right about *what* to do, but *when* to do it is a subject that needs continual revision as unforeseen conditions develop.

If you should buy this book six months or a year after I have finished writing, it is possible that we may have moved past the time when some of these investments were appropriate. We may have developed other strategies which will enhance their value.

I fear that you might make expensive mistakes in timing if you just plunge ahead. I am preparing a brief update on this section, to be changed as often as necessary, and will be happy to send you a free copy of the update if you will just write to me in care of The Ruff Times, P.O. Box 2000, San Ramon, California 94583. Ask for the update on *Survive and Win in the Inflationary Eighties*. I feel a responsibility to see that you are current and won't take the right step at the wrong time, and will maximize the opportunities outlined here. Consider that update to be a crucial supplement to the book you paid for.

The update is available to each reader on a one-time only basis. My newsletter, The Ruff Times, is the ongoing update service by which I keep people updated on changes of strategy and where we might stand at any stage of the economic cycle.

Avoiding the Failures Caused by Having No Financial Philosophy

Most people have no basic financial philosophy, no set of basic premises against which they measure their financial decisions. Consequently, they are like the uncertain souls described by Paul who are "tossed to and fro, and carried about with every wind of doctrine."*

Most people listen to one persuasive advisor and say, "I've got to follow this man. He will make me rich," until the next guy who comes along says the exact opposite in equally persuasive terms. They are easily confused because they do not have any clearly thought-out, time-tested framework within which to interpret what they hear.

I would like to present my basic guidelines so you can understand why and how I arrive at the conclusions that end up in my newsletter and my books. Then you can choose.

I try to bridge the gap between the academic economists and the investment advisors. The economists push abstruse numbers around in their computers, using "monetary aggregates" and the "gross natural product" and other esoteric concepts, but usually know next to nothing about markets and the hard world of investments. The investment advisors understand markets, but often do not have the slightest idea how the real world works, and their advice is usually given in a philosophical and economic concept vacuum. Many investment advisors don't understand anything about economics, and most academically trained economists don't even have any investments.

Some of the most ridiculous nonsense I have read about economics and the fundamentals of how the world works comes from financial advisors and brokerage firms. They make monetary decisions, not understanding the economic context of the real world, which is like Rembrandt beginning a painting without first examining the condition of the canvas, or doing it blindfolded.

Only time will tell if I am truly successful at bridging the gap between those two worlds.

Here are my fundamentals.

---

*Eph. 4:14.

Fundamental Number 1. PLAN YOUR LIFE TO AVOID FAILURE. This is the subject of the next chapter, so I'll defer it now.

Fundamental Number 2. INFLATION IS EPIDEMIC. We are in the early stages of a long cycle of generally accelerating inflation, which occasionally retreats for a while before racing for new highs. There are times to bet some money against inflation.

Fundamental Number 3. DON'T BE GREEDY. On Wall Street they say, "The Bulls make money, the Bears make money, but the Pigs go broke." Try to get rich in your job or your profession, and then try to hang on to your purchasing power (plus a little bit) with your investments. Think like a football coach. Your job or profession is the offensive team. Your investment program is the defensive team whose job is to keep the opponent (inflation and taxes) from scoring, while you occasionally score a touchdown or safety. How many times have you gone to a close football or basketball game that was broken wide open by the defense; a hard hit producing a fumble, a deflected pass or a blocked shot resulting in a fast break, a quarterback sack, or an interception? Even in case of a tie, the investor wins. The usual result, however, is a substantial win. *Beat inflation, plus a little bit!* I don't care how, as long as ethical and moral values aren't violated.

Fundamental Number 4. DON'T GO INTO VOLATILE, HIGHLY LEVERAGED SPECULATIONS which can whipsaw you out with a margin call, unless (1) you can afford to lose 100% or more of your investment, without serious emotional or financial damage or (2) you are sure you have the temperament to watch wildly fluctuating markets with equanimity, without stress distorting your judgment. If you can't, you should avoid stocks and commodity futures on margin. If you can short ten pork belly contracts on Friday, and sleep well all weekend, you have the temperament to be in volatile, leveraged investments.

Fundamental Number 5. BE PATIENT. When you have bet on a certain scenario, and things seem to be chopping around not going anywhere, keep re-examining your basic premises, and as long as they hold up, be patient. Don't panic or act impulsively. You often have to wait for months.

Fundamental Number 6. AVOID THE "GIVE-ME-ACTION" SYNDROME. Some people just have to "do something." Be willing to stand on the sidelines when the trends are confused, with the equivalent of cash (Treasury bills or a money market fund) until things clear up. Don't be like the guy who watches the twenty-one table in Las Vegas; even though the dealer is as hot as a pistol, this guy just can't resist. He's gotta have action, so he sits down and blows his dough.

Fundamental Number 7. DIVERSIFY ACROSS THE BEAT-INFLATION SPECTRUM: real estate, diamonds, colored stones, collectibles, gold, silver, or when the time is right, bonds. Don't fall in love with any one thing. I've had people say to me, "Well, I don't want to buy these other things, I just like diamonds," or "I just like gold," or "I just like real estate." The market doesn't care what you like. You have to be pragmatic and objective about your investments, never emotional. If you are not, you probably won't diversify. If you guess wrong, you lose big. No investment is perfect. Something can always go wrong with any good investment. Kodak might find a way of making film without using silver. The government might call in gold. Real estate might be staggered by rent controls or taxes. Diamonds are relatively illiquid from time to time. These possibilities don't invalidate these investments. Not at all, as there is no perfect investment. It just means you should spread your risks by diversification.

Fundamental Number 8. NEVER CONFUSE INVESTMENTS AND CAUSES. For example, some people feel strongly about South Africa, feeling it is important to the future of the United States. I agree our past African policy was hypocritical and stupid, but that doesn't mean South African gold shares are always a good investment. Buy them only when they are at an appropriate point in the investment cycle. The South African cause is separate and distinct from your investment decisions about gold shares.

Many hard-money-oriented investors believe passionately in remonetizing gold, a worthy cause. But that has nothing to do with whether or not you ought to buy gold today. Those are separate matters—decisions which may or may not coincide at any given time.

You may love your country and feel that buying Series E bonds is patriotic. That has nothing to do with whether or not it is a good investment, which it isn't.

Fundamental Number 9. AVOID LOANING MONEY to banks, savings and loans, and insurance companies. I am not so much worried about them going broke as I am that the money is going broke and they will pay you back in dehydrated dollars. Instead, borrow money from them, and use it to make money.

Fundamental Number 10. NEVER BUY A NEGATIVE CASH FLOW. This principle really answers a lot of financial questions. Should you buy income-producing property in San Jose, California, or in a suburb of Detroit, or in downtown Denver? Only if you can get a building cheaply enough to produce a positive cash flow, or if you are getting a run-down building in a good neighborhood that can be fixed up so you can raise the rents and produce a positive cash flow. If you can't buy or create a break-even or positive cash flow, don't buy it. You can rarely do that in the big cities of America. That's my main reason for investing in small town America. That is why I don't invest in raw land, making payments every month out of my pocket. If your disposable income is crunched up by inflation, you might find yourself unable to make the installment payments, and that happens to many over-extended investors during recessions. I want investments that produce sufficient income to make the mortgage payments and expenses. I avoid negative yields.

Fundamental Number 11. BEATING TAXES IS EQUALLY AS IMPORTANT AS BEATING INFLATION. (Inflation, of course, is a sneaky tax on savings.) Unfortunately, most tax-shelter programs and estate-planning techniques designed to beat income taxes, estate taxes, etc., freeze you into investments which get chewed up by inflation, while most successful beat-inflation investment programs result in capital gains taxes and heavy estate taxes when you die.

Chapters 16 and 17 will present a stunning set of new concepts to beat inflation and taxes. They are the core of my asset-preservation program. You can literally use inflation to help you pass your wealth on to your children. Using the fact that inflation transfers wealth from lenders to borrowers, you put yourself in the position of being a lender to your children. Inflation rips you off so they can prosper, and the estate tax man is disinherited. Beating the system is not just a matter of deciding "What investments shall I buy that go up faster than the rate of inflation?" There is much more to it than that.

Inflation takes a 15% or larger bite out of your money, but for the average person who makes enough money to save anything, taxes take at least 30%. When I hear about investments that beat inflation, the capital gains tax factor is usually ignored, as is the estate tax factor. Civilizations that don't pass on their values and their wealth to the next generation are only one or two generations away from coming totally unglued.

Fundamental Number 12. INTANGIBLE IDEAS MOVE THE WORLD, and here is one that has lived through time: "Lay not up for yourself treasures on earth where moth and rust doth corrupt and thieves break through and steal, but

165

rather, lay up for yourself treasures in heaven."* This lofty concept must be reconciled with the Biblical account of the unprofitable servant who got in trouble for not investing the "talents" he was given. His money was given to the servant who got the best return for his master. Taken as a whole, I believe this means that although the pursuit, acquisition, and preservation of money is morally okay, we must never lose sight of more important long-term values. First among those values are God, home, and family.

Many of the nation's social ills arise when families become estranged from each other because fathers become workaholics in pursuit of the dollar, and forget that whatever else they are in this world, they are first and foremost husbands and fathers, whether they like it or not. Then there are mothers who become so involved outside the home that they forget that when they brought children into the world, they accepted the primary responsibility of raising those children. Too often, in the pursuit of the buck, or social activities or causes, they lose sight of what is most important in their lives and forget that their first responsibility is as wife and mother.

I am not being chauvinistic. This cuts both ways for both sexes.

Don't allow the pursuit of money to canker you. When Paul said, "The love of money is the root of all evil,"** he was overstating a basically valid point. If you fall in love with an investment, it can become a spiritual sickness.

What we allow our money to do to us can have great impact on our happiness and spiritual welfare. Poverty is a spiritual test, just as wealth is also a spiritual test. Whether it cankers the soul or expands the spirit depends on how you react to it. I've been rich, I've been poor, but I was happy both ways (although rich was better). My family passed the

*Matt. 6:19-20.
**I Tim. 6:10.

poverty test beautifully. We were united. We pulled together. But I failed the rich test the first time around. In fact, that's probably why we became poor for a while. My values were distorted, my kids were becoming the spoiled rich kids on the block, and I was about to lose the things that I treasured most. One day after we had lost our money in 1968, we were discussing what had happened to our family and how the loss had really benefited all of us. My daughter Pam said, "Dad, I'm glad we lost our money before it did us any permanent harm." Not bad for a nine-year-old.

Don't let financial success bring you misery by eroding your values and becoming an obsession.

Fundamental Number 13. DARE TO BE DIFFERENT. The majority is always wrong! The financial methods that work now aren't the same ones that used to, and the crowd doesn't know that yet. You can't follow the crowd and win. The fact that you have read this far tells me that you dare to be different. "Contrary opinion" is a valid investment tool, although it has its limitations. I'm sure there were lots of great bargains in Vietnamese real estate the day before Saigon fell. Any principle can be extended to its illogical conclusion. But that doesn't invalidate the point that the most money is made by a brave minority who dare to be different. And they will be the most likely ones to not lose everything in the Inflationary Eighties.

Fundamental Number 14. HAVE A SCENARIO, a framework for decision, which you regularly re-examine. Your decisions must always be consistent with that scenario. Here is what I think the future looks like, and what I think you should do.

The Crystal Ball

1981 is a recession year, the second half of a "double dip" that began in 1980. We spent the first six months of this recession arguing whether we were in one, just as we did in

1974. Every time there's a recession, liberal politicians and economists say, "We can't fight inflation at the expense of poor people. We've got to fight recession and unemployment. Crank up the printing press! There is slack in the economy, so we can afford to run deficits to stimulate the economy without causing inflation."

Remember that phrase: "There is slack in the economy." That's like a water skier with a 50-foot rope who starts out in the water 10 feet behind the boat and yells, "Hit it! There is slack in the rope." The resulting legal government "counterfeiting" or new money will lay the groundwork for the next higher surge of inflation when the slack disappears. The odds are roughly 7-3 that we'll come out of this recession with a burst of inflation which will take off sometime late in 1982.

Fundamental Number 15. HAVE BETWEEN $3,000 and $10,000 OF BULLION-TYPE GOLD AND/OR SILVER COINS for each member of the family, if you can afford it. If not, do the best you can. The criteria for selecting those coins is covered in detail in *How to Prosper During the Coming Bad Years,* but I will briefly summarize it later in the book.

This is the world's scared money. Inflation, war, or political turmoil sends the price skyward. The odds are we will see all of these in the Disintegrating Eighties.

Fundamental Number 16. AVOID PAPER AND BUY THINGS, with a few careful exceptions. In the long-term inflationary spiral, the stockpiling of consumer goods, including such items as automobile tires and spare parts, paper products, dehydrated food, light bulbs, and hunting ammunition, will beat inflation over the long-term. These items should all be fully paid for. Obviously, if your funds are limited, you have to start at the bottom of the scale and do the best you can, but any beat-inflation step, no matter how small, is a move in the right direction.

Fundamental Number 17. WATCH INTEREST RATES.

This is easier said than done because it's hard to predict the course of interest rates.

Interest rates are crucial to my decision processes. When interest rates are rising at the same time as the inflation rate, generally gold and silver prices are rising too. When interest rates are rising, bonds are always falling, and the opposite is also true. A coherent beat-inflation investment program could merely catch the major swings in interest rates, moving back and forth between metals and bonds, and do very well indeed, but I still prefer to diversify more broadly than that.

Fundamental Number 18. WATCH THE MARKETS.

Don't watch the markets just to decide whether you should invest in those markets. Watch the markets to determine and confirm your basic economic scenario. For example, if I'm trying to decide whether inflation is peaking and a recession is at hand, I look at the plywood and lumber markets, the beef market, the cotton market, the gold and silver markets, and the Treasury bill and bond futures. If they are all turning downward (except the T-bills and the bonds, which should be turning up) and seem to be in technical retreat, that means that inflation and interest rates will ease and a recession could be near at hand. If, on the other hand, the opposite is true (and I'm not talking about just a one-day or two-day move), then inflation will be on the increase and interest rates and gold will be rising as they respond to these fundamental economic directions. Markets tend to tip off these events well in advance. Well before the bottom of the recession we are in now, all of these markets will turn, telling us that the bottom is at hand. If, when they reach the point where they should turn up, they plunge abruptly and show no signs of bottoming, that will mean that this recession has no bottom, that my forecast of a turnaround into renewed inflation is wrong, and it will be time to start bailing out of my beat-inflation positions and into depression and deflation hedges.

This piece of advice probably won't be of any help to you

without the technical background to understand the markets. But at least you know how I make my decisions, so that if you become a subscriber to *The Ruff Times*, you will understand why I do what I do when I do it.

And here are my last three fundamentals—the intangibles.

Fundamental Number 19. DON'T BE A SITTING DUCK. On the small farm I recently moved to, there was a pen full of rabbits and a 4-foot fence. Living with the rabbits were two mallard ducks who thought they were feathered rabbits. They were perfectly capable of flying. In fact, they often did fly up 10 or 15 feet, but they never crossed the invisible barrier of those 4-foot walls and they always settled right back down into the pen.

We never worried about our ducks flying out. They couldn't. They had built their own fences.

One day, one of the kids left a gate open and the ducks walked out and one was attacked by a dog. He didn't think he could fly, so he was bitten up pretty badly and died a few days later.

Our Member Services Consultants spend considerable time talking to people who complain that they can't do this, or they can't do that, because they are "too old," "too poor," "too scared," or "too something." They also have built their own fences.

The self-imposed limit is man's only unconquerable enemy. Financial and personal survival in the difficult years ahead may depend on whether or not you are willing to break out of your self-imposed limits. Here are some of those fences.

1. The "I've Always Done It This Way and I'm Scared to Change" fence. People with this fence have usually inherited a stock from their parents or their grandparents, or they are widows whose husbands left them some funds invested in long-term bonds or CDs, and they are living off the income. Although they can intellectually recognize that inflation will devastate the value of those investments, they simply can't do

170

anything about it. They are paralyzed by their self-imposed limits. Any change that leads into new territory raises fears that they might make a mistake.

2. The "I Need Income" fence. They say, "All right, I believe you that inflation is going to destroy my annuity, my CDs, and my bonds, but I need income. I have no choice." My answer is: "One fine way to safely get income without your capital being wiped out by inflation in this crazy environment is to buy an income-producing piece of property, preferably in a small town where you can still buy a positive cash flow."

They then say, "I don't want to do that. I don't want to get up at 2:00 A.M. to unclog a toilet or worry about tenants and advertising and all those things. I'm too old for that. Tell me something that will meet my needs without having to do all that. And don't tell me to buy South African gold shares. I don't understand that either."

There isn't any other answer that gives you both income and beat-inflation capital growth potential, unless you are willing to accept high risk. Buying income property is not "speculation." You are investing for income and betting that general inflation will give you capital appreciation at the same time. It's a real safe bet. However, because of your self-imposed limits (fear, inertia, stubbornness, or all three), you will probably sit there quietly and be financially devastated by inflation.

3. The "I'm Too Poor to Do Anything" fence. This is perhaps the highest fence of all. I've been poor twice, probably twice as many times as you have. My mother was a seamstress who literally took sewing into the home to feed us. She gave me love, three square meals a day, and the clothing I needed. She even scraped and sacrificed so I could have the voice lessons that would help me prepare for the professional singing career I planned. We didn't have a car. I had to hitchhike or take the bus everywhere I went until I was

twenty-two years old. I didn't own my first car until I was twenty-five, and that was an old clunker.

After I had my business problems in 1968, we again went through three years of devastating poverty with a big family to support. I could have simply said, "I'm too poor." But I despise excuses in myself or others.

A variation on this theme is the person who is making a middle-class salary, living in a middle-class home, leading a middle-class life, and has too much month left at the end of his money, while next door there's a neighbor making the same amount of money with the same amount of responsibilities who is saving something every month and has built up an investment fund. The difference between the two is the establishment of priorities, and discipline.

Some people get mad at me because they feel they don't have the resources to follow all of my advice. Most middle-class Americans could start accumulating $50 to $100 a month if they were simply willing to give up some other things. Almost anyone can reduce his standard of living in order to accumulate an investment fund. There's no way you will beat inflation until you do.

If you think you are limited, you are. Frankly, I have no sympathy, patience, or respect for those who simply accept the status quo and, like my ducks, have built the invisible barriers which cage them.

We are living in a financial environment that requires fundamental changes of financial strategies—movement into those things which have been considered imprudent and speculative in the past. Today's risky speculation is now yesterday's prudent investment, and vice versa. If you don't accept this and act accordingly, you will be devastated by inflation. The only impenetrable walls are the ones we build ourselves.

Whether or not you make it in the Dangerous Decade, will depend on whether or not you remove those fences, or decide there are no fences at all and that you can do anything that you choose to do.

I'm sure that those of you who have no such fences have been bored with this, but I believe this disease infects approximately half of you, and I am personally frustrated because that half are the least likely to take my advice. Also, they are the ones who most often beg for help. They are destined to snatch defeat from the jaws of victory. If you let imaginary limitations block you from taking good advice, the wild dogs of inflation and economic disruption may bite you, and you may die financially.

If this book does nothing more than persuade you that you can spread your wings, you just might make it through the Inflationary Eighties.

Fundamental Number 20. CONTINUE THE FIGHT TO ELECT MORE FREE-MARKET, HARD-MONEY-ORIENTED PEOPLE to the Congress of the United States in 1982 and 1984. They can't prevent this inflation scenario from developing, but they can help keep the Ship of State from sinking so the nation and its institutions will get through this safely. The Congress is where the action is. We got off to a good start in the last election, but we can't rest on our laurels. More in Part III.

Fundamental Number 21. BET ON THE LONG-TERM FUTURE OF AMERICA, but not its currency. If America has no long-term future, there is no safe haven anywhere. The Arabs are smart. They are betting on inflation and our long-term future by buying our land; they invested a billion dollars in Florida alone in the first six months of 1979. This nation has the best chance of enduring even that with its freedom and its markets intact. Buy tangible assets right here at home. Keep most of your assets right here at home. America is the world's best long-term bet.

CHAPTER 8

Succeeding by Avoiding Failure

Most how-to books on successful living, successfa¹ investing, successful business, or successful marriage tiptoe around the subject of failure out of fear of being "negative." That's a serious mistake. My basic investment philosophy presumes that your chances of success increase if you squarely face and examine the possible paths to failure and insulate yourself against them. In my investment decisions, I try to wear a belt and suspenders, and I get them laid out long before I ever need them. If you can determine those areas where you are most likely to fail and take steps to prevent that failure, your chance of success increases dramatically. As the chance of failure goes down, the chance of success rises proportionately.

There are three kinds of failure which we must treat here.

First, there is the failure of your own financial strategy. People fail because they have an unsound investment philosophy out of tune with the times, or because they take wild fliers on margin which could hurt them more than they think, or because they plunge with too high a percentage of their money. That's like the gambler with a $1,000 bankroll who throws $900 on the table for his first bet. He simply isn't in a position to absorb the inevitable losses when circumstances temporarily run against him. He is wiped out, and out of the game.

The second failure, which will eventually get most Americans, is the failure of many of the systems around you on which you depend for comfortable, convenient, stable, civilized life. For example, inflation is the failure of the money to hold its value. Your financial and personal strategies must insulate you against this failure.

There is also the failure of the government to maintain a climate of freedom and stability so that you can make long-range plans.

There is the failure of the cities to continue to be fiscally sound so they can provide essential services on which you have come to depend.

There is the failure of energy sources to eventually be translated into gas in your car and heat and light in your home, available at the flick of a switch.

Your strategies must acknowledge those real, or potentially real, sources of failure and must structure your life so that if present trends continue, and any of these systems come down around your ears, the effect on you will be minimized.

Failure Avoidance is the main theme of your strategy for surviving the Inflationary Eighties.

My 1968 business failure affected me even more profoundly than I thought it did when I wrote about it in *How to Prosper During the Coming Bad Years*. That bankruptcy was too rotten an experience to be repeated, so I buried myself in a study of that mess and identified the areas of failure in business judgment, people management, and money management. The resulting insights made it possible for me to plan my personal life and my advice to my clients to avoid failure. For example, the whole concept of food storage and survival coins is a fall-back Failure Avoidance position, so that home base is so secure that you can go ahead and take some prudent risks, knowing that you are not completely out of the financial game if they don't pan out. All of *The Ruff Times*' corporate and marketing decisions have provided fail-safe mechanisms so that if something went wrong it couldn't wipe us out. As a result, we were able to build Target Publishers, with almost nonexistent financial resources, into a viable, sound publishing company.

Yardsticks

By what can you measure your financial success over the next several years?

Success will be measured by the sheer fact that you have retained your purchasing power, your independence, your freedom, and your health. Anything over that is a bonus. The concept of an emergency supply of food is not negative. It is an insurance position—the avoidance of failure. Having silver coins to spend in case of a total collapse of the currency through inflation assures that no matter what else happens, you will not "fail" to be able to buy whatever is available in the marketplace.

Ever since 1968 I've instinctively conducted my personal life, my business life, and my financial life with an eye toward avoiding failure. The net result has been success. I have had some financial success, professional success, publishing success, and, in my opinion, a degree of spiritual, home, and family success. The essence of the philosophy is, if you can objectively evaluate every obstacle that might get in your path, prepare a contingency plan, and insulate yourself from a domino, snowball-running-down-hill disaster, then you can afford to be brave in taking advantage of opportunities.

The farmer does that by "hedging" his crops in the commodities market. Harry Browne uses this principle when he suggests you hedge against your beat-inflation position in precious metals by buying long-term stock options, where the amount of money at risk is low, and you are protected with substantial highly leveraged profits if your precious metals position doesn't work out.

When I want to speculate in gold on a highly leveraged basis, I buy options on gold shares, such as ASA (see Chapters 9 and 12), rather than futures contracts. In the futures market, I can get "margin calls" and be locked into "limit down" days where I can't get out and have to keep pumping money into my broker's pocket that I never really wanted to risk. With an option position, my risk is limited to the money I have already shelled out, and the leverage is just as good. I won't ever get a margin call. I have chosen the path with the least failure potential, without giving up any potential profits.

I believe I have identified our society's most vulnerable social, financial, and political systems, such as big cities, the banking system, pensions, the liquidation of corporate America by inflation, taxes and government regulation, and, of course, the money, so you can avoid being dragged down by their failures. However, as we try to save the system with the political activities described in Part III, we must be sure to spend our limited resources shoring up our defenses in those areas where the system is most likely to fail, in order of their degrees of vulnerability.

My survival plan is based on the assumption that if I am wrong about all my investments, I can eat and have a place to live. That is why I have a good storage program, and why I would prefer to be out of debt with my home, even when inflation makes it advantageous to be highly leveraged, because I don't want to lose it if I can't make the payments.

As this is written, I think there is a 70% chance of a gradually accelerating inflation beginning after this recession, and a 30% chance that I am wrong and we will crash through the bottom into a deflationary depression. So what is my strategy? I have 70% of my money in inflation hedges and

30% in deflation hedges, such as bonds. As the odds shift, I'll shift my investment. I won't do as well as if I guessed right with 100% of my money, but I will have avoided the possibility of total failure, and I can sleep.

That means that I can take fairly high risk positions on either side of the equation and come out well, making a shift of my resources as the course becomes clearer, one way or the other.

I have used this principle in my relationship with my wife. I try to anticipate the things that bother her and plan my life to minimize distressing incidents so that my home life is smoother and happier.

I teach my teenagers to look at everything that could possibly go wrong with their lives, and prepare a position in advance to deal with the most likely troubles and temptations that can drop into their lives, and consequently into mine. My daughters Pam and Sharon adopted this principle when they wisely concluded that a dark night in the back seat of a car wasn't the time to decide about their moral standards, so they thought out their strategy in advance when their heads were clear. They tell me this Failure Avoidance planning stood them in good stead, although they are a bit sketchy on details.

In the final analysis, the concept is much like that used by Vince Lombardi when he took over the Green Bay Packers of the National Football League. He decided that if they were ever going to be winners, he would have to start by building a defense. At first, their offense wasn't anything to shout about, but they started winning almost immediately and became a dynasty, based on the reasonable assumption that if the other team can't score (you avoid failure), you can beat them. As the chances of loss (failure) go down, the odds of victory (success) increase. Occasionally, you can run a fumble into the end zone, or score a safety, or get the ball back close to the other guy's goal line, so your offense doesn't have to be as good. It's easier to drive thirty-five yards than to start on your own 20-yard line. In the inflation and taxes investment game, however, a tie is as good as a win, because if you simply break even in purchasing power, you have won.

I have seen many carefully constructed beat-inflation programs shot down by speculative fever, when someone took a high-risk flyer without adequately insuring himself against the chance of failure. It happens in the commodity market every day. One abrupt "limit down" market move can wipe out years of hard work and savings and prudent investment. I paid a lot of money to learn this lesson. As we move into a recession followed by a runaway inflation, the big buzzword of our times will be "failures": personal failures, corporate failures, and small-business failures: Chrysler, Ford, savings and loans, banks, Social Security, cities, and Heaven knows what else. Because most of you must interface with these organizations and structures, their failure will be your failure, unless you failure-proof your life.

Never Catch a Boat That Might Sink

My most useful Failure Avoidance technique is to "miss most boats." Some people jump on any investment boat that's leaving. This bit of homely philosophy has gotten me in more trouble with my subscribers than any other principle, but it has saved me a fortune and a lot of unnecessary anguish.

Let's take a concrete example.

In October, 1979, gold and silver were going nuts. Silver had roared from $6 to around $18 without taking a breath. And gold had moved almost without a pause from $288 an ounce to over $430.

At that time, I concluded that the markets had become totally irrational and were temporarily unsuitable for hedging against inflation and providing emotional security, which is what gold and silver are supposed to do. When your security blanket is having a nervous breakdown, it is no longer doing its job.

I suggested that my newsletter subscribers should examine their emotional makeup and choose from among three alternatives. I said:

There are several appropriate strategies to use with your survival gold and silver coins.
1. Keep them, but only if you are absolutely positive that you can live with the emotional trauma of being paper rich one day and half as rich the next, and it is possible that that will be the case. Not one person in a thousand can go through that and sleep well.
2. Sell enough to get back your original investment, plus about 15% per annum (after-tax) to make up for inflation, then hang on to the rest. You'll have no money in it and wild fluctuations should not be too traumatic.
3. Sell it all, park the funds in Capital Preservation Fund (a money market fund yielding around 12% at the time) until your nerves settle down, then go into bonds, diamonds and colored gemstones as rational, conservative, low-risk, beat-inflation alternatives.

I stressed at the time that this was not an assessment of the market price:

I will emphasize again, this is not an effort to call a top. I don't know which way gold is going now. It could swing $200 or more in either direction, and that's what makes it so dangerous.

The key is temperament. I have watched people ride markets all the way up, then all the way down, then panic out when the market is low. If you can avoid those emotional responses, wait it out.

I then forecast that the time would come that, if you had liquidated at those levels, you would have a chance to buy back in more cheaply at some future time.

After taking off to an $850 top six months later (making me look like an idiot for months), gold had plummeted back to $460, only $30 higher than my October get-out point. That $30 was more than covered by the 12% to 16% yields we earned in the money market fund into which we put your money.

Silver soared from $18 to $50, then plunged back to a low of $10.60, 38% lower than the point at which we got out.

If you had stayed in for a while and tried to liquidate at a profit during the wild rise, you would have found it was not as easy as it sounds.

When you tried to phone your favorite coin dealer, you probably couldn't get through, because his lines were flooded by panicky buyers and sellers.

One large coin dealer in Minneapolis, Investment Rarities—a firm recommended by us (see Appendix)—had so many people trying to reach their toll-free number that they fouled up the entire WATS telephone system for the state of Minnesota, sending electronic gremlins all over the state.

During this wild rise, silverware, silverplate, and old coins had come flooding out of attics and strong boxes, and people were standing in line for hours outside coin dealers. When they finally did get through the door, there was a good chance the dealer had exhausted his capital and wasn't buying, or he was waiting for the next day's quotes, being afraid of getting caught in a dramatic decline, as the silver market was fluctuating as much as $10 in a day, and gold made a $160 round trip one day. Then if he did give you a silver quote, the odds are it would have been 20% to 40% below the spot bullion silver price, because he was selling it off to the refineries who were buying it at discounts of more than 20%, and they were backed up for more than a year. Then you would possibly have had to wait months for your money, because many coin dealers were being forced by the refineries to wait for payment until it was actually refined, so the dealers imposed the same requirement on their customers.

If you were in gold or silver futures, you found that the market would be "up the limit" or "down the limit" for as many as four days in a row and no trades could take place, so you couldn't take profits at the time or price of your choosing, or cut your losses and get out. In addition to that, the margin requirements had been increased so dramatically that you might have been squeezed out of the market for lack of capital.

All in all, it was a wild, irrational time caused by bullion buying out of the Middle East, frenzied get-rich-quick futures trading, and the "Hunt brothers incident."

Because I don't like to catch a boat that might sink, I decided to miss this sailing. For months, as gold went up, I took a lot of flak, both from angry subscribers who had opted to sell and blamed me for missing the boat, and from some other hard-money investment advisors who are always saying, "Buy gold," or "Buy silver," and were looking like heroes for a while, as even a stopped clock is right twice a day.

The net bottom line of all of this is that the "Never catch a boat that might sink" fundamental became more important than the "Hedge against inflation with gold and silver coins" principle. And when principles are in conflict, I choose the more crucial Failure Avoidance concept.

Forbes magazine did catch the spirit of what I was trying to do when they wrote in their July 7, 1980 issue:

> And while he urges followers to keep a year's supply of food in the basement for chaotic times, he is no hard money fanatic and has a shrewd sense of the practical. Last Fall during gold and silver's wild price jumps, Ruff, worried by the insane markets, dropped his long-standing buy recommendations on the two precious metals. Ruff's advice, which proved premature, may have cost nimble readers profits on the way to $850 gold and $50 silver, but it also saved an equal number of amateurs some horrendous losses when the metals crashed back to Earth

a few weeks later. And this Spring, just before interest rates turned down, Ruff urged readers ''To throw caution to the wind and buy bonds.'' His timing was excellent— bond prices rose sharply.

''Never catch a boat that might sink'' saved me six months of investment anguish and the emotional excesses that lead to stupid investment decisions. Besides, if I had been able to sell at the top, it might have convinced me and my subscribers that I am smarter than I really am, and I might have been trying to ride speculative bubbles for the rest of my life, losing my money more often than not. And it only takes one such loss to wipe out years of painfully earned gains.

Only board the boat when the odds are overwhelmingly in your favor and the fundamentals are behaving normally. I have missed lots of boats. I have missed moves in pork bellies, in soybeans, in platinum, in gold, and in gambling stocks. But in the more than five years that I've been publishing my letter, I have never caught a boat that sank.

If I had called the top, it would have been only luck. I acted on principle. Sound principles have a way of working out for the best. Don't be afraid to miss a boat that might sink. If you don't fail, you are still in the game.

The rest of Part II offers some personal strategies to sidestep and avoid the failure of corporate America, banks, energy, government, and the money.

CHAPTER 9

The Flip Side
of the
Liquidation of America

In the chapter entitled "The Liquidation of America," we raised some serious questions about most of the traditional American savings and investment vehicles, such as the fixed-return investments with banks and savings and loans, and debt instruments such as bonds. We also discussed the liquidation of corporate America and probably scared the whey out of you about your pension and the stock market.

Well, the news is not all bad. There are some useful exceptions to the rule, and there are some ways to avoid liquidation and work with these markets in the Inflationary Eighties.

In this chapter I won't discuss the legislative solutions to the underlying problems. That comes later. Here we will use the judo principle—the technique of "going with the flow" and using the strength of your opponent to defeat him. We're going to show you some ways to use inflation to beat the inflation game and have a fighting chance of enhancing your assets, using carefully selected classes of securities.

In *How to Prosper During the Coming Bad Years* I explored thoroughly the use of gold and silver coins, diamonds, and small-town real estate to beat inflation. These are all still excellent long-term inflation hedges. They will "beat inflation plus a little bit," and probably then some. I don't propose to cover all that material again, and I suggest that you pick up a copy of *How to Prosper* and digest that material. It is just as valid now as when it was written, but there are some more exciting alternatives, including some that might give you good income while hedging against inflation.

The great dilemma for most investors, especially widows and retirees, is that in the pursuit of income, they have been seduced into fixed return investments which expose them to the ravages of inflation. It is possible to beat the game both ways.

Before we proceed, however, I would like to resurrect two paragraphs from *How to Prosper* and put the gold and silver subject to rest for now:

> Gold and silver are counter-cyclical to paper investments. That means that price-wise they move in the opposite direction to paper. When paper-based economies are booming and everyone is confident, and inflation is under control and no one sees any real dark clouds on the horizon, the price of these metals tends to decline, whereas, if inflation is running rampant, war is imminent, or people are uncertain about the stability of their political institutions, the price of these metals tends to rise.

> Until the invention of the printing press, silver and gold coins were the only money used by major civilizations. The invention of the printing press introduced paper money, and ever since then, governments have

tried to substitute it for precious metals with varying degrees of success. Paper currencies rise and fall, but gold and silver always come back— generally after the collapse.

Why Not South African Gold Shares?

In the past I've been generally cautious about South African gold shares, not because I disliked the companies, but because I was concerned about the potential for social and racial disruption in South Africa. Our government's official policy toward them was hostile. We were doing everything we could to make it difficult for South Africa to be an accepted member of the community of nations, while the stiff-necked Afrikaaners who run South Africa were creating a lot of their own problems.

The Soviet Union is the world's second-largest gold and diamond producer after South Africa, and much of the foreign exchange they desperately need in order to buy grain on the world market comes from gold and diamond sales. It would be bullish for the value of their reserves in the ground if South Africa could be put out of production, and much Soviet clandestine activity in Africa, in my opinion, has been aimed at that long-range objective. And, of course, South Africa is also a treasure trove of uranium and other strategic metals.

Ordinarily, South African gold stocks and the price of gold tend to rise and fall together. In fact, many shares are "leveraged," and move up or down even more dramatically than the metal. During the 50% collapse of gold prices in 1975, South African gold stocks lost over 80% of their market values. South African gold mines were subject to great political risk due to increased terrorism and a possible onslaught of black unrest within their country. It was possible that South African gold production could be impaired by political and civil disorders, and the gold stocks could collapse while the world price of gold would soar.

Because of these concerns, I consistently recommended gold and ignored the South African gold shares, and we did very well.

Now my attitude has changed. One sound way to invest in stocks, get income and capital appreciation, and beat inflation to survive the Inflationary Eighties is to buy South African gold shares. The risks are more than acceptable. I have reversed my position for several reasons.

I spent a week in South Africa early in 1980 as a guest speaker at a National Committee for Monetary Reform conference. I had lunch with Senator Owen Horwood, the South African finance minister. My wife, Kay, and I took a helicopter ride over Johannesburg and traveled the length of the "reef" from which most of South Africa's gold has been and is being extracted. We hovered at 500 feet over Soweto, the black township on the outskirts of Johannesburg, and swooped low over Pretoria, the capital. I had lengthy conversations with several of South Africa's leading businessmen.

I came home convinced that the South African businessmen were right in their contention that they have *at least* five years of sufficient social stability to provide reasonable safety for the ownership of South African securities.

Some interesting anomalies popped up during my visit. For example, South Africans told me that our newspapers exaggerate their problems. I read the South African papers every day I was there, and their papers were a lot scarier than anything you've read about South Africa in *The New York Times* or the *San Francisco Chronicle*. The papers are full of reports of such things as gentlemanly debates between blacks and white Afrikaaners in the Parliament over whether or not the blacks can use the Parliamentary dining room. There were reports of massive boycott demonstrations by "colored" (Indian and mulatto) students protesting unequal expenditures for education. There was a daily column by Dr. Christiaan Barnard, the famous heart transplant surgeon, raging against government racial policies. The newspapers are full of racial turmoil, but it is an amazingly healthy kind of ferment. The government either does not or cannot cut down on open, public dissent. There is no question that the momentum is toward the elimination of racial restrictions, despite the thunderings of those stubborn Dutchmen who control the government. I found no racism among the influential South African businessmen I interviewed. They all felt that their country is moving rapidly toward the elimination of racial barriers. And without exception, they would welcome the elimination of the apartheid racial laws.

As we hovered over Soweto, we got a feeling for the South African dilemma. There are approximately 4 million whites and 20 million blacks. Most of those blacks came to this part of Africa later than the whites, drawn by the prospect of work in the gold mines. Soweto has a population of about 1 million, all living in small, identical, government-built homes, paying rent of approximately $5. a month. They have plumbing and water, but no electricity. The dilemma is pretty well summed up by the fact that the blacks know that they do not have equal housing with the whites, and the whites feel that all that the blacks do have is provided by white tax dollars, and that they are carrying four-fifths of the nation on their backs with very high tax rates, and they are doing the best they can. Also many blacks are living in comparative luxury, when contrasted with the villages they voluntarily left to work in the mines.

While on a visit to the mines, we were shown classes where blacks from all over Africa were being trained to work. There were six students in one class who spoke six totally different languages. They had to be taught a common "mine language" so they could communicate on the job. Some come from bush tribes where only the women work, and they literally have to be taught the idea. They contract for a certain period of time, then return to their own countries, after which most return across the border to again find work.

The blacks have a tremendous vested interest in the financial success of South African industry. The Zulu chieftain who spoke to the NCMR conference said to me that he thought the worst enemies of the blacks in South Africa are the American leftists who are trying to cut off American investment in South Africa. The ones who would be hurt the most would be the blacks themselves. The proposed sanctions against investment in South Africa would have more adverse effects in Detroit than in South Africa, as strategic metals from South Africa are essential to industrialized economies around the world.

The businessmen I spoke to were immensely encouraged by recent developments on the African continent. The history of black rule in Africa seems to consist of a Marxist revolution, followed by black rulers utilizing free enterprise to line their pockets. The dictator of Mozambique, Samora Machel, is plunging toward capitalism to try to salvage his devastated economy, and is actively negotiating commercial, industrial, and political relations with South Africa. The settlement in Rhodesia and the general conciliatory attitude of Zimbabwe's Prime Minister Robert Mugabe toward the whites is encouraging to the South Africans, who feel that such accommodation is the wave of the future in Africa. In any event, they seem to feel, and I am inclined to agree with them, that South Africa has bought itself several years of relative stability.

When I asked about the inherent risks in buying South African stocks, the answer was, "The risks are already discounted in the price. You can buy South African gold mining shares yielding as much as 24%." They felt that the future risks were sufficiently discounted, because you could get your investment back in dividends, even if everything fell apart in three to five years. But they don't expect things to fall apart.

All the South Africans I spoke to seem to feel that their racial problems will be solved, that the forces are irresistible in that direction, that the black leadership in South Africa is rational and nondoctrinaire, and that there is little or no communist influence in their country's black population.

My opinion? I think they are a bit naive, but they are right about the gold shares, providing you catch the right cycle in the gold market.

My last impression is that South Africa is critical to the well-being of the West. South Africa controls the sea lanes around it through which a significant percentage of the world's oil must pass. It is rich in gold, silver, platinum, chromium, uranium, and other strategic metals. In fact, by some quirk of geology, many of the critical metals which South Africa produces are also found in abundance in the Soviet Union, and almost nowhere else. Together, these two nations literally control the defense establishments of the world.

South Africa is first in the supply of no less than eleven of these minerals and holds the dominant position in the export of at least eighteen. In terms of production, the country ranks number one in the case of ten of the minerals and ranks two and three in the case of three or four other minerals. It is the principal exporter of platinum, vermiculite, vanadium gold, manganese, ferrochrome, andalusite/sillimanite, diamonds (gem), chromium ore, manganese, and ferromanganese.

Johannesburg is a modern, bustling city with skyscrapers and shopping malls that reminds me of nothing so much as a combination of Minneapolis and Denver. We saw magnificent homes with swimming pools and tennis courts, nothing higher than $150,000, even after prices have doubled in the last nine months. The real estate market seems to be reflecting a sunnier outlook for the future. When a nation is in imminent danger, the first market to give way is real estate. There is no sign of this in South Africa.

I am immensely impressed with the energy, thrift, and

entrepreneurial skill of the people I met, and with the importance of South Africa to our well-being, and I am convinced that the Carter Administration's attitudes toward South Africa were stupid and damaging to the black people we are trying to help. The Reagan Administration probably won't make the same mistakes. Left alone, I believe South Africa will solve most of its racial problems in the next ten years. If we agitate, we could cause a tragedy in South Africa. It is moving in the direction of equality. If it is an evolutionary process, then South Africa will be saved for the Western world. If revolution is forced upon South Africa or encouraged by us, we could lose a crucial corner of the world and would not know the real importance of what we had lost until we had lost it. We cannot allow South Africa to be anything other than a capitalist, free enterprise country.

South Africa is the sixth strongest military power on earth. It cannot be defeated by any combination of its neighbors, and it may even have an atomic bomb.

All of these factors reinforce my opinion that investment in South African securities does not have a high probability of producing an unpleasant surprise for an investor in South African companies during the Inflationary Eighties.

The Bad News Seesaw

Gold is a "bad news bear." When everybody is worried about war, inflation, or political instability, the price of gold goes up. As I mentioned earlier, South African gold stocks will tend to parallel the price of gold, rising or falling approximately the same percentage, and some will substantially exceed the rate of increase in the price of gold, for reasons I'll explain in a moment.

The price of the shares is undervalued in relation to their dividends, simply because so many people are afraid of them. This gives you an outstanding opportunity to buy an actively traded stock at such prices that the dividend yield would return all of your money in four years if the price of gold, the dividend, or the price of the stock did not go up.

I do expect the stocks to rise to a price-earnings ratio more in line with their real worth, but that's not crucial to making money in those stocks.

Let's recapitulate the concepts already covered, and add a few more.

1. As the rate of inflation increases, the price of gold will increase spectacularly. Two thousand dollars to three thousand dollars an ounce in this decade is not unreasonable, possibly by mid-1983. This will result in spectacular increases in earnings and yields of South African gold mines, which tend to pay out a significant percentage of their earnings in dividends. This will drive up the price.

2. The Johannesburg stock market is active and has sufficient trading volume to provide good liquidity. Stocks can be bought and sold almost as quickly and easily as you can buy and sell on the New York Stock Exchange.

3. There's not a lot of gold in the world. All the world's gold supply could fit into a cube 90 feet square, and even if the South African mines were to go all out, production-wise, plus continuing the recycling of the "dumps" (the great piles of worked-over ore that surround those mines, even in downtown Johannesburg), they would not be able to significantly dilute the supply above ground. More and more people are becoming convinced that inflation is inevitable, epidemic, and incurable and they will be hoarding gold, and I believe that the demand will grow at a rate exceeding production, obviously driving up prices in the Inflationary Eighties.

It is not only conceivable but likely that before 1985, the dividends paid by some South African gold mines will exceed today's price of the gold shares.

4. Many managers of large pension funds, mutual funds, and private fortunes are now beginning to seek out investments that have good track records as inflation hedges and are moving away from the traditional "prudent man" type in-

vestments. As an example of this trend, Robert Salomon, partner in the prestigious Wall Street firm of Salomon Brothers, recently stated:

> Gold in all forms has produced investment yields far outpacing paper stocks and bonds. Gold has yielded an annual return of 28% over the past five years while stocks performed at an average of 6.4% each year. New investors are finally waking up to reality, and this will be a strong, bullish factor for gold as long as inflation is a threat.
>
> As inflation has become institutionalized, those institutions, pension funds, bank trust departments, insurance companies and commodity and mutual funds, have begun to conclude that the stock and bond markets have not exactly been a prudent place to have their money invested. In the newfound search for investments that will exceed the rate of inflation, some institutions are now purchasing the stocks of gold mining companies. Not very many, but it's a start. When you consider that it was just over a decade ago that institutions such as pension funds were first permitted to own stocks at all, rather than their old prudent standby, bonds, institutional ownership of gold bullion cannot be too far away, as well as a vast increase in the ownership of gold shares.

Thomas Wolfe, former director of the Treasury Department's office of gold and silver operations, believes more institutional buying of gold and gold shares is inevitable, as pension fund managers tend to be faddists.

5. We have had two examples in 1980 of the potential for huge losses in bonds by long-term investors, a concept that was unthinkable only a year or two ago. Wildly swinging interest rates have caused such incredible fluctuations in bond prices that everyone is terrified of them. Of course, that creates in-and-out trading opportunities, but that's small com-

fort for the widows and orphans who bought bonds for income to be held to maturity. The institutional money that would have gone into bonds has to go somewhere. Some of it will go into gold.

6. The U.S. stock market has gone sideways for fourteen years, as discussed in Chapter 3, but with gold's newfound respectability broadening the demand, the long-term trend for this beautiful, yellow metal can only be up, and the gold shares will not only participate but are already leading the charge into the eighties.

To titillate you with the names of some of the born-again gold bugs, the list includes Alaska's pension funds; the Suburban Bank Group of Palatine, Illinois; AETNA Life and Casualty; and the Endowment Fund of Pennsylvania's Gettysburg College.

7. When you are buying for "survival purposes," as opposed to investment or speculation (a distinction I made in my previous book), you should buy gold coins, for example, Krugerrands, Maple Leaves, and the various Mexican gold coins. These should be physically stashed away somewhere to protect you against the possibility of war or runaway inflation, based on the assumption that one day you might have to physically go out with them in your hand and buy something. If you want to hedge against inflation, or invest long-term, you buy the physical metal. If you want to invest short-term for capital appreciation, long-term for income, or very short-term for speculation, you're better off buying the mining shares because of their liquidity and dividends.

You need not become an expert gold share analyst to invest in South African gold shares. You just need to understand certain simple basics so that you can give your broker some guidance. There are several ways to invest.

ASA Limited

Perhaps the easiest of all is simply to buy the shares of ASA, an investment trust, listed on the New York Stock

Exchange. ASA stands for American South African and, true to its name, ASA is required to maintain at least 50% of the value of its assets in South African gold share holdings. ASA is a South African corporation, and one of the few nondomestic listings on the New York Stock Exchange. ASA also has substantial holdings in DeBeers stock (diamonds) and a number of firms with large coal and uranium holdings. When you buy ASA you're getting diversification among a number of mining companies, and you own a stock that will generally parallel or exceed the price swings in gold. It's like owning a South African mutual fund.

My subscribers caught a heck of a runup in ASA stock and options in 1980. We bought at around $40 a share, and the price moved up to $91 before falling back to $40. ASA's disadvantage is that if you're looking for income, ASA's dividend yield averages only about 7.5%.

One ASA advantage is that you don't have to go through any of the complexities of buying South African shares on the Johannesburg Stock Exchange, even though it really isn't that hard. You can buy and sell ASA with a simple call to any broker in America where you've established an account. It doesn't matter whether the lines at the coin dealer are a mile long or not. You can still buy and sell your gold shares with a simple phone call.

Every time I think I'm prescient and courageous for my gold recommendations in the last six years, I'm a little humbled when I think of the interview I had with Jim Dines, the gutsy, original gold bug, on my new TV show. I asked Jim how long he had been recommending gold and gold shares. His answer was "Twenty years." He had put his clients into gold in Swiss banks when it was $35 an ounce. And he was pushing ASA when it was $2.50 a share. He has ridden out all the declines and taken the abuse that came during those declines.

Most investors don't have the time or the expertise to try to make specific decisions concerning stocks, and it was for this group of investors that mutual funds were created. As gold related investments have expanded in the recent past, there are a growing number of U.S. gold funds from which to choose. In descending order of performance over the past five years, some of the top funds are:

1. United Services
2. Strategic Investments
3. International Investors
4. Research Capital
5. Golconda Investors

As gold goes, so will they. The main characteristic of the funds, as opposed to ASA, is that they charge annual management fees of up to 1.5% of the fund's assets, and some have brokerage commissions as high as 8%. ASA is probably cheaper. Ask your broker for more details on these funds.

Buying ASA, which is a closed-end fund, or shares in one of the other gold mutual funds spreads the inherent risks of ownership, requires little of the investor, and guarantees liquidity. Not being tied to the fate of only one or two companies and their respective performance, investment fund shares should be regarded as an investment in the upward trend in the price of gold. Ideally, shares should be purchased when the price of gold is depressed by recession, a peace scare, or idle talk about comprehensive solutions to the problem of inflation. As in any market, buy when "the blood is running in the streets."

Rolling Your Own

If you have decided to make your own decisions on individual stocks, you need to decide whether you are investing for income or speculating for capital gains based on the movement of the shares. There are some shares that will give you more bang for the buck. They are generally not those that give you the most stable dividend returns. This is caused by differences in the mining company's cost of producing one ounce of gold.

The basic principles are fairly simple. Let's take an old-line, low-cost "heavy-weight" mining company that can produce one ounce of gold at a cost of $200 an ounce. If the price of gold is above $200, the mine is profitable. If it is below $200, the mine is not profitable. If gold is $600 an ounce, their profit is $400 an ounce. If gold moves to $650 an ounce, the mine's $400 an ounce profit is increased by $50, or 12.5%, and you can expect the share prices to move roughly 12.5%, give or take a few points. That mine is probably paying out a significant percentage of its profits in dividends and will be a fine income producer, to be held through thick and thin. Just as an upward swing in the gold price will have less effect on the price of the shares, the same is true on the downward side, so you can ride out the swings and enjoy your dividends, which should beat the rate of inflation, and then some. That big old heavy-weight mine will give you a good income and a lot less excitement than the "marginals."

Let's look at a "marginal" mine where it costs $500 to produce an ounce of gold. If the gold price is under $500 an ounce, you can bet that the price of that mining company's shares will be terribly depressed. But as the gold price approaches $500, and there is now a prospect of "no earnings" turning into earnings, these shares can move wildly. When the price of gold is fluctuating at about $500 and the mine is producing gold at a cost of $500 an ounce, the stock will usually be extremely volatile, reacting nervously to every blip in the gold price, as investors are trying to decide whether gold is headed for higher ground or lower ground. But as the price moves above $500, to $550 an ounce, this obviously becomes an exciting prospect for future income, as the dividends are as leveraged as the company profits and the price can soar. If the price goes from $550 to $600, a

$50-an-ounce profit turns into a $100-an-ounce profit, a 100% increase in the earnings, and gives you the prospect of a 100% increase in the share price.

Comparing our two mines, the heavy-weight low-cost producer would see some price appreciation with a $50 move in the price of gold, but not a heck of a lot. Our marginal mine seeing a $50 increase in the price of gold would probably go crazy price-wise, provided we picked one with the cost of production near the price of gold.

To sum it all up, if you want more bang for the buck, more potential profits, as well as more gut-wrenching swings to the down side, buy the "marginals" with a production cost near the price of gold. If you are interested in income over the long haul, buy the heavyweights and sock away your 20% or even greater dividends. The dividends of the future could easily return the purchase price of the stock.

Here is a list of South African shares by classification, all of which are actively traded. Some are pure gold shares, but some have a uranium kicker, making them even more interesting.

PURE GOLD SHARES

MARGINALS	MEDIUM-WEIGHTS	HEAVY-WEIGHTS
Durban Deep	E.T. Cons.	Winkels
E.R.P.M.	Kinross	Free State Geduld
Grootvlei	Doornfontein	St. Helena
Marrievale	Libanon	Western Holdings
South Roodepoort		East Driefontein
Wit Nigel		Kloof
Bracken		West Driefontein
Leslie		
Loraine		
Welkom		
Venters		
S.A. Lands (Sallies)		

MARGINALS	MEDIUM-WEIGHTS	HEAVY-WEIGHTS
Elsburg	Blyvooruitzicht	Buffelsfontein
Harmony	South Vaal	Hartebeestfontein
Stilfontein	Randfontein	President Brand
Western Areas	Zandpan	President Steyn
		Vaal Reefs
		Western Deep Levels

Heavy-weights: This category has a low cost of gold production (less than $150 an ounce). These mines usually have a life of at least twenty years.

Medium-weights: The cost of gold production is somewhat higher at $150 to $250 an ounce and the life expectancy is slightly lower at ten to fifteen years.

Marginals: A high cost of gold production (above $250 an ounce) is the hallmark of these mines, and the life of the mine depends on the gold price.

New Mines: These mines have just commenced, or are about to commence, major production tonnages. Some mines in this category are Deelkraal, Elandsrand, and Unisel.

The marginal mines' share prices tend to outperform those of the heavy-weights in a bull market. Conversely, the marginals' share prices tend to fall faster in a bear market.

A sensible strategy for the more affluent, enabling you to work both sides of the street, is to invest in the heavy-weights whatever percentage of your assets is necessary to give you the income you want or need. When you believe that gold is generally in an uptrend, invest the balance of your funds in the marginals. The heavy-weights could be held through anything short of a major deflationary depression. The marginals should be bought when the fundamentals are all working in favor of gold, and should be considered long-term income-producing holdings only when gold finds new support levels well above the production costs of those mines, and dividends are established or increased.

Remember, today's marginal mine is tomorrow's heavy-weight.

Marginals are most volatile when the price of gold is trading in a range that swings it above and below the production costs of the mine. The higher the price above production costs, the less volatility. A mine should be classified as an investment heavy-weight only if it has an expected life of at least ten to twelve years, at a production cost 50% or more below the gold price at the time of purchase.

How to Buy South African Shares

Your next problem is how to go about buying these shares. There are two basic approaches. One is to use an American broker and have him buy the shares for you. The other is to go directly through a South African broker, perhaps using a South African Investment Advisor and the Financial Rand, which I will explain in a moment. There are advantages and disadvantages to both techniques.

Aside from owning shares in a fund or ASA, there are two other methods of owning South African shares. The most common way is to own American Depository Receipts (ADRs). They are available for most South African gold shares. The New York bank issuing ADRs purchases the required South African gold shares and holds the actual share certificates in their London or South African branches, and issues dollar-denominated ADRs to cover the shares held overseas. It must be remembered that an ADR is not a share certificate in the truest sense. If the U.S. government decided to impose strict foreign exchange controls, it could effectively block the assets behind the ADRs. In such circumstances it may be extremely difficult for the investor to dispose of the shares supported by the ADRs as they would be held in trust in an overseas bank and subject to the foreign exchange control regulations.

If you're going to buy ADRs, you needn't concern yourself with currency transactions, but if you're going to invest a large sum in South African shares ($100,000 or more), there are savings to be achieved by using the Financial Rand.

The Financial Rand

In order to lure foreign investors to South African markets, South Africa has a two-tiered currency, the Commercial Rand and the Financial Rand. The Financial Rand is used for the purchase and sale of assets only by nonresidents of South Africa. In order to promote investment on the Johannesburg Stock Exchange, the Financial Rand normally trades at a discount of approximately 20%, meaning you can buy more shares for the same bucks. When dividends are paid, it's at the Commercial Rand rate, thereby returning the discount to the investor. It is the stated policy of the Reserve Bank to eliminate the Financial Rand once it moves to approximately the same value as the Commercial Rand, so this is one deal that won't last forever. It may sound a bit crazy, but it certainly achieves the desired goal of bringing capital to South Africa.

Incidentally, when dividends are paid by the mines, the South African government automatically deducts a 15% nonresident Shareholders Tax, which Americans can take as a tax credit on their American tax return.

Buying Cape Stock With Financial Rands

"Cape Stock" is the generic term given to shares purchased on the Johannesburg Stock Exchange (JSE).

If the investor decides to purchase his shares directly on the Johannesburg Stock Exchange, he can instruct his U.S. broker or bank to buy "Cape Stock." The broker or bank buys the shares on the JSE and establishes the exact Rand value. The broker or bank then purchases the exact amount of Financial Rands and immediately sells the dollars to cover this transaction. This dollar value, plus the brokerage fees, are debited to the client's U.S. account.

Holders of "Cape Stock" can receive their dividends in Rands or negotiable dollar drafts, if they apply to the Registrar of the share company.

The investor has to pay the 1% tax and the nominal brokerage fees on the Financial Rand/dollar transaction, in addition to the normal brokerage commission. This may at first sight appear to be more expensive than the ADR method. However, some banks make a charge for issuing ADRs and have also been known to charge for the collection for dividends. This practice tends to offset the other fees in using the "Cape Stock" method.

The following firms should be able to assist you in your search.

Rotan Mosle, Inc.
Gold Specialist
10 East 53rd Street
New York, N.Y. 10022
212-750-0813

Rauscher, Pierce, Refsnes, Inc.
2 Houston Center
Suite 3400
Houston, TX 77010
713-652-3033

Paper Metal

Another way to speculate or catch the investment swings is with gold or silver certificates, marketed by some banks and foreign exchange houses. When gold and silver go up, the certificates go up also, and they can be bought or sold with a simple phone call to the firm that sold them.

Many hard-money advisors and their followers treat paper investments much as they would a leper, but there are some eminently good reasons why anything beyond a survival position should be in paper. You needn't be concerned with transporting unwieldy chunks of your net worth, and you don't have to worry about storage or insurance, pay sales taxes, or pay big commissions. The certificates can even be used as collateral for loans, and the point has already been made that paper is far easier to sell.

These are really gold and silver accumulation plans and can best be compared to a Christmas Club savings account. You make regular deposits and, over time, you will have accumulated more money than a less structured approach is likely to produce. There are two primary strategies to consider: (1) Dollar-Cost Averaging—the regular investment of specific sums over a period of time and (2) Unit Purchase Averaging—the regular purchase of a fixed number of coins, bullion, etc. Both these methods work best for our purposes in declining or stable markets. Whatever the market, you want to build a pyramid that has its base on the bottom, not a top-heavy pyramid that results from buying all of the market's strength and little or none of the weakness.

Before I mention specifics and firms you might contact for more information, let's look at the advantages of the certificate accumulation plans.

Liquidity, under all market conditions is a big plus, for reasons previously cited.

Commissions are low and, unlike saving up to buy a bag of silver or ten Krugerrands, you buy in convenient increments—rather than not at all, as is usually the case.

The accumulation programs listed later in this chapter have minimum initial purchases ranging from $100 to $2,500, and allow minimum additions of $50 to $500, opening up gold to the small investor.

Unless the investor ultimately takes delivery of the gold, there is no sales tax, as the gold is stored in London, Zurich, or Delaware.

Convenience is perhaps the biggest advantage to owning precious metal-backed paper. You may or may not be assessed a storage fee, but at least you won't have to get down to a coin shop or otherwise take delivery, and purchases or sales can be accomplished over the telephone. It's especially convenient for those with accounts at brokerage houses, all of whom seem to be going in the European direction of one-stop supermarket shopping for financial services.

Paper gold and silver can even be used as collateral for loans, it's ideal for trading the gold-silver ratio (Chapter 10), and, being paper, it's acceptable in many retirement and pension plans that don't allow for hard asset diversification.

Although this isn't a complete list by any means, here are the major plans and some of their features.

Although some of the Swiss banks have had programs similar to those now emerging in this country, the pioneer in the United States market was Deak-Perera in 1975. Deak's Precious Metals Certificates are also available in platinum and palladium, the only plan that offers diversification in these metals. If you have large holdings in precious metals, owning these exotics is a sound diversification idea, as they are influenced by many of the same fundamentals that affect gold and silver. Deak's minimum initial investment is $1,000, and you can add to your position in amounts not less than $100. There's a 3% commission on purchases, from $100 to $1000, and lower commissions on larger purchases. The commission on selling is 1%. The metals are usually stored in Switzerland but can be stored in the United States if you prefer. You can do all of your buying and selling by phone, and you also have access to Deak's foreign exchange, banking, and physical metal services. To get details, contact their Washington office:

> Deak-Perera
> 1800 K St. NW
> Washington, DC 20006
> Toll Free 800-424-1186 (USA)
> 202-872-1233 (Washington, DC)

From the same folks that brought you their money market funds and other financial services, Dreyfus Gold Deposits has a minimum first purchase of $2,500, a $100 minimum on additions, and plans to offer silver in the near future. Their commissions do not exceed 2% and, for those who want the convenience of money market transfers, you can freely switch among the various Dreyfus Funds at no cost. Contact them for details:

> Dreyfus Gold Deposits, Inc.
> 600 Madison Avenue
> New York, NY 10022
> Toll Free 800-223-7750
> Call Collect 212-935-6666

In line with their aggressive marketing posture across the financial spectrum, Citibank of New York is perhaps the plan you're most likely to have been exposed to. Their initial minimum is $1,000, additions must be at least $100, and their highest commission is 3%, going lower as your purchases grow larger. Many brokerage firms without their own accumulation plans have chosen to offer the Citibank product, now available in gold and silver. Write to them at:

> Citibank, N.A.
> Gold Center
> 399 Park Avenue
> New York, NY 10043
> Toll Free 800-223-1080 (USA)
> Call Collect 212-559-6041 (New York)

Among the brokerage firms with accumulation plans, Merrill Lynch is way out in front of the competition. Their Sharebuilder Gold Plan offers the lowest minimums on entry and additions. One hundred dollars is the entry minimum, additional purchases must be $50 or above. Commissions are 5.5% on a

$100 purchase, but go down to 2.2% by the time you've spent $1,000. There are no storage or insurance fees and, as with the other plans, you're buying at better prices than the individual investor could hope to. Merrill lumps all orders together and buys at about 50 cents over the second London fix. Write to:

> Merrill Lynch
> Sharebuilder Marketing
> One Liberty Plaza
> 5th Floor
> 165 Broadway
> New York, NY 10080
> Toll Free 800-221-2857 (USA)
> Toll Free 800-522-8882 (New York)
> 212-637-2848 (New York City)
> Or call the nearest office.

One of the better and most varied Swiss bank accumulation programs is Goldplan, which has regular and irregular investment plans, and even has an automatic withdrawal program for investors who need income from their gold holdings. The details are available from:

> Goldplan A.G.
> P. O. Box 213-K
> 8033 Zurich
> Switzerland

As you can see, gold's growing respectability has resulted in the product being tailored to meet the demands of more investors. These are all large institutions and they do, in fact, have the metal to back up the paper. That's more than can be said for the well-known Washington financial institution that no longer backs its paper with anything other than empty promises.

In the previous chapter we discussed some of the fundamental factors that have made most U.S. stocks poor performers in the past. Although the stock market indexes and many individual share prices may have some inflation-beating potential over the next few years, stocks as a category remain a guaranteed loser to long-term inflation. Inflation destroys capital and stocks represent capital; it's that simple.

Those of you with a penchant for reading between the lines probably know what I'm going to discuss next. "Most stocks" and "stocks as a category" can only mean that certain stocks have characteristics that are likely to make them less prone to the ravages of inflation. These stocks represent tangible assets that, if history is any guide, will appreciate at a rate that approaches or exceeds inflation. Like all stocks, they require individual analysis of their management, earnings, performance, and vulnerability to the cyclical performance of the market. The primary characteristic shared by these stocks is their holding of "real assets," generally given to mean natural resources.

Oil stocks are one of the most obvious examples of stocks that have done well over the last few years. Oil is a resource that industrialized economies must have, it's a nonrenewable resource (much like an option, a "wasting asset"), and its supply has proven uncannily vulnerable to the whims of oil-rich countries that can make the rules—as long as they have what everyone else must have to survive. The same is true of other firms holding basic resources, especially those in sectors that will likely prove to be the growth industries of tomorrow. In addition to oil, you can also bet that gas, coal, uranium, hydrogen, solar, strategic metals, and their related service and equipment industries also show strong potential for growth in the future. When analyzing a stock for purchase in these and other sectors, the prospective buyer should ask himself the following questions:

1. *How fast is this company growing?* What are the projections for growth in this industry? Unless a company's profits and/or the value of its assets will grow at a rate that outpaces inflation, and are likely to stay ahead, purchase of the stock is not likely to reward you in the future.

2. *How sensitive is a company to changing interest rates?* The housing and automobile sectors of the economy have shown us over the last year just how much control interest rates have in these areas, and the same is no less true of utilities and financially oriented stocks. A year or two ago, a 20% prime rate was a preposterous thought; today it's past history and, at that, history that has repeated and exceeded itself—all within one year's time! Interest rates affect all of us, but you don't want to own stock in companies that are most affected by the preposterous becoming reality. I have said that we'd look back on 10% inflation with nostalgia, and the same can be said of a recent prime rate of 21.5%.

3. *How is this industry affected by government regulations?* Is it being propped up by government? Lockheed and Chrysler have gotten most of the publicity, but other industries have received their "bailout" gratuities in more subtle forms. The steel industry's government-sponsored protection from foreign competitors is one of the more obvious restraints on free trade, and this trend toward government lending a helping hand will get much worse before it gets better. If government is "helping" a company get back on its feet, or talking about making regulatory demands on an industry, look elsewhere in your search for stocks.

4. *Does the company have control over their source of raw materials?* Growing shortages and cavalier pricing policies on the part of suppliers can wreak havoc on

an otherwise failsafe firm. Processors and sellers should ideally have some control over their raw materials. It's known as "vertical integration," and it's the reason that independent gas stations have been disappearing, due to tight supplies of gasoline. Evidence of vertical integration sure beats being without a product.

5. *What is the labor component of the company* you're considering for investment? Labor unions have never been hesitant about asking for more, and the harder inflation makes it on everyone, the more strident they must be in their demands.

There are many other benchmarks that can be used to evaluate a stock, but the inflation factor cannot be overlooked in today's environment. The following list of stocks is by no means comprehensive, but they're all representative of growth industries or have strong natural resource positions and give you the right answers to many of the above questions.

Amax	Air Products
Masonite	Babcock & Wilcox
St. Joe Minerals	UNC Resources
Kerr-McGee	Mountain States Resources
Foster Wheeler	Energy Minerals
Boise Cascade	Premier Resources
Combustion Engineering	Webb Resources
Weyerhauser	Amerada Hess
Union Carbide	

As in gold stocks, if you don't wish to make your own choices, go with a mutual fund that has an aggressive outlook. Again, the funds mentioned below haven't cornered the market on keeping up with inflation, but they're a beginning. Check with a broker for current ratings of the various funds.

44 Wall Street Fund
150 Broadway
New York, NY 10038

American Investors
88 Field Point Road
Greenwich, CT 06830

Pennsylvania Mutual
127 John Street
New York, NY 10038

Sherman Dean
120 Broadway
New York, NY 10005

Twentieth Century Growth
605 W. 47th Street
Kansas City, MO 64112

Able Associates Fund
174 Birch Drive
Manhasset Hills, NY 11040

Rowe Price New Horizons
100 E. Pratt Street
Baltimore, MD 21202

Energy Fund
522 Fifth Avenue
New York, NY 10036

Stragetic Metals: the Oil of the '80s?

Strategic metals—currently the catchiest two words in hard money investments and the hottest thing going in the hard money investment advisory field—offer huge potential for both profit and loss.

Like any other hot market, such as diamonds and gold in 1977-1978, the scam artists are jumping in and it's hard to separate the good guys from the bad guys because they won't stand still long enough for us to put white or black hats on them.

In any event, I think strategic metals can be a fine investment but the unaware, uninformed investor is going to get taken by the same guys that used to sell "London commodity options" and diamonds to the ignorant, greedy, and uninformed who are vulnerable to a get-rich-quick scam.

If oil is the lifeblood of today's industrialized world, then strategic metals are the bones and muscles, without which modern communications would not exist, all industry would grind to a halt, and Western Civilization would, in effect, be in reverse at full throttle. No jet planes, no television, no pocket calculators, no flashlight batteries, no more technology of any kind. There seems to be general agreement that strategic metals are about 40 metals (and minerals) essential to industry and defense, and whose availability in quantity is dependent—in some cases, wholly dependent—on foreign sources. "Critical" metals, on the other hand, are also required in defense and industry, but, domestic supply is sufficient. We rely on foreign sources for more than 50% of our supply of 23 of the 36 minerals that our government classifies as most critical to our industrial economy. Strategic metals include but are not limited to: antimony, bismuth, cadmium, chromium, cobalt, germanium, indium, manganese, mercury, molybdenum, rhodium, selenium, tantalum, titanium, tungsten, and vanadium.

Not only do these metals sound exotic, most of them come from often unstable or hostile places such as Namibia, Zaire, Zambia, Zimbabwe, plus the Soviet Union and South Africa. The current glut of oil demonstrates a commodity's eventual resistance to increases in price, but there's been a tenfold increase from the days of cheap energy to today's much higher priced surplus.

The same principle applies to strategic metals, the primary differences being that the market is much smaller, the uses are at least as diverse, and our dependence on foreign sources is worse. For example, in 1980, we imported 42% of our manganese and fully 100% of titanium, strontium, and columbium. All of which brings us to The Resource War.

This inherent vulnerability of the U.S., coupled with some alarming trends, have made our future too precarious for comfort. Aside from the African nations on which we are largely dependent—most of which are prototypes for political instability—much of the remainder of our dependence falls on the Soviet Union. And you don't have to be a paranoid with a "The Russians are Coming" button to fear that they won't always do us favors. The Soviet appetite for conquest remains unsatisfied, and making the United States a "resource hostage" would be more effective and much neater than military action. As Leonid Brezhnev remarked to the President of Somalia in 1973, "Our aim is to gain control of the two great treasure houses on which the West depends: The energy treasure house of the Persian Gulf and the mineral treasure house of Central and Southern Africa." In addition to exporting revolution to these areas, the Russians have started withholding many of the metals they used to export, and in some cases have become net importers. Buying in world markets only helps to raise the value of their holdings in the ground. There are some hopeful signs, however. In March of this year the Reagan Administration announced that $100 million would be spent to begin to rebuild the National Defense Stockpile, the first additions to the stockpile in the last 20 years. The total cost of bringing our inventory up to national security requirements is estimated to be $20 billion; and will require many years into the next century. The current program is a halting first step in the right direction, after a long history of walking backwards. Let's look at the investment opportunities presented by this crisis.

Fundamentals

When recessions develop, prices of most strategic metals go down and inventory accumulates. With a few exceptions, this accurately depicts today's market.

Some metals, however, are less subject to industrial activity, usually those that are produced in small quantities as by-products of base metals, such as germanium (a by-product of copper and zinc refining) used in lasers, fiber optics, semiconductors, etc. Demand is strong, new supplies are down, and the prospects for higher prices are excellent. The more exotic the metal and the scarcer it gets, the more it is governed by speculative price expectation than by strict con-

213

siderations of supply and demand. A fundamental like cost of production becomes irrelevant when something is required regardless of price. Political factors are crucial for such metals.

Cobalt is perhaps the classic example of a case when a good State Department source would have been more valuable than the demand expert at Pratt & Whitney, each of whose jet engines requires 910 lbs. of cobalt. The U.S. imports 97% of its cobalt needs, and in 1978, 60% of U.S. supplies were cut off when one Zairean mine in Shaba Province came under military attack. The supply "at any price" phenomenon took hold, and in six months the spot price of cobalt went from $6.85 to $50. Proponents of the Resource War theory point out that Russian purchasing agents were quietly accumulating large supplies of cobalt in advance of the invasion. The National Defense Stockpile will begin to accumulate ten million pounds of cobalt, partly paid for with sales from the U.S. stockpile of silver and partly bartered for food.

If all this sounds like a cinch, be careful. It ain't that easy. London is the center of these markets. They don't trade on a formal exchange, they are cash markets (no leverage), liquidity is poor in many markets, and investor information is hard to get. These markets are still dominated by professional traders, people who know that all rhodium is not created equal (South African rhodium is purer than that from Russia), and that titanium that's been on the shelf for years is not the same titanium that Boeing or one of the other aerospace giants will want to buy back from you. It's not practical to take physical possession of strategics because once a metal leaves the network of official papers and approved warehouses, it can be difficult, if not impossible, to resell.

Additionally, the entry level of most programs is beyond the reach of many investors. Although single units of some metals could be purchased for less, as a practical matter, $25,000 is about the minimum an investor should be able to devote to a diversified long-term (2-5 year) investment. The portfolio approach is a hedge against one bad choice or the discovery of a substitute for a single metal. In addition to being a long-term investment, strategics are a long distance investment you won't see unless you choose to visit Rotterdam or London.

There are commissions on both ends of the sale, storage and insurance costs (usually 2-3% of the metal's value). There are also the usual price risks of bad judgment in buying something in extreme oversupply, or at a cyclical peak, or for which new supplies or a substitute has been found.

Despite some of the drawbacks I've mentioned, including a runup in price of over 800% (the Strategic Metal Index) since 1972, limited and tenuous future supplies probably mean an excellent investment opportunity for those who aren't discouraged yet. I think there is a lot of money to be made.

The following firms are among those involved in serving investors, a new field where being in business a year is being a veteran. We believe them all to be reputable, but no recommendation is intended nor implied.

Kearney Metals and Minerals, Ltd. (P. O. Box 784, Novato, CA 94948, 415-892-8441, TLX 172176; Bermuda Office: P.O. Box 1629, Hamilton 5 Bermuda, 809-295-6009, TLX 3292 SMLBA) is a Bermuda corporation that manages discretionary accounts of $50,000 minimum, and brokers metals in individual amounts that vary according to the metal being purchased. They also offer an interesting tax advantaged program.

Strategic Metals and Critical Materials, Inc. (90 Broad Street, New York, NY 10004, 212-425-2360, 800-221-4120) is one of the Sinclair group of companies, and they offer a full range of metals on a fully paid basis. They recommend that clients achieve the greatest amount of diversification possible, their preferred minimum being $25,000. They also sell strategic metal stocks.

Strategic Metals Corporation (500 Chesham House, 150

Regent Street, London W1R 5FA, England) offers the following programs: The Strategic Metal Index; minimum investment of $250,000. The Strategic Metal/Managed Account; minimum $10,000. Individual Metal Purchases; minimum $10,000-$30,000 depending on the metal.

There's been a lot of interest in strategic stocks, usually companies whose main business is mining gold, lead, copper, or zinc. Because the strategic metal part of most of such firms' business is minor, it's a watered-down version, not the "pure play" that would most directly correlate to higher strategic metal prices. Oregon Metallurgical (Ormet) is perhaps the classic example of what happens to the pure play that everyone discovers at the same time. Their shares went from $5 to $61 during the last year, and U.S. Antimony, another relatively pure play, went from $1 to a high of $10. Volatility and speculative excess will likely result from more investor interest in this area.

Caveat Emptor

Earlier I indicated that involvement in strategic metal investments is inappropriate or impossible for many people. One firm recommends a net worth of at least $500,000, 5%-10% of which might be invested in strategic metals, however, many are seduced by the neat package strategic metals represent. After all, isn't this "the gold of the '80s," "to the '80s, what oil was to the '70s," and a "groundfloor opportunity" to get rich and patriotically rebuild our National Defense Stockpile at the same time?

Strategic metals could be all of these things to you, but it could also represent a total loss if a telephone pitchman can get between you and your money. Selling the idea that the Resource War is for real, that the National Defense Stockpile could be repatriated, and that volatility breeds profits should not be hard. With government agencies and the Reader's

Digest to back up their claims, strategic metals are a perfect vehicle for the unscrupulous: they're a big-ticket investment vehicle and, being a long-term investment, the client's encounter with reality will, in most cases, be a few years off.

The techniques of the telephone pitchman were the same as the rip-offs in gold, silver, heating oil, etc. Plant the greed seed, find out if the prospective client can invest $10,000-$20,000, mention what happened to cobalt when Zairean supplies were cut off, talk a bit about world stockpiling, and call as many times as it is necessary to wear the client down. The boiler rooms are just cranking up.

Here are some questions to ask. Who are the promoters and what have they been doing over the past ten years? Many have rather colorful backgrounds. Check out the references. The Better Business Bureau is certainly worth a phone call. The investor turned investigator is at a real disadvantage in researching a person's background, but for a few hundred dollars a private investigating firm can save you thousands. If in doubt, find out.

Information

The most complete book on the subject of strategics is *Guide to Non-ferrous Metals and Their Markets,* by Peter Robbins and John Edwards ($32.50, Nichols Publishing Co., P.O. Box 96, New York, NY 10024). A more highly visible book—due in part to its gold foil cover—is *Get Really Rich In The Coming Super Metals Boom,* by Gordon McLendon. This is available in hardback ($12.95) from Simon and Schuster and in paperback, Pocket Books ($4.95).

The McLendon book is more a treatise on what government has managed to do to our money over the years than it is a guidebook to riches via strategic metals, but there is much to be gained from the author's personal experiences in the field.

If you're really serious, subscribe to ''The Metals Investor,'' a monthly newsletter written by John Pugsley (711 W. 17th St. G-4, Costa Mesa, CA 92627, $250 for 12 issues); "London Metal Bulletin" (Metal Bulletin Inc., 708 Third Ave., New York, NY 10017, $241.50); New York Metals Week (McGraw Hill Inc., 1221 Avenue of the Americas, New York, NY 10020, $347).

Strategic metals meet many of the criteria attached to investments with great potential, the foremost being necessity, almost irrespective of price, scarcity, and—a geopolitical kicker—vulnerability of supply. Stockpiling by governments, the influx of investor demand, and the likely emergence of resource cartels should contribute to the future steady appreciation of these metals. Perhaps even more important, demand because of the growing trend toward ever higher technology, the home computer revolution, and space-age communication systems are only beginning.

Recession would depress prices in most strategics, but would just present some spectacular opportunities. (Remember, most strategics are by-products of base metals, very little mining of which would be taking place.)

At this time, strategic metals are an exotic investment product that may indeed be the equivalent of gold at $35 an ounce. But like gold at $35 an ounce, it's not readily available to the average investor, and its illiquidity is unattractive to many. The field is already attracting some of the "sure thing" sales types. The years ahead, however, will probably bring us many of the forms of ownership that we've grown accustomed to in gold: certificate programs, mutual funds, and futures contracts. Bache is the first of the major brokerage houses to enter the field of strategics, there is a strategic metal fund pending before the SEC, and even the suede shoe smoothies will probably be correct in the long run.

In the short run, slack economic conditions worldwide suggest that you may not miss out if you don't send your money to someone tomorrow or the next day, but I suggest that you educate yourself and monitor strategic metals. Those who do their homework early may be grateful for early involvement in strategic metals.

Annuities—a No-no

Millions of people have socked money into fixed-income annuities, deferring the tax on the income until their retirement years, hoping to receive a payout on retirement and live comfortably. Don't kid yourself. Years ago, perhaps up until the late sixties, this retirement vehicle had merit. However, when inflation escaped its chains, not only did the income cease to keep up with inflation, but the purchasing power of the principal began to erode dramatically.

In 1967, had one put $10,000 into an annuity and taken it out today, that same $10,000 would purchase only $3,938 worth of goods. To put it another way, the $10,000 would have to have been put into some nifty investment that earned an average of $1,183 per year so that principal and interest today would amount to $25,390 and that's just to stay even in purchasing power. Today you need close to 20% to break even. We haven't even computed the taxes to be paid when you draw out the money.

If after-tax dollars have been put into an annuity, meaning it is not "tax sheltered" or "tax deferred," you probably are better off withdrawing the funds and investing them in hard assets, such as survival coins, numismatic coins, colored gemstones, or diamonds. Of course, you're liable for the tax on earned interest and capital gains when you liquidate the annuity, but this probably is a small price to pay compared to what will happen to the money in typical annuity plans in the Inflationary Eighties.

Recently, more flexible tax-deferred annuities have entered the marketplace. A one-time payment will buy an annual income for life close to the payment. Some offer bail-out provision with no penalty if the rate declines below a certain level. Generally, the first year or two are at a fixed rate of interest. As of this writing, the rate is better than T-bills. If you can determine that the money is invested in inflation hedge assets and that you may be receiving an accordingly fair return on your capital, this type of annuity may be okay. Read the fine print as future guaranteed rates may be considerably lower than the initial rate. Even though the bail-out provision is attractive, do you want to pay all the tax at once when at least in the next three years you know you'll be pushed into a higher tax bracket? I believe you're better off in inflation-hedge assets that will produce a long-term capital gain, but if you feel you have plenty of these and you're in a high tax bracket, the above plan offers some diversification.

If you're employed by a nonprofit organization such as a school or hospital and are contributing to a tax-deferred annuity, you should ask yourself if the tax deferred status is worth it. A pre-tax contribution, even if matched by the organization, may not be enough to offset inflation. In the unlikely event that it is, you may wish to continue your contribution to enjoy the net savings on your income tax. Your age as well as your contributory years should be weighed. For example, if you're 59½ or older, or when you terminate your employment, the money may be rolled over, tax deferred, into a desired IRA plan. You may at any time receive your contribution, but unless you meet the aforementioned qualifications, you may be subject to a penalty as well as a liability for income tax on the principal and interest, but it still may be worth it to beat inflation in the long run by getting your money into hard assets.

What about a Swiss franc annuity? You may have entertained the thought, as, long-term, the Swiss franc is thought to be stronger than the dollar. Did you know that in the three-year

220

period ending December, 1980, gold has risen 140% more than the franc? I prefer the metal, or the gold mining shares.

Company Plans

Some companies offer stock savings plans from which you benefit. Does the company contribute enough to offset the inflationary impact? Is your company strong enough that the stock will achieve a high enough price to offset inflation? Or might your company have a difficult time earning real profits in an inflationary environment? One of my employee's relatives was going to make a partial withdrawal of Sears & Roebuck stock in January, 1973. The company officer talked him out of it, because he'd have to pay income tax on his withdrawal. Too bad, because in January, 1973, with the Dow at 1,000, Sears stock was $125. In early 1981, with the Dow at 1,000, Sears stock was under $15. Even adjusting for a 2-for-1 split, the value is about $30, a 76% loss. Find out your average cost per share, add the value of what you get from your company's contribution, compute the average-per-year rate of growth, and compare it to the rate of inflation. It probably compares unfavorably.

IRA and Keogh Plans

Many people not covered under corporate retirement plans often get turned on about IRA and Keogh plans. These plans seem to be attractive for the individual who agrees with me that the value of a Social Security pension is questionable.

Under an IRA (Individual Retirement Account) an employed individual may set aside, tax deferred, up to a maximum of $2000 a year. If the spouse is employed, an additional $250 may be set aside. There is not much benefit in making the contribution for the spouse, as you have the expense of setting up and managing two accounts, and the money is split fifty-fifty between the accounts, leaving very little in each account for investment.

Keogh plans (for the self-employed) allow for greater deductions from income, as well as a greater contribution toward retirement. Present law allows one to contribute 15% of net business income, up to $15,000 a year. A large portion of that $15,000 might otherwise have gone to Uncle Sam in taxes.

First the good news. Every dollar contributed to IRA or Keogh plans is tax deferred. Capital gains and interest from investment are sheltered from taxation until you pay taxes during the retirement years as you withdraw money from the plan, when it is assumed you will be in a lower tax bracket.

Now the bad news! Most IRAs and Keoghs are guaranteed instruments of inflationary purchasing power confiscation. Those placed with banks, savings and loans, and insurance companies with fixed rates of interest are subjected to inflation erosion. The principal in this type of account in the last three years alone has lost over 39% in purchasing power (as measured by the increase in the Consumer Price Index from October 1978 to October 1981). The fixed-rate interest earned has not even come close to making up the difference. And with inflation escalating us into higher tax brackets, a phenomenon called "bracket creep," there is no assurance you will be in a lower tax bracket later on.

Now some more good news! The logical alternative to terminating such accounts and paying the penalty and tax (further eroding the money already set aside) is to transfer the plan to a hard-money-oriented custodian who holds the assets in trust in the truest sense of the word. If it is a bank, the assets of a trust cannot be attached along with the assets of the bank should the bank go broke. The plan should be set up to allow investment in stocks, bonds, mutual funds, money market funds, Treasury bills, gold, silver, diamonds, colored gemstones, or numismatic coins, so that assets may be bought and sold to fit the current economic scenario.

With the proper trustee, the individual makes all investment decisions, places the orders for the assets to be purchased, and gives written authorization to the trustee to disburse funds from the account. The assets are stored in the trustee's vault.

The trustee will charge a set-up fee and an annual administration fee, so attention should be given as to whether the fee is worth paying to keep the plan in force. The overall tax savings should be taken into consideration, as well as the individual's investment expertise.

The older the Keogh, and the more funds there are in the account, the larger the penalty and tax liability if the plan is simply terminated. Setting up a plan transfer, however, is relatively simple.

Many individuals with Keoghs find it to their advantage to incorporate, as 25% of the individual's total compensation can be set aside tax-deferred when adopting both a pension and a profit-sharing plan. The corporation makes the contribution, not the individual.

The pension and profit sharing contributions are a deduction for the corporation, thereby reducing corporate income taxes. The greatest advantage with corporate plans is that a corporate employee or officer, can become a trustee, so close control can be maintained. The assets can be stored in a vault on business premises, in a bank custodial account, or in a bank safe deposit box rented in the name of the corporation. One needs a good attorney to design the plans and to present them to the IRS for tax deferred qualification.

For information regarding hard-money-oriented trust companies, you may contact:

The Trust Department
First State Bank of Oregon
1212 SW 6th Avenue
Portland, OR 97207
503-243-3517

Ron Holland, President
Retirement Consultants, Inc.
Rt. 2 Darby Bridge Road
P.O. Box 314
Taylors, SC 29687
800-845-3970

Section 314B Miscellaneous Provisions of the new tax law prohibits investment in collectible or tangible assets in self-directed retirement accounts after December 31, 1981. I'm leaving the above material in my book just in case 314B gets repeated. We are lobbying vigorously for that repeal.

In the event 314B stands as law, that doesn't mean all is lost. Actually, from a long-term tax planning standpoint, we might be better off putting 70% of our IRA or Keogh money into inflation hedge assets that pay interest or dividends and 30% into stocks representing tangible assets. Remember, when we sell these stocks, we should have a long-term capital gain if we hold them outside our pension plan. We lose that tax benefit by buying capital gain assets to hold in the retirement account, as the gain comes out as ordinary income, but if we do some decent tax shelter planning, we should be able to solve that problem.

Picking the Winners

Over a long period of time, what assets might be expected to best outstrip inflation? I expect gold to be $2,000 to $3,000 an ounce by the end of 1983, and silver over $100 an ounce . . . numismatic coins should rise 300% to 500% in the next three to five years . . . the dividends on some South African gold shares probably will be higher than current share prices . . . who knows how far colored gemstone or diamond prices might go? All I know is that they will be up. I think you should diversify as broadly as your funds will permit. I can't think of better assets to purchase for appreciation to help us triumph over the Disintegrating Eighties. If you can buy these in tax deferred plans, so much the better. If not, these assets are probably still better bets than money in annuities, and most company stock plans.

When it's time to own gold (like now) it's time to own gold mining company shares. The shares pay handsome dividends and 100% of the dividends could be reinvested inside our retirement account as Uncle Sugar is deferring his take. So, buy gold shares for your IRA. Instead of silver, buy Sunshine Mining Co. bonds. You might want to consider some of the resource stocks mentioned in Chapter 9.

The major stock brokerage firms have self-directed IRA and Keogh plans. Plan establishment and administration fees are very reasonable. The plans are as flexible as any in that you are making the decisions and placing the order for the asset. Your own temperament for the market will tell you if you belong in this type of account.

CHAPTER 10

Only for the Rich?

Recently we did a detailed analysis on why some people do not renew their subscriptions to *The Ruff Times*. Like any good business, we worry if a customer is dissatisfied, despite the fact that we have a very high renewal rate.

As we interrogated those who had chosen not to remain with us, one frequent comment was: "*The Ruff Times* is written only for the rich, not the little guy."

Gary North put it well in a recent issue of his fine newsletter, *The Remnant Review* (see the Appendix) when he described the same problem, and stated that a lot of this frustration arises from the unalterable facts that (1) obviously the more money you have, the more of my advice you can take, and (2) the game of beating inflation, taxes, and government is so stacked against you that sometimes there just aren't a lot of options to select from in the search for solutions if you don't have much money.

Recently, I was interviewed on a radio station in Chicago

ice that was mostly poor and black. The
questions implied that I was a bad guy
ve any good suggestions to help the poor
it is sort of like killing the messenger who
ews that the cards are marked, the dice are
loa...   odds rigged, and the house wins most of the
time, bla...   him for your losses. Why blame me because I
can't answer a question which has no answer?

If I write about apartment buildings or diamonds or bags of
silver coins and you don't have enough money to buy one,
you could understandably react by feeling frustrated and mad,
and I'm a convenient target for your rage. I understand that,
but it really isn't quite rational.

The mythical "average" *Ruff Times* subscriber is in his late
forties, has two or three years of college education, and makes
around $35,000 a year. He has between $10,000 and $50,000
in savings and investments, and an inflated equity in his
home. It wasn't many years ago that he would have been
considered one of the more affluent members of society. Now
he is almost lower-middle class, and government is taking a
larger and larger portion of his income as the IRS rate
structure assumes he's rich, ratcheting him into higher tax
brackets, and inflation is devastating the traditional investments that he is making (*i.e.*, blue chip stocks, bonds, CDs,
cash value insurance, etc.). He has this hard, cold knot of
fear in his stomach warning him that the affluence he pursued
and thought he had found is turning to ashes in his hands, and
his retirement will be nothing better than genteel poverty.

This book is an effort to help a broad spectrum of readers.
There are millions of you whose assets and income fall well
below our mythical "average." There are also some who
have assets in the millions of dollars. Some of the people who
control the world's largest fortunes are regular and enthusiastic readers of *The Ruff Times*. By the same token, there are a
lot of little old ladies on social security who are also looking
for help.

A book dedicated to the preservation of savings and assets will be of more value to someone who has more savings or assets to preserve. The only legitimate question is: Is it worth the price?

Actually, the less you have, the more important it is. The rich can better afford to make expensive mistakes and recover from them. Most people would be just as happy on $5 million as on $10 million if they lost half of it. But if they only had $5,000 and lost half, they would be devastated.

I think it's a bum rap that "Howard doesn't help the little guy." Let's examine the advice I give to help him.

Failure Avoidance

My most important objective is the preservation of whatever you have, as opposed to the aggressive accumulation of wealth. If, as a result of this book, you simply get out of those investments that are being devastated by inflation, then I should be entitled to just a smidgen of gratitude for having saved you from inflationary losses. The insidious nature of inflation is that you lose purchasing power while the numbers appear to be growing. You can get raises and capital gains that, after taxes and inflation, actually result in large losses of purchasing power, while generating phony taxable "profits." One of the things I'm most proud of is that we have awakened a lot of people in this country to this sick situation. The rich can afford the expensive attorneys and estate planners. The middle and lower-middle classes can't afford that kind of advice. I believe that we have helped those people to have insights into their planning which can help them avoid these costly hidden mistakes.

Let's look at another typical misconception—that the advice to buy gold and silver can only be followed by wealthy people. You can buy two Krugerrands for under $1,000. You can buy a 2 Rand for about one fourth of that. You can buy two or three rolls of American silver dimes for under $100. You can buy food storage, one bucket of wheat at a time, for under $20 a bucket (45 lbs.).

Just because you can't do everything, or do it all at once, is no excuse for doing nothing or being angry. It misdirects your energy to vent your frustration on me because of your financial shorts. If you rationally conclude that this book is wrong, I can understand that, even though I don't agree with it. However, for you to read this and not enjoy any benefit from it because of your misconception that these things can only be done by the "rich" is foolish. You are a sitting duck. With this attitude you will miss a lot of fine opportunities for both profit and the preservation of your precious capital.

Let's list a few things that you could do if you had less than $5,000.

1. You could start accumulating some food storage.
2. You could buy silver coins—a roll, or a partial bag. Or you could do what my foster son David did. He spent a few hours going into banks and buying and checking rolls of half dollars, and managed to reap from his day's activities nine 40% silver Kennedy half dollars, worth $27. Total capital required? About $20 to buy the rolls. Total investment in that $27 worth of coins? $4.50. I just ran into a fan of mine on an airplane who informed me he had paid for his *Ruff Times* subscription with this strategy. If you have more time than money, and want to build a survival silver coin position, you can do it, too. Dimes and quarters have been pretty well picked over, but there are still enough silver halves around to make it worth a try. (Look for 1965 through 1969 halves!)

   If your time is more valuable than money, then your kids might do it for you. You could put up the capital and share the profits and get them into the feel of survival coin accumulation.

3. You could buy some bullion-type gold coins ($180 to $700 each).
4. You could become a collector of inexpensive semi-precious stones, baseball cards, comic books, or numismatic coins.
5. You could grow a garden and become self-sufficient and independent, drying your produce in your oven or in the sun. There are such books as *The ABC's of Home Food Dehydration* (see the Appendix) which show you exactly how to do it.
6. You could become politically involved and try to bring about change. You can ring doorbells or stuff envelopes for the campaign of some free-market, honest-money oriented candidate who might help to bring about some change. Ultimately that might do you more good than having all the gold and silver in the world.
7. If you have an unutilized inflated equity in a home, you can borrow against it and put it to work with a beat-inflation program.

What couldn't you do if you had only $5,000? You couldn't buy a good one-carat diamond, and you probably would find it difficult to buy a big apartment house, but using the creative finance ideas described in Al Lowry's wonderful book *How You Can Become Financially Independent by Investing in Real Estate,* and in *How to Prosper,* you can go out with only a few thousand dollars and make a downpayment on a small house or duplex, fix it up, raise the rent and the market value, and trade for a bigger property. Great real estate pyramids have been built on less than $5,000. We have a marvelous opportunity for creative financing in this disrupted marketplace that is now a buyer's paradise, as this book is written.

As I write this, I am getting more and more frustrated, and

not just a little bit angry as I think through some of the letters I've read from a handful of disgruntled subscribers who were expressing their frustration over this imaginary "problem." I think it's a cop-out. I have little sympathy for those who insist on remaining sitting ducks. What they are basically saying is: "I don't believe in myself strongly enough to be willing to get off my tail and act."

CHAPTER 11

Silver Threads
Among the Gold

The Hunt brothers, Bunker and Herbert, have become household words, largely because silver—their favorite commodity—went from $5.96 an ounce in early January of 1979 to $48 on January 21, 1980. From there it declined to $10.80 on "Silver Thursday," March 27, and the Hunts got blamed for everything but Mt. St. Helens. During that period, because of the huge damage to the confidence and pocketbooks of the usual gaggle of silver traders, and the resulting reduction in trading volume and liquidity, I became cautious about silver. However, because silver is basic to my beat-inflation strategy, as described in *How to Prosper During the Coming Bad Years*, let's examine why silver did, and what it may do in the future.

Silver has always been the poor man's gold and, because both have long served as money, the ratio between the two has interested traders because of its potential as an investment guideline. The gold-silver ratio is the number of ounces of silver required to buy one ounce of gold. The current ratio can be obtained by dividing the morning London gold fix by the morning London silver fix. If the price of gold is $600 an ounce, and silver is $15, gold is forty times more expensive than silver, so the ratio is 40 to 1.

The ratio can be traced back over 5,000 years to the Egyptian Pharaoh Menes, who fixed the ratio at 2.5 to 1. It was later fixed at 15 to 1 by the Romans and stood at 10 to 1 when Columbus discovered America. When the Comstock Lode was discovered in 1890, it took forty ounces of silver to buy one ounce of gold. Six years later, despite a free market ratio of 32 to 1, the gold-silver ratio was officially fixed at 16 to 1 when the United States went on a bimetallic standard in 1896.

Although gold and silver have both been used as money, silver has many more industrial uses, which makes it more vulnerable than gold to price fluctuations during economic ups and downs. With industrial demand almost nonexistent during The Great Depression, the free market ratio went to 70 to 1 at one point, until the "official" ratio was pegged at 27 to 1. Official ratios aside, the average free-market ratio for the past century has been about 32 to 1. The importance of the gold-silver ratio as an investment guide is probably overstated, but it can be helpful.

Gold and silver are both precious metals, both have served as money, and unlike paper money, each has always emerged triumphant as a store of value. Both will always benefit from inflationary pressures, but silver has the upper hand from a fundamental standpoint. Gold's main role is monetary, whereas silver's is primarily industrial. Severe economic downturns theoretically should have a greater relative depressing effect on silver's price, but even a stagnant economy continues to find new industrial applications for silver. Silver has many more uses than gold, and it has unique properties for which we're not likely to find a substitute soon, if ever. For example, silver conducts heat and electricity better than any other metal; it is the most light-reflective metal; it is second only to gold in its ability to resist corrosion; it has photochemical properties that are essential to photography, catalytic properties essential to the oil industry, as well as medicinal and other medical applications. Its broad-based demand is growing all the time.

With demand strong and growing, how does the supply side of the equation look? It looks very promising indeed, if you own silver. The most attractive fundamental about silver is sometimes referred to as The Gap. We have used silver faster than we can mine and reclaim it every year since 1957. Because silver is found on or near the earth's surface, most silver deposits have probably already been discovered. Even without inflation, the projected shortages would make silver an excellent long-term investment, even though the 1979-1980 panic liquidations of silver temporarily narrowed the gap for 1981. But inflation will continue to be a factor, and it was this attractive set of fundamentals that aroused the interest of the Hunt brothers back in 1973.

Having been in oil over the years, the Hunts are well acquainted with the investment potential of nonrenewable resources. Along with the attractive fundamentals, their hard-money outlook led them to believe that silver also would be a prime beneficiary of a strong inflationary trend.

Silver hovered around $3. an ounce in 1973 when they purchased 35 million ounces in the futures markets and took delivery. The Hunts have had their speculative flings, most notably in soybeans, but they've shown themselves to be investors—not speculators—in silver. Their holdings certainly command respect as a potential depressant on the market, but their actions have always run contrary to the rumors that they were on the verge of unloading their silver. I think that will continue to be the case. Any downward effect such rumors have had in the past has only presented them with better buying opportunities. They love such rumors and may have started some. As silver's foremost cheerleaders, the Hunts haven't been at all bashful about saying that a gold-silver ratio of 10 to 1 would be a more accurate reflection of their relative values. That would mean that if gold were selling at $1,000, silver would some day be selling at $100. I think it's possible. Rumors aside, the Hunts have been on the "buy" side of the market all along. Their patience was temporarily rewarded in 1979, but it also laid the groundwork for a drama unequaled in recent market history.

In early 1979, silver was just above $6. an ounce, and the margin deposit on a 5,000-ounce futures contract was $1,000. As the price rose, first to $7., then to $8. and beyond, increased volatility led the Exchange to require higher margins. The margins went to $1,500, $2,000, then $7,500, and on September 18 (when silver went to $15.90), the Comex increased the margins to $50,000 for the nearby or "spot" month, $20,000 for other months. Such changes would normally apply only to new businesses, but the Exchange changed the rules in the middle of the game, and these requirements were made retroactive for those who already had positions; many were required to sell.

Now, why would the Exchange pull such a dirty trick on those already in the market? Why would they make such an obvious effort to drive the market down? Naked, unadulterated, save-our-skins survival, that's why!

It seems that a large number of members of the New York Commodity Exchange (COMEX) had taken big short positions anywhere from $7. an ounce on up to $13, and as the market went up, they were getting clobbered. The combination of the Hunts' buying, plus rumors about the Hunts' buying, had sent the markets skyrocketing. Gold also was going nuts, dragging silver with it. Silver was under incredible upward pressure. This bull market had fooled almost everyone.

The Exchange Board of Governors (made up partly of those traders in trouble) was faced with an interesting dilemma. Should they allow their much prized free market to function without interference and further damage the financial position of its members? Or should they take a chance on manipulating the market, with all the legal and regulatory risks that might follow? Silver had moved so fast and was "up the limit" so many days that there was no way out for the shorts. Many of them had reached the point where, if they were required to liquidate or cover their positions, they would have been bankrupt, and the COMEX could have been destroyed. What was developing was an incredible, classic "shootout on Wall Street." It was total war between the Hunts and the traders, and the Exchange had decided to take no prisoners.

The net effect of the changes was that many of the less well-heeled silver "longs" were forced to become sellers and had to liquidate positions because they couldn't meet the higher margin requirements and, in many cases, they simply took their profits and left the market. The market still rose, however, as many big players who were long met the new margin requirements and held their positions. Volume fell, and a thinning market led to more volatility, but the market still climbed upwards. Silver closed in October at $16.56 and in November at $18.82. It sailed through $25 the day after Christmas and closed out 1979 at $34.45.

When higher margins, position limits, and retroactive changes didn't turn the market around, the COMEX said, "No more Mr. Nice Guy!" Eliminating physical delivery and barring new purchases but allowing new sales finally turned the market around with a crash, but not until it went to $48 an ounce on January 22. Two months later, silver was at $10.80, and Bunker and Herbert Hunt had a cash flow problem on their hands. The Hunts lost, the Exchange won, and the rule changes set a precedent that put the big players on notice that they should look to London to do their future business, because the U.S. exchanges could get away with changing the rules in mid-game to protect their own hides. Remember, the Exchange rules are set by a committee: the Board of Gover-

237

nors. They are members of the Exchange. Most of them are traders. Many were short silver.

In October, when silver was around $17 an ounce, I put out the word to my subscribers that the markets were going to be incredibly volatile. I explained what was going on, both in the pages of my newsletter and on our two-minute recorded twenty-four-hour update lines. I cautioned, "When the bull elephants are fighting, the mice should head for the underbrush."

A few weeks later when I went down to Dallas to accept an award from the Bonehead Club, Herbert Hunt came up to me and asked, rather smugly, "Why did you tell your people to get out of silver at $17?" (Silver was about $35, then.) I answered, "Because I didn't know exactly how this battle between you and the Exchange was going to turn out, and the fight isn't over yet." He smiled and said, "Oh, yes it is." And that's how we left it.

Obviously, the battle wasn't over. The Exchange won that round. When silver crashed to $10.80, most of the traders were able to cover their short positions and get out with a whole skin. They were also able to paint the Hunts as the only bad guys, when they really were not. The Hunts were believers in a long-term inflationary spiral. They believed passionately that silver was the investment of the future, and they wanted all they could afford to get. Their biggest sin was being big—very big. They have huge amounts of wealth to hedge against inflation and they decided to do it with silver. They were not attempting to "corner the market" in the classic sense, although their actions might have resulted in just such a corner. They weren't interested in unloading at a profit. They simply wanted to own as much of the world's silver as they could afford to buy. They weren't interested in selling and taking profits. They did underestimate the power of the Exchange to manipulate the market by changing the rules. When the Hunts cried "Foul" over the rule changes before a Senate Committee, they didn't get a lot of sympathy.

What they did wrong was get greedy. What the Exchange did wrong was get greedy and change the rules. It was a classic battle over money. There was no high principle involved whatsoever, and the whole incident is one of the shoddier experiences in the history of American markets. This episode tarnished silver in the eyes of many, but it may also have represented what we'll remember as one of the all-time buying opportunities for silver—"the last train out," or maybe the next-to-last.

The damage is that people are now afraid to trade silver futures. They are now relatively illiquid, because volume is so thin. Often they are up and down the limit, and it is difficult to get in or out at the time and price of your choice. Perhaps the greatest injustice is that the Hunts were blamed for the whole fiasco, and the Exchanges have not been, and probably will not ever be, held to account for their actions.

Buying Silver

If it's such a good idea to own silver, how do you go about it, assuming you haven't already followed my advice? Silver has always been my number two recommendation, after food. I prefer bags of "junk silver" (pre-'65 dimes, quarters, and half dollars, representing $1,000 of face value). Before the runup in 1979 I recommended one "survival" bag per family member. However, the higher prices rendered this advice impractical for many of you. I'm now recommending one-half bag per person for the new investor. There are many other ways to own silver, but you should consider them only after you've purchased a "survival" position. Your survival coins are your calamity hedge and, even if you never need them some day for spending money, they will also serve as an excellent, if somewhat volatile, inflation hedge.

Silver bullion is a more concentrated way to own large quantities of silver, and this is the conventional method for holdings abroad. It comes in 1,000-ounce bars and in some smaller sizes, and you can get more information from:

Deak-Perera
1800 K Street NW
Washington, DC 20006
Toll Free 800-424-1186 (USA)
202-872-1233 (Washington, DC)

Silver Certificates

Silver certificates are receipts for silver held in your name by a bank, already described in more detail in Chapter 9. In addition to being more suitable for buying or selling in fast moving markets (and less unwieldy under any and all conditions), they are a way to avoid sales tax, and avoid storage and theft problems. These certificates are also available for gold, platinum, and palladium.

Highly leveraged speculation in silver is another game entirely, and your only reasonable choice is the futures market. Silver futures contracts are not for the faint of heart or light of wallet. As is the case in all commodity trading, you shouldn't be in the market with money that is not purely risk capital, money that you can afford to (and probably will) lose, and an ample supply of guts.

For well-heeled investors who wish to acquire large quantities of bullion, taking delivery in the futures market is an inexpensive and safe way to make large purchases. Unless the cash market is trading at a premium, you should buy the current month's contract. Buying farther-out months only means that you'll pay more for the same amount of silver. For those of you who are relatively new to commodity trading and also wish to scale down your risk, or who cannot afford 5,000 ounces, "mini-contracts" of 1,000 ounces are available. They're traded on the Mid-America Commodity Exchange. Ask your broker about them if you wish, but if you can't afford the standard-size contract, you have no business buying any futures contract.

Silver-Backed Bonds

Early in 1980, Sunshine Mining Company, one of America's largest silver producers, issued silver certificates which mature on March 15, 1995. These are really silver-backed bonds. Their face value is $1,000, but according to the preliminary prospectus, the principal amount when due at maturity will be the greater of (1) $1,000 or (2) the price of 50 troy ounces of silver bullion. If silver goes up above $20 an ounce as I have forecast ($20 × 50 ounces = $1,000), the bonds will be worth a lot more than $1,000. Sunshine Mining Company may, at its option, honor the requests of the bondholders electing to accept the 50 ounces of silver in bullion rather than the dollar equivalent of the 50 ounces of silver. In other words, if silver is selling at more than $20 an ounce, and the silver certificate holder accepts, Sunshine may choose to deliver 50 ounces of silver, in lieu of the cash equivalent.

The company may "call" or buy back all the bonds early if it chooses, on or after March 15, 1985, and pay the principal indexed amount (50 ounces × the price of silver) plus accrued interest, but only if that indexed figure equals or exceeds $2,000 for a period of thirty consecutive days. That would occur at $40 an ounce or above.

This issue is listed on New York Exchange bonds as Sunsh 8½ 95. At the closing of the market on December 15, 1981, the bond was selling at 141⅜ (1410.37) yielding 6.0% to the investor. When the rest of the bond market was crashing during the big interest rate runup of late 1980, Sunshine bonds hung in there, bucking the trend because of the silver backing.

Observe how closely Sunshine bonds parallel the price of silver and how well they outperformed other bonds, even after a decline in silver.

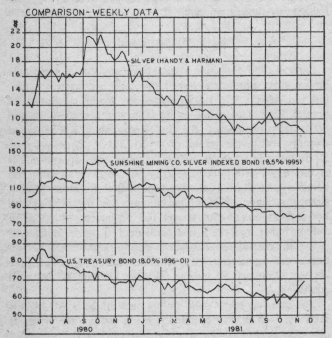

COMPARISON - WEEKLY DATA

SILVER (HANDY & HARMAN)

SUNSHINE MINING CO. SILVER INDEXED BOND (8.5% 1995)

U.S. TREASURY BOND (8.0% 1996-01)

The November 20, 1981, yield on an 8.0% long-term Treasury issue was approximately 11.7%, but the long-term capital gain potential with Sunshine makes the investor willing to accept a lower yield, confident that the purchasing power of his principal will not be eroded by inflation, and the low yield represents a genuine, after-inflation, spendable profit.

This is a unique investment, offering interest income, a floor price ($1,000), and almost unlimited capital gains potential. If silver goes to $100, as is possible, the bonds would be worth $5,000. If they are called in early, you would get at least $2,000 worth of silver.

If the price of silver peaks at $100 or above, before the call in 1985, as it could do, I will be advising you to sell, as the bonds would be selling at $3,000 to $5,000 each. It's beautiful!

Priorities

You should own both silver and gold, but silver first. I think silver will ultimately prove to be a better long-term investment than gold, although I prefer gold for trading purposes because of the thinness of the silver market.

The gold-silver ratio I discussed earlier can be used as one factor in determining timing when deciding between gold or silver, over and above your "survival" holdings, preferably the certificate. The ratio approached 15 to 1 in January, 1980, when silver peaked and was just over 46 to 1 in March. Due to the government auction and slow investor and industrial demand, the ratio has traded as high as 50 to 1 in 1981. Just as you can't expect to catch market tops and bottoms, you can't hope to trade the extremes of the ratio. You can, however, shift from silver into gold as the ratio widens. All you need to remember is that, historically speaking, an abnormally high or low ratio indicates one of these metals is inexpensive *in relation to the other,* and your holdings should be shifted into that underpriced metal. This presupposes, of course, that you believe the threat of war and the continued high and rising rate of inflation favor both metals, and that *they are both going up.* A ratio greater than 38 to 1 means that you might sell some gold and buy silver; less than 20 to 1 is a signal to sell silver and buy gold. Over time, your precious metals holdings will increase in value, and I would also expect the ratio to narrow in favor of silver. Intrinsic value has a way of asserting itself over the long run.

243

Outlook

What is the future for silver? A real collapse of silver prices could only result from two primary factors: (1) reduced inflation rates that would coincide with a prolonged recession or an even greater deflationary collapse; or (2) new supplies entering the market that would also depress silver prices, the most significant threats being the 140 million ounce U.S. stockpile and the 63 million ounces owned by the Hunt family. India has many private silver hoards on a grand scale, but only severe famine—as opposed to the ongoing variety—would cause them to sell, and not much at that, because the people who own it are not the ones who get hungry.

Inflation will continue and accelerate, and a massive deflation will not threaten silver prices until inflation has run its irreversible course, although prices under $8 are likely before this recession bottoms out in 1981.

Except for their forced liquidations, the Hunts are not short-term silver traders. Their holdings represent an overhang that certainly could depress prices but, as Bunker Hunt has said many times, "If you sell, you get into a tax problem." You can safely ignore the threat of a large Hunt sale. Their silver and just about everything else they own, down to the Rolex on Lamar Hunt's wrist, is the collateral that got them the $1.1 billion loan that solved their cash flow problems last March. While the reported terms of their loan seem to suggest that some liquidation will be required to service this debt, I'd be more inclined to expect them to pay their bills from sources other than silver. Their recent sales of horses have been highly publicized, and there are indications that they're selling everything from stocks to ancient coins in order to keep their silver. As one knowledgeable source reports, "They're working very hard to liquidate other assets." The Hunts may have violated some of the rules governing commodity money management, but it doesn't appear that they're going to abandon silver just because there have been some rules changes in their favorite game.

There are some other factors affecting my silver outlook. In view of the public's uncharacteristic selling at market tops in October, 1979, and again in January, 1980, 1980 was the first year since 1957 that new production and reclaimed supplies exceeded demand. Tea sets, jewelry, silverware, and thousands of bags of coins came out of closets and chests all over America, causing a six-month backlog at the silver refiners. These supplies have now been processed and absorbed by the market. With inflation easing somewhat (if only temporarily), industrial demand off during a recession, and a massive overhang surrounded by much uncertainty, I wouldn't expect much upside potential for any inflation hedge like silver, which has a primary dependence on industrial demand, until the recession ends. Early 1982 will be accumulation time, with relatively low prices holding throughout the first six months. Your silver crop should come in in 1982-84.

If the Arab interest in the market continues to grow, the aberrations of 1979 and 1980 could look tame. You may not be able to participate on the scale of the big players, but it will certainly make good sense to bet with them, not against them.

If you don't own silver, get some—now.

Look in the Appendix for a list of dependable dealers.

CHAPTER 12

Rich Man's Gold

Whenever I discuss gold, someone invariably asks, "But what about silver?" When silver is foremost on my mind, someone asks about gold. If I fully cover both, somebody says, "What about platinum?" I know you can't please all the people all of the time, but today the fellow who wants to know about platinum gets an answer.

Like gold and silver, platinum is classified as a precious metal, and it's the best known and most widely used of the metals commonly referred to as the "platinum group," which includes palladium, rhodium, ruthenium, iridium and osmium. At $600 an ounce, rhodium has the dubious distinction of being the world's highest priced metal. All members of the group share the common qualities of resistance to heat, corrosion, and oxidation, high density, electrical conductivity, malleability and reflectivity.

Like so many other metals we need to keep our economy running, platinum and its lesser known siblings come primarily from South Africa and the Soviet Union. These two politically questionable areas accounted for over 95% of the 1980 world production of 6.7 million troy ounces, with South Africa accounting for about three-fourths of world exports. Canada was the world's next largest producer with less than 1% of the 1980 output, all of it a byproduct of copper and nickel mining. An example of our vulnerability to a cutoff of platinum imports is the amount of domestic production, a grand total of 6,000 ounces in 1980, a byproduct of copper mining. U.S. recycling of platinum far exceeds annual mine production—345,000 troy ounces in 1980—and this trend is rising, although it didn't make more than a dent in the 1980 consumption of 2.2 million ounces.

This 2.2 million ounces was down 20% from 1979, mostly because the auto industry has been running on fumes for the past two years. Platinum will ride the same inflationary wave that sometimes governs the price action of gold and silver, but, like silver, its overriding fundamental is industrial demand. The sluggish U.S. economy and even more depressed European economies, coupled with deflationary expectations in many quarters, has in 1981 resulted in the unusual phenomenon of platinum trading at less per ounce than gold, but more about that later.

As I suggested a moment ago, platinum's fortunes rely in large part on the health of the automobile industry, which uses approximately half of the total platinum purchased in this country each year. If you've ever had to replace a catalytic converter, platinum is the reason it cost so much. Pollution control systems required on autos made since 1975 contain about half an ounce of platinum group metals. Platinum is also used in electrical contacts and relays, as a catalyst in the chemical and petroleum industries, in glassmaking, jewelry, and in dentistry and medicine. If you've got a heart pacemaker, it's platinum that's preventing you from rusting from the inside out.

248

There are two primary benchmarks in platinum pricing, a producer price fixed by Rustenberg, the South African firm that is the world's largest producer, and the free-market price, reflected by the London Metal Exchange and by platinum futures contracts on the New York Mercantile Exchange.

The two-tier price structure of platinum gained a lot of attention in 1979 and 1980 as the free market price ultimately reached a high of $1045 in March of 1980, while the producer price lingered just above $400. This disparity in price is due to the long-term contracts that large platinum producers—primarily Rustenberg and Impala—have with big users of the metal, such as General Motors and the other big automotive companies. The long-term contracts protect the platinum producers during periods of price depression, and they assure adequate supplies of metal to users when prices are rising and supplies are tight. If the platinum users desert producers and buy on futures markets when prices slump below their contract prices, as prices have done this year, they run the risk of jeopardizing their future supplies from producers. The restraint shown by producers during the frenzied rise two years ago will help to ensure that the producers receive the prices they set. The degree of market control exerted by producers has led some observers to suggest that there may be a new OPEC on the block—and this time the P stands for platinum.

Ownership

My opinion may run contrary to some of the advertising you've seen, but physical platinum ownership isn't for everyone. Investment in ''white gold'' should be considered only by those with survival holdings in ''junk'' silver and gold, plus comfortable positions in excess of these core holdings. Because platinum is not a monetary metal, and lacks the universal recognition of gold and silver, platinum should not be considered part of your "survival" holdings in precious metals. It's too rare to qualify as "real money" in an economic breakdown.

There's no magic balance sheet number that qualifies you as a platinum buying prospect, but for the person with large precious metal holdings—$50,000 strikes me as a reasonable although arbitrary number—platinum has intriguing long-term prospects that warrant your consideration for diversification, especially while platinum is selling for less than gold.

The amount of platinum you want will pretty well determine the form of ownership you choose. If you want to add to your physically held precious metals a bit at a time, the Credit Suisse, Engelhard, and Johnson Matthey bars are the most practical. They're available in 1, 5, 10, and 50-ounce bars, and also in sizes less than one ounce. The smaller the size, the greater the premium will be. It's always a good idea to compare prices, but this is especially true when shopping for platinum. Under an ounce, your liquidity will be reduced to the point where you're buying a novelty item, not making an investment. If you want to diversify a much larger metals portfolio, and can afford to acquire 50 ounces all at once (about $20,000 in December of 1981), the cheapest way is to buy the nearest month platinum futures contract trading on the New York Mercantile Exchange. (Be sure to compare the nearby contract to the cash price, as "distant nearby" months may cost more than buying from a coin dealer.) Buying a more distant contract month just means you're paying unnecessarily more for the product, as distant month prices reflect a carrying charge premium.

The most commonplace way to take delivery when the contract expires is to take possession of a depository receipt. At that time you'll have to pay the difference between any margin you already have on deposit and the value of the 50-ounce contract. Taking delivery in this manner is inexpensive (usually one and a half to two times the normal commission, which averages about $90) and a good way to maintain your liquidity. When you want to sell, you simply sell one near month contract, and on the delivery date, deliver the depository receipt. Storage and insurance fees will approximate $5. per month, but it would probably cost you at least this much to store it elsewhere anyway. If you like the convenience of the precious metal certificate programs, the only major firm now offering platinum certificates is DEAK-PERERA (they also have palladium if you want to get really exotic). Merrill Lynch and others are considering adding platinum to their certificate programs, but in the meantime, you can buy Deak's Precious Metals Certificates in minimum initial purchases of $1,000, additions can be made in $100 minimum increments, and the metal will be stored in their depository in Zurich or domestically at the Bank of Delaware. For more details on Deak's program, write or call Deak-Perera, 1800 K Street, NW, Washington, DC 20006, (800) 424-1186 (USA), (202) 872-1233 (Washington, DC).

Those of you with experience in South African gold shares may be aware of another "platinum play." There are a couple of platinum shares you might want to investigate if you want to diversify your gold share portfolio. Rustenberg (OTC) is usually regarded as the Cadillac of platinum shares, and when Merrill Lynch issued a recommendation in early 1979, Rustenberg went from $2½ to $8 in October of last year. Impala is the other big name in platinum shares, and either of these might give you a commensurately greater swing up or down than would the metal. There are a few other stocks, a couple of them being Canadian nickel mine issues that produce platinum as a byproduct. Ask your broker for more details if you're interested.

Platinum vs. Gold

Gold seems to be a convenient measuring stick for a lot of things—silver, barrels of oil, purchasing power of the dollar—

and the gold/platinum relationship is another of the so-called "traditional" indicators. I say so-called because the one indication, the gold/silver ratio, has been particularly undependable during the past two years; and now in 1981 platinum has sold for a lot less than gold, which is quite unnatural.

Unlike the gold/silver ratio, whose lineage can be traced back for over 5,000 years, platinum was not discovered until the early 1700s. The Spaniards then mining gold and silver in Mexico and South America called the new white mineral "platina," which translates to "little silver." They didn't know what to do with platinum in those days, and it was sometimes referred to as "fool's silver." In approximately 1775 the French developed a process that allowed for the separation of platinum from surrounding minerals. Unlike gold and silver, platinum never acquired much status as a monetary metal; it was used in coinage on only one occasion, when the Russians made platinum-based rubles from 1828 to 1845. Until platinum's industrial uses began to evolve, platinum's high density and malleability resulted in its use as a base for gold-plated counterfeit coins. If you've bought any platinum lately, you know that we've come a long way from the days when platinum was used as a cheap filler in fake coins.

The broad and growing industrial applications for platinum have resulted in a situation where platinum traditionally sells for a higher price than gold. This spread widened to almost $400 in March, 1980, and has been narrowing ever since. This year, with gold in decline and the economy slack, platinum has traded as much as $50 below the price of gold. Platinum's price should lag behind gold for awhile, but when there are signs of economic resurgence, platinum's stronger fundamentals should reassert themselves—platinum should again become more valuable than gold. Based on above-ground supplies, it's estimated that there's enough gold to satisfy 50 years of demand, while there's only about a 5-year supply of platinum. The current reversal of the premium relationship (December 14, gold $415., platinum $410.) means that long-term platinum buyers may purchase pretty cheaply. The last time investors had the opportunity to acquire platinum cheaper than gold was in 1977. There is no reason why platinum's unique fundamentals won't again reassert themselves, unless you assume the economy will never revert to the boom-bust cycle.

Platinum futures are not for the novice commodity trader, but this unusual platinum/gold spread presents an opportunity for battle-scarred veterans. Buying platinum futures and selling gold (two for one, as platinum is a 50-ounce contract to gold's 100) should ultimately result in a profit in platinum that exceeds the loss in gold. This is a long-term trade that should be considered only by those with experience in commodities. If you fit the description, you'll want to enter this trade at the greatest discount to gold possible. This past January, 1981 found platinum at a $55 discount, and, in late September of 1981, on the washout following the announced silver auction, platinum again traded almost $55 below the price of gold. A $45-$55 discount seems to be a strong level of current support.

The largest "open interest" (number of contracts outstanding) in any month in gold is now almost 40,000, the biggest month in platinum is only about 4,600 contracts. This is a very thin market, the volatility is extreme, and getting whipsawed is commonplace. Don't start with platinum if you've never traded futures before.

Outlook

Now that the guy who wanted to know about platinum has some answers, what are the prospects for platinum living up to its high expectations?

First, there's no reason to get excited about platinum until gold and silver are again in an uptrend. In the meantime, platinum should continue to trade at a discount to gold. As of June 1, 1981 platinum supplies held by dealers, importers, and refiners were 33% larger than levels of a year earlier, and the continued bad economic news and low levels of auto production aren't likely to spur demand for awhile, at least until mid 1982.

One factor that many proponents of platinum point to is the U.S. National Defense Stockpile, which is 857,000 ounces short of its goal. Stockpile purchases will probably give impetus to prices of some metals on the General Services Administration's list, but sources close to the decision-making process suggest that platinum is too far down the list to benefit from stockpiling. "They'll be out of money before they get to platinum," was how one expert put it.

The Japanese, who have long been major consumers of platinum for jewelry, are likely to be an even bigger force in the platinum market in the years to come. Beginning in 1983, Japanese auto emission control laws will require catalytic converters on their cars, and regulations in this country are expanding to include diesel cars and trucks. The new approach to government in Washington has already resulted in many favorable regulatory changes, and if rolling back emission control standards is among future changes, this could be a significant depressant on the price of platinum. It's not likely, but it's worth keeping in mind if the auto industry got some leeway on catalytic converters.

If you decide that the high-priced spread is for you, buy it at a discount to gold, and only after you own basic positions in gold and silver. Platinum may be gaining acceptance, but it's still a Rolls-Royce when most people only need a Chevrolet.

CHAPTER 13

Failing or Failure Proofing Through Leverage

Archimedes, the Greek who discovered the principle of the lever, said, "Give me a lever and a place to stand and I can move the earth."

Leverage is probably the most powerful of all financial principles. Through leverage, fortunes are made. That's the good news! The bad news is that through leverage, fortunes are also lost! Whether the two-edged leverage sword helps or hurts the one who wields it depends on his understanding of the principle of the lever. Like fire and debt, leverage is a wonderful servant, but a fearful master. I want to show you how to use leverage to the fullest, while limiting the risk of damage.

Leverage is the principle of multiplying one's strength beyond one's natural capabilities.

In the financial sense, this means using a small amount of your own money to control a much larger investment. The lever which multiplies your financial strength is borrowed money. The trick is to use leverage to build fortunes, while at the same time avoiding the horrible consequences of losing fortunes by being highly leveraged and guessing wrong on the direction of an investment. Unfortunately, many people who use leverage lose money they don't have and didn't intend to risk, and end up going bankrupt.

Perhaps the most common example of leverage is real estate. Very few people who buy property pay cash. They stumble onto the principle of leverage simply because they don't have any other choice. If they want to buy a building, a residence or an investment property, they will have to borrow the money. Making a down payment and monthly payments over many years is a form of leverage that made possible the American dream of home ownership. Let me give you an example I used in my previous book, HOW TO PROSPER DURING THE COMING BAD YEARS.

"You have $100,000 to invest. If you buy a piece of property for $100,000 cash, and eventually sell it for $130,000, your $30,000 profit is a 30% profit on your $100,000 investment. However, if you buy it with $10,000 down and a $90,000 loan and sell it for $130,000, your $30,000 profit is a 300% return on your $10,000 invested, and you could have used your other $90,000 to buy nine such income properties, and you can make ten times as much money, and spread your risk."

While adding some tax shelter, I might add!

To elaborate a bit, your percentage of profit would depend on the degree of leverage you used. If, rather than putting $10,000 down, you had put $20,000, the $30,000 profit would have only given you 150% return on your money. If you had bought with nothing down, your leverage would be infinite, even though your actual cash profits would be a bit smaller because you would have larger finance costs.

Real estate leverage has worked best for most Americans because it carries a very low risk. In a long-term inflationary environment, and even under the worst disinflationary conditions such as we suffered in 1981, real estate prices rarely drop much. Even if they do, the bank won't call your loan as long as you make your payments. Even if the value of the mortgage holder's security (the market value of the building) should decline sharply, they are legally obligated to leave you alone if you simply meet your payment schedule. The only way leverage could hurt you in this situation or force you to sell is if you did not make those payments.

Leveraged Losses?

Real estate is an imperfect example of the leverage principle precisely because it does not adequately demonstrate the risk side. Let's go to a typically risky kind of leverage: the futures market. There you can put up from 2% to 5% of the value of a futures contract and either make or lose a lot of money, depending on the way it moves. For example, you can, as of this date (November 18, 1981), buy 100 ounces of gold, with a market value of about $40,000, for approximately $1,500 downpayment or "margin". You send your broker $1,500 and tell him to buy you one 100 ounce gold contract for delivery in, say, February, 1982. If you hold the contract until the delivery date, you'll have to come up with the rest of the money due on that contract. If the price of gold had risen to $500 an ounce, that contract would be worth $50,000 and your initial deposit of $1,500 (this would vary from broker to broker) would have given you a $10,000 profit; the difference between the $40,000 value of the contract at the time you bought it and the $50,000 value of the contract at the time you took delivery, or, much more likely, sold the contract. If, however, the price of gold had dropped from $400 to $300 an ounce, you would have committed yourself to buy a contract at $40,000 an ounce that now has a market value of $30,000. You would have not only lost your original $1,500, but another $8,500 besides. As a practical matter, when gold had

257

declined enough that your margin had been reduced to about half of what you put up, your broker would have given you a "margin call", the only totally unqualified piece of advice you'll ever get from your broker. Unless you want to have the broker sell you out to protect himself, you'll have to come up with more margin money. If you don't, he'll sell you out whether you like it or not. If gold should suddenly drop far enough to wipe out all of your margin and then some before he could execute a sell order, you'll get billed for the additional losses. You can end up losing more money than you put up. The leverage works exactly the same on the loss side as it does on the profit side. You can lose several times your initial investment, either because your broker sells you out because of an abrupt drop, or because you put up more margin money in the mistaken belief that it had bottomed and would go no lower. A margin call is an agonizing choice but that is the risk you accept in futures market because of the high leverage. Obviously, if you use less leverage by putting up 10% or 20% or 30% of the value of the contract, then you watch the market decline with less likelihood of the agonizing decision of a margin call, but the dollar loss potential is the same, with less profit potential as a percentage of return on investment.

There has been more than one occasion when gold futures have plunged "limit down" for several days. This means that the price fell more than the amount set by the exchange as the trading limit. All trading then stops. You can't get in or out until the price rises to within the limits, or until the next day. If it happens several days in a row, as it has on more than one occasion in gold and silver, all you can do is watch helplessly as your losses mount. If you don't keep shelling out more margin money, your broker will sell you out the minute trading opens again.

The main principle to remember when using leverage in any investment is, the smaller the percentage of money you put down, the greater your chance of big profit or loss.

I use leverage in the conduct of my business also. By myself I can't do the accounting, the data processing, the printing, the typing, the marketing, the secretarial work, the day-to-day administration, set policy for my publishing company, do the research and write THE RUFF TIMES. So I have "leveraged" myself by utilizing other people's strengths to do the job. There is a cost attached to that—the cost of renting the facilities, hiring and equiping the people who will provide that strength. But through the principle of leverage, I will be able to accomplish more than I could do myself. I will share some of the rewards in the form of salaries. I might share some of the rewards in the form of profits paid to shareholders who will provide the money to finance all of this. But in the final analysis, I will be better off and make a lot more money than if I did it all by myself.

Let's get back to real estate leverage for a moment.

What are the safety factors and the danger signals in real estate leverage?

The principal danger signal is that if you are leveraged too highly, or, are paying too much interest for too large a loan, the income from the property might not service the debt, and you could have a negative cash flow, meaning you'll have to pull money out of your pocket every month to keep the investment alive, because the income won't be sufficient to meet those expenses. Your leverage should be set at that level which will give you at least a break-even cash flow. In calculating your cash flow, you might want to take into account additional "silent cash flow" in the form of taxes not having to be paid on your ordinary income because of the tax shelter of owning the property.

Leveraged Inflation Hedging

An inflation hedge is defined as any investment whose price can be expected to move in the same direction as the inflation rate, only more so, but leverage can turn an investment which is not an inflation hedge into an inflation hedge. Real estate has been and will continue to be a good inflation hedge, but, if the inflation rate was 15%, meaning that the dollar was self-destructing and losing purchasing power at 15%, and real estate was only going up 10% per year, obviously it would not be a very good inflation hedge—if you paid cash.

Here's a simple example:

```
       $110,000  sale price after one year
less   $100,000  purchase price
       $ 10,000  profit
less   $ 15,000  15% loss of purchasing power on $100,000
                 investment
      [$ 5,000]  net loss in real terms
```

If you used 75% leverage, the picture would look like this:

```
       $110,000  purchase price of property (25% down pay-
                 ment, $75,000 mortgage)
       $100,000  selling price
       $ 10,000  profit
less   $  3,750  15% loss of purchasing power on $25,000
                 investment
       $  6,250  net profit in real terms
```

Put another way, your $10,000 return on your $25,000 downpayment is 40%, and that beats the heck out of 15% inflation. Even if you use only 60% leverage, the profit on $40,000 down would be 25%. Taxes and commissions were left out for simplicity.

The advantage of leveraged real estate is the relatively low risk, assuming that you buy at a decent price and structure the financing properly, as recommended in HOW TO PROSPER DURING THE COMING BAD YEARS.

Through commodity futures you can get leveraged profits or losses from 100 ounces of gold for a $1500 downpayment. But how could you get on limited profit potential in gold with the same percentage of leverage, while having no margin call risk?

Gold is so intimately tied into the inflation rates that if you

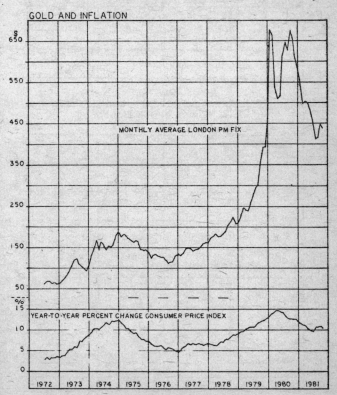

GOLD AND INFLATION

MONTHLY AVERAGE LONDON PM FIX

YEAR-TO-YEAR PERCENT CHANGE CONSUMER PRICE INDEX

can catch the trend of inflation, you are almost sure to catch the trend of gold. Rising inflation rates mean rising gold. Steady or falling inflation rates mean gold either drifting downward or plummeting because gold exaggerates.

There are two companies listed on the New York Stock Exchange whose fortunes are intimately tied to gold. Their stock moves dependably in the same direction at the same time. They are somewhat leveraged, in that they tend to move

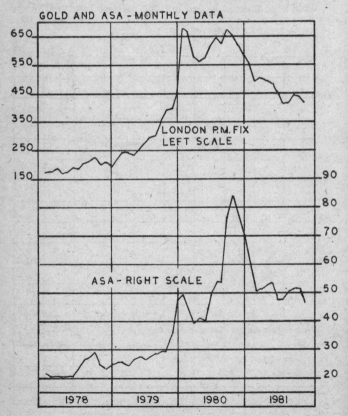

GOLD AND ASA - MONTHLY DATA

LONDON P.M. FIX
LEFT SCALE

ASA - RIGHT SCALE

further and faster than the metal itself. The companies are ASA, an investment trust which invests in South African gold mining company shares, and Homestake Mining, America's largest gold mining operation. These are both large, stable companies with excellent dividends and earnings histories. When you buy these shares, already discussed earlier (pp. 195-97), you, in effect, own some of their gold in the ground. If gold goes up 10%, Homestake and ASA will probably move 15%, if their historical trend continues. By buying the shares, rather than gold bullion, you get a little better leverage.

Homestake and ASA, however, give us a unique leverage opportunity in that they both offer "options." ASA options are listed on the American Stock Exchange, and Homestake options on the Chicago Board, and there are daily quotes in the WALL STREET JOURNAL. An option is simply the right to purchase a given stock at a given price before the option expires on a given date. At the risk of boggling your mind, let's take a look at the option listing for November 18, 1981.

OPTION & STRIKE NY CLOSE PRICE		CALLS—LAST			PUTS—LAST		
		JAN	APR	JUL	JAN	APR	JUL
HOMSTK	40	2½	4¾	6	3¼	4¼	4⅝
37⅞	45	1⅛	2¾	4¼	6⅝	7¼	7¼
38⅞	50	7/16	1⅝	2¾	11⅛	12	11
38⅞	55	¼	⅞	2⅛	16⅛	15¾	17
38⅞	60	3/16	9/16	s	21¼	22	s
38⅞	70	⅛	s	s	32¼	s	s

Now let's untangle that complicated batch of numbers. Under the name of the stock in the far left hand column you see 38⅞. That is simply the closing price of the stock on the previous day. The next column lists the "striking price" of the options, ranging from $40 a share to $70 a share. That simply means that at that price you have bought the right to purchase the stock. If you bought a Homestake 40 call option, that means you purchased the right to buy shares of Homestake at $40, gambling that the price would go above $40 giving you a good profit. The first three columns headed "January," "April" and "July" are for "call" options.

A "call option" is a bet that the stock will go up. For example, if you have a "call" on 100 shares of stock (the size of each option contract) on or before the third Friday of January (all Homestake options expire on the third Friday of the expiration month), there are some interesting possibilities. When you buy an "April Homestake 50" option (the right to purchase the stock at $50 before it expires in April), you are betting that the stock will rise above $50 by then, and you are willing to pay a little premium for that leverage. As you can see, that option is trading at 1⅝. That means that whenever the price of the stock rises above 51⅝, which is the "striking price" of the option, plus what you paid for the option, you start generating handsome profits. Everytime the stock goes up another $1.63, you will add another 100% return on your investment.

Conversely, if the stock should go down, unlike a futures contract your option can't be worth less than zero. Your loss is limited to the money you put up for the option. You can lose 100% of the money you put up, obviously, if the stock never rose above the level at which it would be profitable and if you held it until it expired worthless. As a practical matter, if the stock rose close to the option striking price well in advance of the expiration date, your option would rise in anticipation that the stock would continue rising. It's a very volatile market. The closer the option expiration date, the cheaper the option is, because you are now in a race with the calendar. As you can see, the July Homestake 50 call option is 2¾, but January is only ⁷⁄₁₆, because of the increased safety factor of time. If you got a fast move in the stock that ran it up quickly, you'd have better leverage in the January call. If it didn't move real quick, you have a surer loss, also.

The basic risk-evaluation facts are these:

1. Options are safer than futures contracts bec. won't have a margin call. You can't lose more than yo for the option.

2. You get the best leverage with the closer expiration months because they are cheaper. You get the best safety by buying the farther out option months because that gives you some leeway to be wrong on your time table, but you pay more for that option as the price of safety.

3. Any option striking price which is higher than the current price of the stock is referred to as "out of the money." Your safest bet is the first option "out of the money", although you will pay more for it because you are again paying a premium for safety. For example, if Homestake is selling at 38⅞, the first option "out of the money" is Homestake 40. Because of the better chance that Homestake will go to 40 than to 50, you'll pay more for that option. The most conservative way to play the options is to take the first option out of the money, and buy the farthest out month. When an uptrend is so clearly established that you feel you can safely bet on it, then you get the most "bang for the buck" with the highest risk by taking the second option out of the money, in this case, the Homestake 50, and buying the nearest month—that is if you are not allergic to cold sweats and nightmares, and groove on risk. It is a pretty exhilarating game.

4. The key advantage of options is that once the price has risen above your striking price, the stock does not have to double in order for you to double your money. It merely has to move above the striking price by an amount equal to what you paid for your option. If you paid 1½ for your option, every $1.50 move adds another 100% to your investment. You have a floor because you can't lose more than you put up, but you have no ceiling on your profit potential. Obviously, success or failure depends on whether or not you catch the direction of the stock. If you do, there is no better way to make a whole lot of bucks.

The free market of investors and speculators evaluates the prospects for Homestake and determines what that option is worth.

The best hit I ever made in all the years I've been in the investment business was in May of 1980 when I jumped into ASA options, based on the assumption that gold was going to go up. ASA was trading around $39 a share and we jumped on the ASA 45 option. ASA eventually went to $90. I got out around $75.

At the time we went into the market, gold was at approximately $480 an ounce. I thought it would go to $850 by the end of the summer. Well, it only went to $700 and it took until September, but that's not bad. At about $650 gold, ASA was at $75, and I decided to get out. With a $20,000 investment I paid for an indoor swimming pool, a racquetball court, a new apartment, a security fence, a stable and a tennis court. If I'd been wrong about the direction of gold, I would have lost about $20,000. The risk/reward ratio was super. I did about as well as I would have in futures, but if I'd been wrong, my futures loss would not have been limited. For leverage speculation in gold, it's the only way to go.

Now we get to the $64 quesion. WHEN and AT WHAT PRICE do you buy either Homestake or its options?

As a general principle, when I signal that gold is about to make a powerful up move, or is in a solidly established move upward, that will be the time to jump into the options. When I tell you that gold is near its lows and in an accumulation phase, you can safely buy the stock as a long-term, mildly leveraged investment in gold for the relatively conservative investor who wishes to hedge against inflation and enjoy some interesting dividends. You don't touch the options until you are pretty darn sure a trend has been established and it is apparent that the gold market is beginning to signal the end of the recession and a resurgence

266

of inflation, and that depends on when you buy this book. That's why we have offered a free update. See page 160 in this book.

A word about the last three columns in our example of the option newspaper listing on page 263. Those are "put" options, where everything is a mirror image of what we just talked about. You're betting on a decline in gold. I personally have difficulty playing the option market from the "put" side, simply because I don't like to bet against a long-term trend. The long-term trend is inflation and I'd just as soon stand on the side lines until it's time to move. Gold's upward moves should be much more explosive than its declines, and the very nature of the option market requires relatively explosive moves. The odds favor the "call" side. So for practical purposes, I ignore the "put" side. Obviously. a lot of other investors don't agree with me; that's why "puts" are listed in the newspaper. But I prefer not to entangle a relatively clean and simple concept by getting into a detailed discussion of "puts."

Riding the Rates

The spectacular rise in Treasury bond, T-Bill, and CD futures, have generated a lot of futures horror stories on THE RUFF TIMES Member Services hotline, just as bad as the gold futures horror stories, so we have developed some similar Failure Avoidance strategies for less risky leveraged speculation in interest rates.

The key to safer leveraged gold investments was to find stocks that move with the gold price, and have listed options. The key to safer interest rate leverage is to find stocks with listed options that move with interest rates. Here's two we found: AETNA (insurance) and CHASE MANHATTAN (banking).

Look at the chart below. The correlation isn't perfect, but

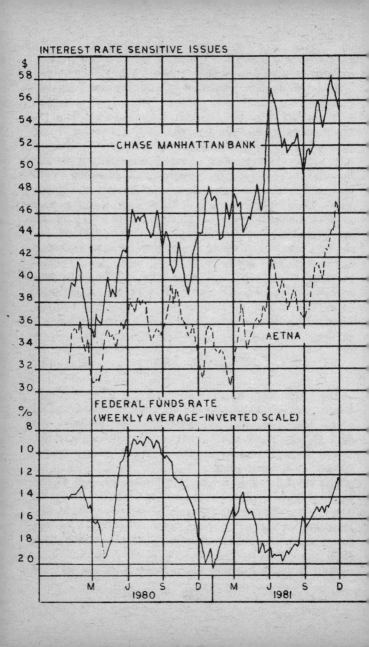

it's pretty darn good. When interest rates go down, these stocks tend to go up and vice versa.

To show you the safety advantages of options over futures, let's study two hypothetical speculators with the same idea at the same time, one in options, one in futures.

Let's assume that back around May 29, 1981, JOE and BOB decided that interest rates were finally going to decline. Both of these interest rate optimists jumped in on May 29. Joe chose to buy options in interest rate sensitive stocks.

Being either unworried or unaware of the possible adverse consequences, Bob bought a bond futures contract, putting up the $2500 initial margin required on a December T-bond futures contract. Joe spent roughly the same amount on December call options, buying the nearest "out of the money" and the most distant month available. He bought Chase Manhattan December 50 calls at 2⅛, listed on the American options exchange, Chase Manhattan stock was selling for 51. Eleven option contracts were purchased for $2337.50. They were worth a lot less several times along the way, but because there were no margin calls, he hung in there. By November 27, and 11 options, at 6⅜, were worth $7012.50. Joe tripled his initial investment, with $4675 in profit, a 200% profit in six months.

If Joe had chosen Aetna on the same date, when the stock was at 37⅛, the January 40 call (American options exchange) was 2⅜. Ten options could have been bought for $2375. On November 27, Aetna closed at 47⅛. The call option was 7¼. The total value of his position was $7250, profit $4875—up 205% from initial investment. As was the case with the Chase options, there were some paper losses along the way, but no margin call panic sales.

Now let's see what happened to Bob. He bought one December T-bond contract for his $2500, at a closing price of 66-20 (that's 66 and 20/32nds). On two days the following week, Bob had small paper losses, but by the market close on the first day of the third week, he had paper profits of over

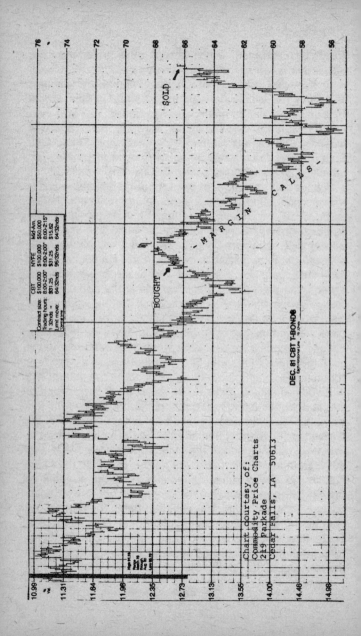

BOUGHT

SOLD

MARGIN CALLS

	CBT	NYFE	Mid-Am
Contract size:	$100,000	$100,000	$50,000
Trading hours:	8:00-2:00*	8:00-2:00*	8:00-2:15*
1/32nds =	$31.25	$31.25	$15.62
Limit move:	64/32nds	96/32nds	64/32nds

DEC 81 CBT T-BONDS

Chart courtesy of:
Commodity Price Charts
219 Parkade
Cedar Falls, IA 50613

$2,000. He remained convinced that interest rates were no-where near as low as they would be by December. Within the next two weeks his paper profits had turned into a loss, and his broker was calling, demanding that he bring his account up to maintenance margin levels—a margin call. Still convinced that interest rates were going down, he met the margin call, feeling it was only a matter of time before interest rates vindicated his outlook on the market.

Only a matter of time—and money, as it turned out. The market continued to defy his expectations. As interest rates went up, bonds went down toward their eventual bottom just above 55 in September. One of two things had to happen. (1) He either got "stopped out" of the market for a substantial loss, or (2) *he* continued to meet margin calls to maintain his position, ultimately paying out over $11,000 above and beyond the initial investment of $2,500. Chances are that most people would have cut their losses somewhat in advance of this point, but that is what it cost Bob to continue to back up his opinion on interest rates in the T-bond market.

Assuming Bob had the financial staying power and the stomach for this setback, this example is not without a twisted sort of happy ending. On November 27, when his fellow interest rate bull was taking profits of about 200%, Bob, the hapless futures trader, was liquidating his position at 66-11, a loss of $281.25, excluding commissions.

Joe and Bob had the same opinion on interest rates at the same time. They were both right in the long run. It was the short run that killed Bob. Joe opted for a choice that also limited the risks.

If you believe interest rates are headed lower, Aetna or Chase look good. I would probably choose Aetna over Chase, because Chase has big exposure to defaults on Polish loans. Choose the closest call out of the money, and the second available month.

Now, to drive this all home, let's take a tour of a commodities exchange.

271

We are visiting the floor of the Chicago Mercantile Exchange, and our host is Marshall Wright. Marshall is not only my broker who executes my futures trades, but he's also a great friend. He and I talk several times a day as I assess the markets. Recently, some of my staff and I were in Chicago and visited the Exchange floor. It was a real eye-opener for them to discover that the commodities markets are an integral part of the free enterprise system. I didn't want you to miss this discovery, so I have arranged a tour through the pits for you. I also want you to understand the commodity futures markets, so you will know whether or not you want to get involved in this high-rolling, volatile game. Most of you should not try, and I hope this tour entertains and enlightens you, and gives you the cold sweats at the very thought of buying a futures contract without a lot of dough, a lot of knowledge, and the nerves of the Wallendas on the high wire. If you don't qualify and plunge anyway, you will disintegrate faster than the Eighties.

Marshall, we're in your hands.

MW: Then let's get started. Howard, when we open the doors to the trading floor, the decibel level will leap, so let's talk here in the foyer. This is one of the last existing bastions of free enterprise. This is a "primary market," meaning that I cannot sell or buy anything for you on this Exchange unless somebody is willing to take the opposite side of the trade.

HJR: In other words, if I wanted to buy one contract of 100 ounces of gold, there would have to be a willing seller?

MW: Right. Starting more than 125 years ago, farmers brought their grain here to a farmers' market on the corner of LaSalle and Jackson. Some farmers wanted to sell their crops before harvest to a miller or baker who wanted to ensure his supply of grain months from now. This was the start of the trading of "futures," contracts which would not actually be consummated for several months.

HJR: And the consummation of the trade would be the actual delivery of the grain?

MW: Correct. As we walk through the floor, you will hear the euphemism "cars." Agricultural contracts are based on a railroad carload, such as 5,000 bushels of wheat or 40,000 pounds of live cattle. We now trade gold financial instruments and foreign currencies. It sounds funny, but when we trade 25,000 British pounds on a contract, we still call it a car, even though 25,000 pounds of British sterling is a very small pile of paper.

HJR: Why would someone want to buy or sell his crop before harvest?

MW: Let's say a General Mills' buyer believes that grain prices will go up between now and the time he needs it. He would like to buy his grain at today's prices so that he can predict his profit margin. On the other hand, the farmer may expect a glut, so he would rather sell now for future delivery.

HJR: I guess his banker would also be more willing to loan.

MW: This is a big component of the agricultural market. The farmer "hedges" his crops on the futures market. The bank will hold the hedges as security and maybe loan him an extra 10% or 15% of the money he needs in order to plant his crop. Now let's go through these doors and dive in to this chaos.

HJR: The noisy confusion is overwhelming. Can you untangle it for us?

MW: The people you see running around in yellow coats are "runners" who work for the members of the Exchange and for the various clearing firms or brokerage firms. They are physically carrying the customer orders back and forth between the phones and the Exchange members in "the pit." Those in red coats are Exchange members, called professionals or locals, and are the only ones permitted to trade here. They trade for four different kinds of people: the "hedgers," such as General Mills or the farmers; the "speculators," who have no use for the product but are trying to make money by trading; "arbitrageurs," who we will discuss later; and, of course, their own accounts. A broker takes an order on the phone which is carried by the runner to the pit, where the member executes the order.

HJR: Who are the people in the light blue coats?

MW: They work for the Exchange. They immediately report every trade to a position right next to the pit where they are entered into the computer. Look over there. One is being reported right now. Within 30 seconds the world will know that a September gold contract just traded at $644.

HJR: Marshall, would you explain how someone can buy a commodity he doesn't really want, or sell one he doesn't own?

MW: "Going short" is selling contracts you don't own. Compare it to buying a magazine on subscription. You have, in fact, "gone long" on that commodity, meaning you bought that magazine for future delivery at a specific price, even though a specific issue of the magazine may not be delivered for a year. On the other hand, the publisher, having sold you a magazine that doesn't even exist yet, is "short." He is betting that he has accurately estimated the cost of producing that magazine. If he guesses wrong, he could pay more than he thought for paper, editorial costs, and wages. So a trader who felt that prices would drop, would sell a contract which he did not own, for delivery, say, on November 4, and he must buy a contract before November to either cancel out his position, or actually deliver the product. More than 97% of the futures transactions are liquidated before delivery is required. If you have sold one contract, then you must buy back one contract ultimately. Your net position is zero. You hope prices will fall so you can buy a contract at a lower price than you sold, and the difference is your profit.

HJR: Let me see if I have this right. If you sold one 100-ounce September gold contract today at $644 an ounce, you are obligated to deliver $64,400 worth of gold in September. And if gold fell to $500 an ounce sometime between now and September, you could then buy one contract for $50,000 and your profit would be $14,400. Because you now have obligations both to deliver and to accept delivery of 100 ounces of gold in September, it all cancels out. Whether you bought it first and sold it later, or sold it first and bought it later is irrelevant. The difference is the profit in either case. And incidentally, you didn't put up the whole $64,400. Only $5,000 "margin" was required.

MW: That is correct.

HJR: If the original purpose of the Exchange was to provide an opportunity for the farmer to sell his crop and for General Mills to buy it to grind it into flour, and if, as you say, 97% of the trades never result in delivery, hasn't the Exchange lost sight of its original intent?

MW: Absolutely not. In real life, General Mills might be willing to pay $4 a bushel for wheat and the farmer would really like to sell his wheat at $5. They would probably never get together if it were not for the speculators. When wheat is trading at $4, and the speculators collectively feel that the market is probably going higher, they start buying. Now there are more buyers than sellers, and they drive the price up to $5., at which point the farmers start selling. The traders would probably sell, driving the market down to $4 a bushel, at which point General Mills starts buying again.

HJR: Then price is the way we reach a balance between supply and demand!

MW: No question. The futures market works if the professional traders, plus the speculating general public, produce enough transactions so that the market "flows," and there are always buy and sell offers so the Exchange can meet the original intent of the farmer and General Mills.

HJR: Then the speculator makes it all possible. He isn't doing anything immoral.

MW: Of course not! This is one of the last bastions of free enterprise, and an honorable one. General Mills and the farmer would find it very difficult to contract with one another without the speculators in the middle. Incidentally, there has never been one contract defaulted to a client or a speculator here in over 110 years.

HJR: You mentioned "arbitrageurs." Would you explain who they are and what they do?

MW: The arbitrageurs are over there on the phone banks, right next to the pit, so they can have direct eye contact with the members who represent them. On the other end of the phone line is a man on a trading floor in London or Zurich. Let's say gold is $650 in Chicago and London is trading at $646. The arbitrageur, says to his man across the floor in the pit, "Sell 1,000 ounces at $650." He simultaneously buys 1,000 ounces in London at $646. He has made $4 an ounce on 1000 ounces, or $4000.

HJR: That sounds too easy. What's the catch?

MW: His timing must be perfect. Let's just say that he bought gold in London at $646, and an instant before he sells at $650 in Chicago, the FDA announces that gold causes cancer, and in seconds gold drops $10 to $640. He then owns 1000 ounces of gold at $464, with nothing on the other side to "arbitrage" it, unless he sells at $640 and takes a $6 per ounce loss, or $6,000.

HJR: Does he perform any useful function?

MW: Because of him, the markets in Hong Kong or in Zurich or in London will never get grossly out of line with one another. If Chicago is $5 higher than London, then he sells in Chicago and buys in London. Chicago comes down, and London goes up, until those two markets are literally forced back together. He keeps all the markets around the world trading within a very narrow range of one another, and provides liquidity.

HJR: A trader in the pit or an arbitrageur must take an emotional beating.

MW: You pay a tremendous emotional price. A fantastic

amount of money changes hands. Assuming an average price of $60,000 per contract, and an average of 15,000 gold contracts per day, that's almost a billion dollars. It is not unusual for a member of the Exchange to trade millions of dollars worth of gold in one day. At least 8 out of 10 commodity traders lose money. It is very, very difficult for a speculator to handle the emotional factors without a lot of guts. Amateur speculators need a competent broker to help them handle the emotions stirred up by the volatility of highly leveraged speculation.

The market works only because the hedgers and the speculators and the arbitrageurs and the professionals, acting in their own self-interest, can come together in the pit and trade so smoothly that at the end of every day, when the buy and sell transactions are balanced out, there is a ''zero sum'' market. We will not open the market the next day until all of the trades have evened up. We traders provide stability for the whole commercial market which can now hedge or buy insurance in the futures market. They pass this risk from themselves to the speculator, or arbitrageur, who is willing to accept the risk of a loss in the interest of making a profit, he has stabilized the entire food complex and the wood complex and all of the other commodity markets. He takes the risk away from the producer or the merchant.

HJR: Why are they waving their arms like a convention of deaf people?

MW: That arbitrageur giving hand signals toward the pit is giving an order to his member, who is standing there yelling, and holding out his hands with his palms facing inwards. He is trying to buy contracts. If he's holding his palms away from him, then he's trying to sell contracts. If he says the price first, he is buying. For example, I want to buy ten gold contracts at $649. I say, ''649 on ten.'' And if the man on the other side of the pit wants to sell ten at 650, then he will say, ''10 at 650.'' If he says the price first and he's holding his palms in, he's buying. If he says the price last and his palms

277

are out, he's selling. In this noise, it would be easy to misunderstand without sign language.

HJR: There must be a tremendous amount of trust on the floor.

MW: There is. If you are offering 10 contracts at 650, and I say, "Buy 'em. Buy 10 at 650," you will write down on your trading card, "I sold 10 to SAGE," my floor trading name. I see your trading name is RUFF, and on my card I write that I bought 10 contracts at $650 from RUFF. We both turn our cards in to the computer, which compares your card and my card and spits out a set of completed trades. In this Exchange, there are 150,000 to 250,000 separate trades a day.

If an error occurs, the computer rejects it. Let's say that you offered "10 at 650," and I bid "649 on 10," and I decided not to wait for 649, so I say "buy them at 650." But in the meantime, you accepted my bid at 649. The computer then spits out an "out trade," meaning that the cards don't agree. "Out trade" clerks would settle that trade between us before the market opens the next day. The customer is protected. He is always right if the member has erred.

HJR: What kind of people should or should not attempt to speculate?

MW: A good speculator first needs the financial wherewithal because of the high leverage. People without a lot of liquid risk capital should never trade gold futures. They should buy Krugerrands or junk silver coins. They should not use leverage where they are subject to margin calls. It's too emotional.

HJR: Could you explain again how the trader could lose a lot more than he intended if he got caught in a limit move?

MW: If you buy a 200-ounce gold contract, you will realize the consequences, good or bad, of owning 100 ounces of gold. Even though at $650, the 100 ounces is worth $65,000, you will put up only $5,000 in "margin." If gold goes up or down $1 an ounce, you have made or lost $100.

HJR: If gold moved up $50, you would have doubled your

money because you would have made $5,000, just as if you physically possessed the whole 100 ounces.

MW: Conversely, if gold went down $50, you would have lost $5,000, and wiped out your margin money. Let's say that the Iranians suddenly released our hostages, or good news broke out somewhere in the world and the cash market dropped $75 overnight, from $650 an ounce down to $575 an ounce. The limit in the Chicago Mercantile Exchange for gold futures is $50 on any given day, meaning that if the market moves $50 in one day, trading stops to allow emotions to cool off to keep a more orderly market.

HJR: What if the market wants to move more than $50, regardless of your rules?

MW: Then the market would be locked "limit down." No trades would occur. We could not liquidate your position.

HJR: Then if it dropped $50 more tomorrow . . .

MW: You are locked into more losses. If you didn't come up with more cash in response to a "margin call," we would have no choice but to sell you out whenever we can and bill you for the additional losses. You must have enough money so that you are not forced out of the market against your will.

HJR: I, along with others, got caught in 3 or 4 "limit down" days in a row in Carter's Save the Dollar program November 1, 1978.

MW: Correct. There was almost a $50 move without a trade from $250 back to the $200 areas. The limit then was only $10.

HJR: What qualities of personality or temperament does a trader need?

MW: Successful floor traders are not intimidated by the amount of money changing hands in the pit. They must also be able to calmly withstand emotional inputs from news and rumors. The biggest emotional hazard to a non-professional speculator is that on a leveraged basis your equity may change by a very large percentage during any given day. One gold contract requires a "margin" of only $5,000. If gold went up or down $35 in one day, your profit or loss would have been $3,500, or 70%. Even if you played it safer and put up more than the required margin, say $15,000, your equity would have changed 23% in one day. A 23% movement in your portfolio even in one month, let alone a day, would be a great emotional hazard to the average person.

HJR: Do you have anything else you would like to add?

MW: The Chicago Mercantile Exchange represents some of the truest principles of free enterprise. The last year and a half has brought a tremendous amount of legal activity by the government to step in and "protect" the speculator, the same activity that has completely stifled American business and industry over the last ten years. I hope you sense the beauty of what you are seeing today—this fantastic microcosm of activity which represents supply and demand, weather, news and all of these honest, economic factors. Government regulation threatens this. Free enterprise itself is at stake.

* * *

I hope this scared the hell out of you. If it didn't, you just might make a good commodity speculator. If not, stick with options.

CHAPTER 14

Numismatic Coins

There is a persuasive case to be made for buying collectible items during the Inflationary Eighties. As traditional investments are ravaged by inflation, and especially as interest rates in the marketplace generally rise above that which can be legally offered by financial institutions, people look for various kinds of inflation hedges and shelters, and collectible items are the traditional beneficiary of these conditions. During the inflationary boom of '73 and '74, every kind of collectible from antique stamps and gold coins on down to old bottles had amazing increases in price, and this is still continuing. Almost anything "they ain't makin' no more of," which has an active collector market, has gone up, and will probably continue to do so.

Some of these came down temporarily when inflation eased, but rare coins held their own much better than most investments, and they offer marvelous opportunities for the astute investor.

Numismatic coins are coins that are no longer being minted and so have acquired scarcity value. With some exceptions, the best numismatic investments are those which have been around for some time. You can, of course, buy numismatic coins that also have a high bullion value, for example, Morgan silver dollars and the U.S. $20 gold Double Eagle. But there are a lot of coins which have very little bullion value at all which are now worth as much as $100,000 for a single coin.

The market value of a numismatic coin is based on demand, availability, and quality. There is a broad-based market for numismatics with a published "bid-and-asked" price. Unless you intend to be an "international man" who travels outside the country and has financial holdings in other nations, you would probably be better off sticking with the U.S. coins, because daily price quotes for these are available in this country.

If you wish to become such an investor, you need a little expertise, but there are three ways to get around that problem. One is to buy and read all the best books on the subject, and there are several. The other is to find a coin dealer with integrity and depend upon him to supply you with the proper coins. Number three is best of all. Do both.

Five hundred to a thousand dollars can get you off to a pretty good start, although, the more money you have, obviously, the better buying opportunities you have.

If you have $500 or $1,000 to invest at the time this book is written, I would suggest U.S. gold coins—the $20, $10, $5., $2.50, $1., and $3. coins.

The price of rare coins will vary according to their condition and you should concentrate on the highest quality coins. Put your money with the best merchandise, even if it costs a bit more. Resale is such a strong factor that you should avoid anything that is not high-quality material.

If you have a coin with bullion value, then you have a floor on the price, represented by the market price of gold or silver. With a good coin you may pay a huge premium above the bullion value, but don't make light of collector demand premium. It is the same factor that makes a Rembrandt worth several million dollars, even though the paint, canvas, and frame may be worth only pennies. Most coin dealers will mark their products up from 10% to 15%, so you have even more incentive to select coins which have great liquidity. They will tend to appreciate most rapidly.

It's not uncommon for numismatic coins to move up 30% annually year-in and year-out for as much as a decade. For example, in 1968, a $20 gold "high relief" struck in 1907 was selling for $500. Now it is close to $7,000. Higher grades of this coin which sold for $1,000 in 1968 now sell for $17,000 to $18,000.

In February, 1979, Numisco, Inc. (see the Appendix) displayed a $5,000 sample portfolio of numismatic coins at our annual *Ruff Times* National Convention. At the time of our next convention, a year later, this portfolio had appreciated to more than $15,000, beating inflation by quite a bit.

At the time I wrote *How to Prosper During the Coming Bad Years,* a bag of uncirculated Morgan silver dollars was worth about $12,000 to $15,000. They have since been worth as much as $45,000.

Sample Portfolio

If you have $10,000 to invest in a numismatic program, I'd put $2,000 of it into silver dollars, $3,000 of it into U.S. gold coins ($20, $10, $5.00, $3.00, $2.50, and $1.00 coins), and the other $5,000 spread through U.S. "proof sets," U.S. commemorative coins, and rare single coins, all in choice condition.

"Proof sets" are U.S. coins which were minted for investors and collectors in 1936 through 1942 and again through the

'50s and early '60s using a highly polished die. They are sharper than circulated coins and have a mirrorlike, highly reflective surface.

You might want to buy rolls of silver coins, such as the "Walking Liberty" half dollars, Franklin half dollars, Mercury dimes, and silver Washington quarters. In early 1981, prices were roughly $300 to $500 for certain low-mintage coins that have excellent potential, but of course, any price I quote here is subject to change, depending on when you read this book.

The only real source of such coins is coin dealers. The chances of an individual stumbling across a rare coin in his change from a candy counter is virtually nonexistent. The minute a coin becomes circulated it loses a substantial amount of its value anyway, so even if you found an old date or some old coins tucked away in the attic of an old house, the likelihood of them having great value is remote. Only the choice, uncirculated coins have significant value.

Coin shows offer a wide variety of coins from a number of dealers. Although these shows are pleasant and educational, unless you have developed some expertise, particularly in the area of grading, you should be extremely cautious about making initial purchases there.

All U.S. numismatic coins are listed each week in the "Gray Sheets," along with the bid and asked prices in the wholesale market for coin dealers. They are similar to the New York Stock Exchange quotes in your morning paper.

If my basic premise is correct about inflation on the prowl in the Inflationary Eighties, the continued appreciation of numismatic coins will be tremendous.

The line between numismatic and bullion coins may be blurring, simply because many of the bullion-type coins, such as junk silver, are being hoarded by people who subscribe to newsletters like mine. These bullion-type coins may never see the light of day and may become scarce. Also, a lot of them were sold to the refinery and melted down in the Hunt silver panic. But the supply of real numismatic coins of high quality is also rather thin. That's why the price can explode so dramatically when inflation takes off.

If you think the price of gold or silver is too high, you might be happier buying numismatic coins without any precious metal content. If you think the price of gold will continue rising, then you would want to buy numismatic coins with a lot of gold content. If you have sufficient funds, you probably should balance your investment program between those two kinds of coins.

Rare coins are both private and portable. If privacy is important to you, consider the fact that the coin market is one of the last truly free markets left. It is not subject to government regulation or record-keeping requirements, except the normal business practices and fraud statutes that cover all businesses. Because it is a cash market, it is relatively easy to consummate confidential transactions. If the government should call in gold, numismatic gold coins will probably be exempt, as they were in 1933.

Commemorative Medallions

Commemorative medallions from private prints are generally very poor investments. The mints sell as many as they can so the medallions have no scarcity value. You are generally paying a substantial premium over-and-above the silver content. If you like them, buy them from some poor guy who has to liquidate his holdings for some reason. You'll get them a lot cheaper than buying them from the mint.

Rare coins are a concealable asset of high value and small size. They are a liquid asset with an international market, and they are frequently exempt from import-export currency regulations. There are no restrictions on taking them in or out of the United States. While America is being liquidated, rare coins will still stand tall.

CHAPTER 15

A Girl's
Next-Best Friend

Here's a sparkling idea for surviving the Inflationary Eighties.

Over the years I've watched the colored gemstone markets with a great deal of interest and considerable trepidation. My major concern was that the difficulty of judging the value of a stone puts the amateur gemstone buyer at the mercy of the seller. There are some nice people in the investment gemstone business whose honesty is not in question, but I had no way of judging their expertise. I also wondered about their restraint if we should have a shortage of good-quality stones at any given time. They are in the business of selling stones, no matter what kind of quality is available in the marketplace. The colored stone market is much like the numismatic coin market, in that you should always buy the better quality goods, so it is "Buyer beware!"

I now believe colored stone prices will go to the moon as a result of inflation. To give the subscribers to my newsletter an education on the subject of colored stones, I interviewed Bill

Pinch, one of America's foremost gem and mineral experts, back in October, 1979. Bill is in charge of all gemstone buying and appraising for Investment Rarities, one of our recommended vendors (see the Appendix). He has done appraisals for the Smithsonian and other institutions. His suggestions, now updated for the eighties, are no less relevant today.

HJR: Bill, gemstone prices have literally exploded and seem to have a wonderful future. Would you give us a rundown on their past and future market record, and some of the do's and dont's of colored stone investing?

BP: Gems have been traded and sold for over 7,000 years, and, to my knowledge, there has never been a significant drop in the market. They only appreciate.

HJR: What percentage of appreciation have we seen?

BP: Depending on the gem we are talking about, a 50% to 100% increase in 1979 and 1980.

HJR: Do you feel good about diamonds as an investment?

BP: Oh yes, I feel good about diamonds, but only on the top end of the quality scale: D, E, and F in color and VVS-1, or flawless, very high quality stones.

HJR: Why should one then decide to invest in colored gemstones, rather than diamonds?

BP: Diamonds, across the board, have become so expensive that most people can't afford them. They have discovered colored stones as the poor man's diamond. Colored stones are starting to move partly because of the rapid increase in diamond prices. Also the more expensive precious colored stones—sapphires, rubies, emeralds, cat's-eyes, chrysoberyl—are increasing very rapidly in value.

HJR: The price per carat of some precious colored stones is right up there with diamonds, isn't it?

BP: Yes, it is. Of course, D-flawless diamonds are often over $50,000 per carat. I've seen flawless, top color emeralds bringing $25,000 to $30,000 a carat wholesale. I have seen fine rubies that are bringing $35,000 to $100,000 a carat. These are good investments, but you don't have to invest that much to make money. A few hundred dollars can get you started.

HJR: Then this could provide an opportunity for the small investor that he could never afford in diamonds?

BP: It provides an excellent opportunity. Investors are just beginning to buy the lesser semiprecious colored gems, which are very beautiful and now are being marketed very heavily in Europe. American prices are much lower than they are in Europe.

HJR: What kind of increase can we expect?

BP: We could see a 50% increase per annum in stones like tourmaline. Tourmaline comes in a number of colors. The beautiful pink is called rubellite. Tourmalines also come in deep reds, greens, blue-greens, blues, and sometimes even yellow. They vary in price according to the brilliance of the color of the stone, the most valuable ones being the deep pigeon-blood red stones, which retail for $600 a carat and wholesale for about $300 a carat.

HJR: How much are some of the smaller tourmalines?

BP: A small investor could buy plain green stones for around $90 to $100 a carat, maybe a little less. They are an excellent investment.

HJR: How liquid are colored stones?

BP: Right now, the very expensive precious stones are more liquid than the semiprecious gems, but most stones could be sold in a reasonably orderly market. When prices go up, jewelers need to replace their stock, so you might sell to one of them. A word of caution about selling to jewelers, however. Jewelers buy from the wholesalers, and if the jewelers can't buy for less than they pay the dealers, they aren't interested. That makes it very important to buy a stone at close to the wholesale price, because that's how you will sell it.

HJR: Are you more likely or less likely to have a hassle over the value of a diamond than you are over a colored gemstone? Don't diamonds have greater liquidity?

BP: Yes, because certification of a diamond is pretty well accepted throughout the world. The Gemological Institute of America (GIA) issues a grading certificate on diamonds. With colored stones, one company gives a good certification paper, but it is not universally accepted yet. When there is a lot more standardization, you will find the interest in colored gemstones really picking up and prices rising even faster.

HJR: How soon do you think it will be before there is general standardization?

BP: It should start early in 1981, and will probably take three years to really get rolling. It certainly is going in that direction. Gemologists realize it is badly needed.

HJR: What other advantages are there to buying small stones for investment?

BP: First of all, they are beautiful. You can't enjoy a stock certificate on your wall, but you can set a gem in a beautiful ring. This doesn't increase its value, but it's much more enjoyable. The metal and the small stones around it generally are not counted in the value when the ring is sold. Usually, the price is based on the stone only.

HJR: Which particular kind of stone will appreciate best over the next few years? Is there danger in picking the wrong one? Might topazes do better or worse than tourmalines, for example?

BP: They are all going up. For this reason, I would suggest that the buyer get a portfolio of mixed stones.

I would include some tourmalines, possibly some red garnets, maybe peridot, malia garnets, and tanzanite. Also, I would put a sapphire into the parcel. If you have enough money, you should add a ruby and an emerald too. You might include a tsavorite garnet. It is a green garnet—an intense, beautiful green. It is a fairly new, very desirable gem. You can pick one up at $1,000 to $2,000 a carat wholesale. I've seen them sell for $5,000 a carat in the retail market.

HJR: You have referred to "precious" colored stones. Which ones are in that category?

BP: The precious colored stones are rubies, sapphires, star rubies, star sapphires, emeralds, chrysoberyls (which include cat's-eyes, chrysoberyl, and alexandrite) and precious topaz in the fine, imperial colors. All the rest are considered semiprecious gems.

HJR: Are there any special problems in the care and storage of colored stones?

BP: There are very few problems. They come in little gem papers and can be kept almost anywhere. The only problem is theft, and one could use a safe-deposit box to prevent that.

HJR: Any problem with scratching?

BP: I wouldn't put a lot of gemstones together in one parcel. We generally try to keep stones separated to avoid chipping.

HJR: Is there a problem with either synthetic stones or doctored stones?

BP: There are a number of ways to tamper with stones, such as treatment with radiation, followed by heating. This is done to blue topaz, but that is well known and seems to be acceptable. I see no reason why it shouldn't, because 95% of the aquamarines on the market have also been heat-treated, which turns them from a greenish-blue to a pure blue. Many sapphires coming out of Ceylon are being heat-treated also, which gives them a richer blue color and greater value, and yet the GIA can't determine whether or not this has been done to many of these stones. Actually, this doesn't have an adverse effect on the value of stones.

HJR: Blue topaz gemstones are not universally accepted, are they?

BP: That's true, but I believe them to be a fine investment.

HJR: Can some unscrupulous businessman buy the cheaper

stones and treat them with radiation or heat and have an automatic increase in the value of the stone?

BP: It is not as simple as it sounds, and it doesn't always work. Any reasonably knowledgeable expert can tell which stones are valuable and which aren't.

HJR: It has been alleged that heat is being used on poor quality sapphires, which are really worth just a few dollars a carat, to create a color that looks like that of the untreated stones, which are worth thousands of dollars a carat.

BP: The statement isn't quite accurate. It isn't "a few dollars a carat" to "thousands of dollars a carat." I've dealt with a dealer in New York City who has sold me sapphires and said, "These are treated stones, but look at them. There is no way you can tell. I know they are because I bought them in Bangkok as treated stones." But a fine color-treated sapphire is worth every bit as much as a natural fine color sapphire. There won't be a flood of them on the market, as there aren't that many. Treating them isn't very profitable. For every one that comes out a good blue, there are several which are ruined.

HJR: How do you judge the quality of a stone?

BP: The 4 c's of judging a diamond are all equally important (color, clarity, cut, carat). A tiny microscopic flaw can reduce a diamond from flawless to VVS and lower its value considerably. With the colored precious gems, however, this is not the case. The most important factor in judging any colored gem is color. A flaw which can be seen with the naked eye in a ruby or emerald might affect the value, but not a lot. Emeralds which have no visible flaws are rare and, of course, command higher prices, but many fine color emeralds have "gardens," which are a number of small flaws, and still command thousands of dollars per carat on the wholesale market. Look at some jeweler's emeralds or rubies to get a feeling for clarity and color vs. price per carat. Also, many of the rubies and sapphires, even some emeralds, frequently are not symmetrically cut. This is because almost all these stones are cut in Thailand or Sri Lanka (Ceylon) or Colombia, which we, the dealers and wholesalers, have no control over. This does not usually affect the value, unless the cut is really bad.

HJR: How about other methods of treating stones? Is this very common?

BP: Surface coating is common in lower-quality emeralds. Wholesalers and the natives in Zambia and Rhodesia oil the rough stones. It gives them a more intense green color. However, when you are dealing in fine quality emeralds, you never see anything that is oiled or treated.

HJR: Are there any other problems with emeralds?

BP: There are some man-made emeralds so natural looking that, in order to determine whether they are natural or synthetic, they must be examined under a high-power microscope for "three-phase inclusions." These are tiny negative crystals with a little bit of water and a bubble and a little crystal of halite or salt. Only the natural stone has that.

HJR: What about the problem of overgrading—being sold a stone that is represented as being a better grade than it is? Is this very common in the industry?

BP: Yes, it is far too common. The buyer must be careful. Most colored stones like sapphires and rubies are sold according to quality, but with no numerical grading whatsoever. Today the dealers know quality; the knowledgeable buyers know quality and they rely on their own judgment.

HJR: But if my readers follow my advice and buy some stones, there will be a lot of people trying to buy stones who don't know quality. And isn't it possible that unscrupulous dealers could simply represent the stones as being more valuable than they are?

BP: It is not only possible, it has been happening. I've examined some sapphires that were sold to a customer by one defunct company for about $600 a carat. On the retail market right now, those stones are worth about $30 a carat.

HJR: Are any of these stones heat-sensitive?

BP: One hundred degrees or thereabouts will not affect most stones, but you should avoid extreme temperatures.

HJR: What other pitfalls should the average buyer watch out for?

BP: I don't see any other pitfalls. Just find a dealer who is reputable and whom you can trust, or become an expert yourself.

HJR: How much does a jeweler mark up most colored stones?

BP: A jeweler marks them up from about 60% for a fine ruby to over 150% for the less expensive semiprecious gems. We mark them up 20%.

HJR: Actually, then, jewelers have a better markup on the colored stones than on diamonds. Diamonds are marked up about 100%.

BP: That's right. Sometimes, of course, they will discount.

HJR: Let's take a person with $20,000 to invest. How should he invest it?

BP: I would recommend he put $12,000 to $15,000 into a precious emerald or ruby or a fine sapphire, and the rest into some of the semiprecious gems.

HJR: Why shouldn't we wait until certification procedures make the market safer?

BP: By the time that happens, prices will have increased spectacularly.

HJR: If we get in now before this happens, and should want or need to get out, won't we have uncertified stones?

BP: You can get those stones certified later.

HJR: What will the buyer get which testifies to the stone's value?

BP: It is not really right for a dealer who is selling a stone to hand the customer his own appraisal, nor is it right for the dealer to push one appraiser. All we can do is assure you that it is a very good value. We don't do appraisals on the stones we sell. I've seen in-house appraisals for stones sold by gem "investment" houses which are unrealistic, to say the least. You can get almost any appraisal you want on a stone. A dealer's own appraisal is worthless.

HJR: What about the problem of the "low-ball"? Someone buys stones from you and asks himself, "I wonder if they are really worth what I paid for them?" He goes to some jewelry store to get them appraised, and the jeweler comes back with a "low-ball" quote to make the competition look bad. The low-ball is common with diamonds. Are we going to have the same problem with colored gemstones?

BP: We run into it all the time. If that happens to you, ask the jeweler to sell you a stone of comparable price and quality at the price he has quoted. If it's a low-ball, he'll suddenly be out of stock.

Sometimes you can take a tsavorite garnet to a jeweler who has never heard of one. There are a lot of jewelers who just don't keep up with what is going on in the world. Some are not aware of current price changes because they don't handle a large variety of stones. I am not knocking jewelers. There are certainly some jewelers and some large jewelry trade groups who are very reputable and can give you a fair opinion.

HJR: What developments in the marketplace do you expect over the next few years?

BP: I expect colored gems to take off. The first reason is increased demand and scarcity of quality goods. The second is an increase in diamond prices. When the diamond market goes up, colored stones follow. There is also the strength of the European market. If investors in the United States decided to sell all their stones, the European market is so strong that I don't think prices would be affected very much.

HJR: If a lot of people decide to sell diamonds, DeBeers is sitting there with several billions of dollars worth of liquid assets and could buy stones in the market to support the price.

There is no one who would do that for colored gemstones. Would DeBeers' support of the diamond price, in effect, provide support for the colored stone price also?

BP: There is no cartel like DeBeers, but there are a number of very, very strong gemstone companies throughout the world. The strength to support the market is out there. It's not any one organization, but a lot of people with many, many billions of dollars.

Bill Pinch has also given a few do's and don'ts to consider before you spend any money on colored stones. There is one major "do."

Become knowledgeable by reading books and articles on the subject, visiting museums and gem and mineral shows, and, if you are really serious, take the correspondence courses offered by the Gemological Institute of America. This costs about $400, and can take most of the risk out of a marvelously profitable hobby.

There are several don'ts.

1. Don't buy stones in any foreign countries. The business standards of companies that cater to tourists overseas are sometimes not the best. One of our two recommended gemstone dealers, H. Stern, Inc., is a reputable firm with offices all over the world, but their foreign offices cater to the tourist trade, selling stones in the upper range of what might be considered a fair retail price. They are reputable, and by retail standards, won't rip you off, but subscribers to my newsletter can buy investment stones from them at very close to wholesale through their New York office (see the Appendix). You are not going to get bargains when you are abroad unless you are a knowledgeable buyer doing business on the wholesale level. If you are not, you should do business here in this country.

2. Don't order stones from companies that don't have them in stock, ready to hand them to you as soon as they receive your money. More than one company has taken orders for

rubies and emeralds, used the customer's money to capitalize their purchases, and taken many months to deliver. Some companies have gone broke holding the customer's money.

3. Ignore an appraisal for determining market value. One major lab does good appraisals in terms of quality, and lists a "replacement value" for the stone. Most stones can be bought for considerably less money than that appraisal.

4. There have been "land exchanges" where people have received precious stones in payment for land. I know of one instance where a person traded $100,000 worth of land for colored stones, which, when properly appraised, turned out to be worth less than $3,000. In making any kind of swap for precious stones, be positive you are getting "value for value" by going to the best experts you can find and getting an honest and accurate appraisal before you sign the deal.

5. Avoid most package deals for tax write-offs. For example, one common scheme is to acquire a stone which supposedly has collector value for a museum, to hold it for one year, and to donate it to the museum at an appraised value several times more than you paid for the stone, then to write it off against your taxes. The IRS looks askance at such deals, although sometimes you can make them work. You need to be careful that the stone is of true museum quality. This can only be done by checking with the curator of the museum. Also, be sure that you are not attempting to take a tax deduction based on an inflated, unrealistic appraisal of its retail value. The IRS will shoot you down in flames. Get some good tax advice before you enter into any such scheme.

The chief advantage of colored stones is that the guy who is shut out of the diamond market by cost can buy semiprecious stones. This is why I got interested. I also believe we will see a restructuring and strengthening of the marketplace through technical advances and better certification and identification. Additionally, with the help of a knowledgeable, dependable dealer, people who buy now would, in effect, be buying cheaply enough that the expected inflation in the price of those stones would cover almost anything but the most flagrant mistakes in judgment.

Don't buy stones expecting to make a fast profit by selling in a year or two. Just as with silver and gold, 1982 will be an accumulation period for colored stones. I want people who buy these stones to say to themselves, "I want to hedge against inflation as long as it persists. I am going to hang on to these stones as a way of preserving my wealth and enhancing it at a rate faster than inflation can chew away at the purchasing power of my paper dollars." Remember: "Beat inflation, plus a little bit."

CHAPTER 16

Avoiding Energy Failure

Our energy delivery systems have a high probability of failure, and you must prepare your affairs so you can ignore that failure, as the Dangerous Decade might be characterized by people freezing at home because they have no gas to go anywhere else.

We've already demonstrated in Chapter 5 that we're going to have periodically recurring energy problems over the next several years. President Reagan has given us some encouragement as this book goes to press, as he has deregulated oil, but until natural gas is also deregulated, our problems will continue to grow faster than the solutions can correct them. When and if gas is deregulated, we will probably see increases in domestic production, which will bust the Arab oil cartel and make the energy crisis a thing of the past, but that will take at least two or four years after it happens. There will be no tangible results before the 1982 election, and a backlash against the temporarily higher energy prices that will result from deregulation could cause Reagan to lose control of the Senate, making it more difficult to stick to the oil deregulation plan.

In any event, the next two years will probably give us at least one and possibly as many as three energy crises. It depends on how cold the winters of '81 and '82 are going to be and how much fuel oil is consumed. It depends on what happens when the Ayatollah Khomeini dies and on the outcome of the war between Iraq and Iran. It depends on whether or not the Soviet Union makes political and military moves in the Middle East. It depends on whether Israel has another fight with one of its neighbors, or somebody blocks the Persian Gulf with a sunken ship in the Strait of Hormuz. In any event, we are energy vulnerable and your Failure Avoidance program makes it absolutely mandatory that you prepare your life to be somewhere else when everybody else is punching each other out in gas lines on odd and even days.

I have a list of recommendations and it's not really very long. These are minimum survival strategies that must be implemented between crises. You can't wait until supplies are tight to start installing a 2,000-gallon fuel-storage tank. John Denver, the popular singer, tried to do that at his home in Colorado and almost started a revolution; he did it when his neighbors were immobilized in odd-even-day gas lines, and he made everybody mad—with envy, no doubt. It has to be done quietly while everybody is convinced that the crisis has gone away, and then you can honestly argue that everybody should be glad you're not sitting ahead of them in that gas line, competing with them for scarce supplies.

Let's list the key things that should be done, in order of importance.

Ruff Energy Recommendation #1. Prepare now to be able to heat your home in an energy crisis.

About the only way to be sure is to have wood stoves strategically installed throughout your home. They must be properly installed, because an improperly installed wood stove is a hazard and can result in the death of you and your family.

Modern wood-burning stoves are a far cry from the old Franklin stove. They are airtight and the rate of burn is controlled by regulating the amount of air that enters—an extremely sophisticated form of draft. You can heat with them and cook on them, and one load of wood will last for many hours. I began recommending them before the weird winters of 1976 and 1978. And, as a result, I received a letter from one subscriber in Pennsylvania:

> When the big storm hit, the natural gas pipeline pumps froze as did the waterlines, but having taken your advice, we had enough emergency water supply to last for two weeks, and we simply dusted off our new Gibraltar stove and lived off our food storage. The freeways were blocked for several days and the trucks were not able to get into our town and the stores were bare. Besides, we're two miles out of town and don't have a snowmobile. But we're getting one.
>
> For our family, it was merely a relatively minor inconvenience as we were warm and fed. I cannot thank you enough.

If you live in a moderate climate in the Sun Belt, you would probably get along without a wood stove for heating, but at the very least you should have a good charcoal grill for cooking, and a substantial supply of charcoal, but be careful. Using charcoal indoors without adequate ventilation can be lethal!

There are heating units that can be installed in your existing fireplace to reduce the loss of heat up the chimney. You can't heat a house very well with a typical fireplace. It generally creates a negative flow of warm air. When the fire is burning, the hot air rises up the chimney drawing air out of the room. Cold outside air is thus drawn into the house through cracks and openings, and the net effect is that the rooms away from the immediate vicinity of the fireplace get colder. More heat is lost up the chimney than is gained through radiation into the room. There are attachments that can be installed in your fireplace, such as the Heatolater which will recirculate hot air back into the home. You can actually heat a pretty good-sized home with such a fireplace.

We have twelve fire centers in our house, including stoves, fireplaces with Heatolaters, and a wonderful, old-fashioned wood or coal cook stove actually installed in the kitchen, ready to use whenever we want it or need it.

You can try the simple trick of installing a one-quarter-inch steel plate in the back of your fireplace, one-half inch out from the rear, which will reflect a lot of heat out into the room, and, in fact, will double the heat output.

Just in case of severe oil and natural gas shortages, you might want to buy some portable electric space heaters, as there might still be electricity, even if there is no gas or oil. That could be lifesaving in a really cold climate and a fuel crisis.

Ruff Energy Recommendation #2. Prepare for gas rationing so you can travel in an energy crisis.

It's not a question of whether or not there will be fuel rationing. The only question is *when*. We've already seen informal rationing several times. The odd-even scheme is a form of fuel rationing. It means that on certain days you can't buy at all, and there are long, irritating lines. Presumably, everybody consumes less gas as a result. California drivers were limited as to the amount of gas they could buy at any one stop. The combination of small purchases and long lines were a form of rationing.

Dr. Gary North, a wonderfully acerbic newsletter writer, believes that the new currency of the future, after the dollar has collapsed, will be the gasoline ration coupon. He may well be right.

You can prepare for rationing and/or shortages in several ways, depending on your financial limitations.

Try to have two economical vehicles, using differents types of fuel. The ideal combination would be a Volkswagen diesel Rabbit and some small American or foreign car that burns unleaded gas. That way, the odds are that you can buy one form of fuel or another. The ultimate extension of this principle would be to have a vehicle such as a pickup truck or a motor home with a dual fuel system installed, so it can, with a flick of the switch, burn either propane or gasoline. Every city has people who make such installations. Look in the Yellow Pages under Fuel Tanks.

If you have the money and the yard space, install underground fuel tanks and store diesel fuel for a diesel automobile.

Gasoline is too treacherous to store unless you have a lot of open space and can put underground tanks a sufficient distance from your home so that there is no fire danger. The explosive power of the vapors that can emanate from one cup of gasoline is equal to ten sticks of dynamite and is not to be messed with. Under no circumstances should you store gasoline unless the tanks are installed underground, a safe distance from any inhabited dwellings, by professionals who know what they're doing.

Diesel fuel has low volatility and is safe to store. Both fuels, however, have storage problems. When they sit for a while, they tend to stratify and separate into their various chemical component parts. Diesel fuel will develop little streamers of paraffin that can seriously impair the functioning of a diesel automobile. Also, water accumulates in the tanks and can be a problem.

For some time we have been recommending to our subscribers a product called "Fuel-Mate," which can be bought from independent distributors and added to either diesel or gasoline to extend its storage life from a minimum of six months up to as many as five years. (See the Appendix for information on Fuel-Mate.)

These recommendations represent the ideal program, and it may not be possible for all of you to do everything. A farmer can store fuel a lot more easily than a cave-dwelling apartment owner in New York City or Detroit. You must look at your needs, your financial resources, and your life-style, assess your situation and your vulnerability, and do the best you can.

CHAPTER 17

Death and Taxes

Shakespeare had one of his characters say, "First thing we do, let's kill all the lawyers." I'm not sure they deserve execution, but whatever virtues or demerits have been earned by the legal profession, it is clear that the legal jargon which confronts you while you try to find your way through life in the simplest way possible is darn near grounds for mayhem. It drives you into the arms of expensive lawyers who perform their medicine-man mumbo jumbo, often leaving a troubled client in complete ignorance as to what is really going on.

When an ordinary man wants to give an orange to another, he says merely, "I give you this orange." But when a lawyer does it, he says it this way:

Know all men by these presents that I hereby give, grant, bargain, sell, release, convey, transfer, and quit-claim all my right, title, interest, benefit, and use whatever in, of, and concerning this chattel, otherwise known as an orange, or *citrus orantium*, together with all the appurtenances thereto of skin, pulp, pip, rind, seeds, and juice, to have and to hold the said orange together with its skin, pulp, pip, rind, seeds, and juice for his own use and behoof, to himself and his heirs in fee simple forever, free from all liens, encumbrances, easements, limitations, restraints, or conditions whatsoever, any and all prior deeds, transfers or other documents whatsoever, now or anywhere made to the contrary notwithstanding, with full power to bite, cut, suck, or otherwise eat the said orange or to give away the same with or without its skin, pulp, pip, rind, seeds, or juice.

Life has become so complex that the requirement for attorneys has begun to drain a significant part of the national income, and the cost of legal help is not generally included in the rate of inflation. Either the cost of legal aid, or the cost of the expensive mistakes we make without that aid, is an authentic cost-of-living fact of life. I'm not sure I have any useful alternative to suggest. At the moment, I can do no better than decry the problem, and rely on my attorneys. A really good one is a Pearl of Great Price, and mine is the best.

B. Ray (Bill) Anderson probably writes more trusts for estate planning than anyone in California. He is the prime theoretician and teacher behind and the star of our regional *Ruff Times* Beat-Inflation-and-Taxes courses (see the Appendix). He is thoroughly "hard-money-oriented," and we have worked closely together to solve a very difficult tax-inflation dilemma. He is the author of the best-selling book *You Can Use Inflation to Beat the IRS,* and we've worked together on this chapter. His job was to be legally accurate. My job is to clean up the mumbo jumbo and apply the concepts to the beat-inflation-oriented investor.

You're Richer Than You Think—for Now

If you sit down to figure out your net worth, most of you will find it has grown over the years, and yet, most of you have too much month left at the end of your money. Inflation has made you paper rich while squeezing the purchasing power of your income so that you don't feel rich at all. You feel squeezed, and yet, because taxes don't adjust for the effects of inflation, your home, your land, or your business has inflated you into some serious tax and estate problems.

Not being a high-risk speculator by nature, let's say that you read *How to Prosper During the Coming Bad Years*, followed the advice, and your investments have beaten inflation, and then some. Your real estate, gold, diamonds, colored stones, your gold shares are all up. The good news? You are richer than you used to be. The bad news? Between the capital gains tax you pay if you sell out to switch investments, and the estate tax to be paid when you die, you lose most of what you gained with your brilliant beat-inflation strategy, and the rapacious state and Federal tax men are the biggest winners. You have still been liquidated. It's like a spy and suspense movie where the hero fights and struggles to make it safely to the end of the story, only to be shot in the back at the last minute by his own side.

As I explained in Chapter 3, "The Liquidation of America," the capital gains tax on real profits is often over 100%, and the Federal estate and gift tax rates begin at 18% and escalate to as high as 70%, which can take 100% of your hard-earned profits, after adjusting for inflation. Your estate goes through probate, and the probate fees paid to court appointed attorneys, on top of the estate taxes, mean your heirs will end up with only a fraction of what you owned at your death. In fact, your widow or your children may be forced to sell the estate at a poor time in the market cycle. while under the great stress of bereavement, in order to pay the fees and taxes.

On the other hand, many tax sheltered investments, such as Keoghs, IRAs, tax deferred annuities, etc., can give you some protection against income taxes, but those funds are put into precisely those kinds of investments that get tromped on by inflation, such as CDs, bonds, etc. Your tax savings are more than wiped out by the money depreciation we call inflation.

By the only standard we can legitimately use to define wealth—purchasing power in terms of goods and services—you are getting whipped. If you don't think this applies to you because you're not rich, consider the following.

Do you have a substantial equity in a home, mostly because of inflation? Do you have a small business, a farm, or some rental units? Then you are worth more than you think. You are a sitting duck for the tax man, and you may be able to use some of the following techniques. This will not be light reading, as it's not the simplest thing in the world to explain.

How do we escape this dilemma, which could be described as "Beat inflation, get whipped by taxes; beat taxes, get clobbered by inflation"?

The following techniques are designed to cope with "Taxflation." Understanding these basic concepts is absolutely essential if you want to pass on all your wealth to your children and grandchildren so they can use it to handle their share of the incredible debt we dumped on top of them— remember, my grandson Ryan's $21 million share of the national debt at age twenty-one. You are going to have to be smarter than those people who spend all their time thinking of ways to extract it from you.

The basic methods of beating Taxflation are:

1. Estate Freezing. This is a method of freezing the value of an appreciating asset for tax purposes so that you can enjoy its benefits for the rest of your life without creating a larger tax liability at the time of your death as a result of your wisdom in the selection of an investment. If you have a building worth $100,000 and you die ten years from now, you don't want a million dollar house in your estate, which it would be if inflation accelerates, even with the new higher exemptions under the 1981 tax law. You would rather have only a $100,000 house in your estate. You can freeze that value at this point in time, and allow the appreciation to accrue to your children. This technique can shift the future growth of your assets to the next generation of taxpayers, while at the same time preserving control of the assets and preserving the ability to derive most of the income from those assets. These transactions include such strategies as an installment sale—or the creation of a private annuity. Also, there are interesting techniques called "preferred stock recapitalization frozen partnerships" and interest-free loans.

Estate freezing won't be covered in great depth here because Bill Anderson has written about it so beautifully in his book (see the Appendix). My purpose here is for you to grasp the concept and catch the spirit of it.

2. The Creation of Tax-Exempt Wealth. This technique takes advantage of certain provisions of the IRS code which exempt wealth from transfer taxes, such as the simple procedure of having your life insurance policy owned by someone else so that the proceeds belong to that person and are not a part of your estate.

3. Giving Programs and Creative Charitable Techniques. By this method, you can continue to enjoy the benefits of your estate while no longer owning it.

We have raised some pretty big questions.

Is it possible to transfer property to the next generation and at the same time retain control of and receive the financial benefits from the transferred property? Can you, at the same time, avoid the gift tax on the transfer and successfully resist attack by the IRS? And, last of all, is it possible to do this while beating inflation, and in fact, using it to serve you? Can you switch into hard assets with few or no tax consequences?

Yes, if you know what you are doing.

Frozen Assets

Let's examine the estate freezing concept.

First, you must establish the "fair market value" of the assets to be transferred, using an independent, objective appraiser. Cash, gold, silver, or listed stocks are easy to evaluate. Just look in the paper. Real estate, a business, or a farm will need an appraisal. "Fair market value" is a flexible, vague, uncertain, and perhaps impossibly precise definition, which is flexible enough to be manipulated under the law to minimize the tax impact.

Each of the several kinds of estate freezing transactions has tax advantages and disadvantages, depending on your non-tax or investment objectives. Here are some examples.

The Installment Sale, Example Number 1. Let's assume that you want your kids to inherit 500 acres of farmland. You don't have to wait until you die. That's too late. You want to tranfer this land to your children during your life, with no gift tax, while continuing to farm the land and keep the income. You expect the property value to rise. You may believe that at some time within the next five years it will be worth more. With a runaway inflation in commodity prices, it will probably be much more.

At the present value of $500,000 (500 acres at $1,000 each), if you were to die tomorrow, the Federal death tax on your estate would be a little over $100,000, plus whatever your state grabs. However, if the land value were to triple to $3,000 an acre, the death tax would be approximately $380,000, almost four times higher. How do you avoid the problem?

Sell the property to your children or to a trust which has been set up for their benefit. The children make a nominal downpayment in the same year as the sale, and sign a long-term installment note for the balance. The note is secured by a mortgage or deed of trust on the farm. The terms of the note are fully negotiable (which means you probably can set those terms at will) and include interest at some reasonable rate, probably around 10%. The payments are "interest only" in the early years, and you defer the principal payments until a time which coincides with your income or retirement planning objectives. Then you use the installment method of reporting on your Federal tax return.

You then lease the property from the children for some fair annual rental, based on a per-acre rental of crop-sharing arrangement. You make your lease payment to the children or the trustee, who will, out of those funds, pay you the annual interest payments on the note. You get to use the farm (or the business, or the real estate) for income. The interest payments to you are taxable, but your lease payments to the kids are tax deductible. That's a "wash."

The net effect is that the property is no longer in your estate if you die. You sold it to your kids. Any appreciation in the value of the property due to inflation, or any other reason, after the date of the transfer will belong to your children or to the trust for their benefit. You maintain control and use of the land because of your lease. There is no gift tax because there was no gift. You sold it. You didn't give it away. And you continue to control it.

But, I hear you ask, if you were to die, doesn't your estate own a promissory note equal to the value of the farm? Well, over the years the note will probably be reduced by installment payments, but more important, inflation rates will be over 40% in the eighties. Inflation drives up the price of money (interest rates) along with other commodities. When rates go up, the value of the rate goes down—just like a bond. When inflation reaches 40%, so will interest rates. The fair market value of the note would be about 25% of its face value. You have become a lender to the buyer, your kids. Inflation causes lenders to be ripped off by borrowers who buy appreciating assets with borrowed dollars while paying off the loan with possibly worthless dollars, if the note is long-term enough. If you are a lender to a bank or insurance company, you get ripped off. But in this case, you are being ripped off by your own kids. And they are getting what Uncle Sam would have taken. You now hold a shrinking asset—the note. The children own a growing asset—the farm—with no tax consequences until they sell it. The valuation on the note for estate tax purposes at the time of your death is the "fair market value."

The primary income tax advantage to you, during your lifetime, is that you can defer the capital gains tax until funds are actually received in payments, while putting the property in the hands of another person (your kids or the trustee).

Another Installment Sale, Example Number 2. Let's assume you have an inflated piece of real estate worth about $800,000 that has an income tax basis (the original cost of the property, plus the improvements, less the depreciation) of $200,000. If you sold the property for cash, you would have a $600,000 capital gain. If you are in the 50% income tax bracket, it would cost you $120,000 in capital gains taxes. There could also be additional "recapture" tax costs or "tax preferences."

Let's say you wanted to convert the equity into something such as gold, without having the profits from the sale taxed away, because you want to invest that $120,000, not give it to Uncle Sam. You can't just exchange the property for gold or silver, because the Tax Free Exchange provisions under Section 1031 of the IRS Code require the exchange property to be "like kind" property. The exchange of land for precious metals would not qualify. If you pay taxes on the $800,000 sale, however, you can only buy $680,000 worth of gold or silver. How can you convert your property into gold with minimal tax?

You enter into an installment sale contract with the kids' trust for $800,000, as described above. The trustee now has a new cost basis for tax purposes, which is the same as his purchase price, *i.e.*, $800,000. The trustee, after holding the property for two years, can sell the property for cash with the taxable gain measured only from the $800,000 purchase price. He can then purchase $800,000 or more worth of gold, because his capital has not been sliced up by taxes. The trustee then pledges the gold as "substituted security" with the installment note. No longer is the note secured by the property. It is now secured by gold. The net effect is to convert the total equity to gold in two years. As the gold appreciates, you release the trustee to sell some so that he can make his interest and principal payments.

It would be more convenient, of course, if the trustee could sell the property immediately, rather than having to hold it for two years. There are some possible ways to get around this two-year holding period restriction.

1. The property could be sold to a daughter-in-law or son-in-law instead of your children. This transaction is exempt from the two-year rule.
2. Your brothers or sisters are also exempt from the two-year holding rule in this transaction.
3. The property could be sold to the fiancé of one of your children, who could sell it immediately and then loan the money to the child or the trust for family investment purposes.
4. The trust or the child could immediately lease the property with a two-year *option to sell*, meaning that he or she agrees that at *your* option he will buy the property from you at the agreed-upon price in two years. This gets a little complicated, as you might want an inflation provision to protect you during the two-year period and the lessee-buyer might not appreciate that, and it would be more difficult to turn this transaction into gold, so this technique has limitations.

The point is not that this can be done without difficulty but that if it is important enough to you, you can turn that transaction into gold with no immediate tax consequences if you want to struggle a bit.

The Installment Sale, Example Number 3. Let's assume you own an apartment building with a fair market value of $200,000, 20% being land and 80% being improvements. You have been depreciating it for a long time and your depreciated cost basis is now only $20,000, which means there are not a lot of depreciation tax benefits left. If you sell it outright, you pay taxes on the difference between the sale price, and the $20,000. For tax purposes, your profit is $180,000.

To beat the tax man, you could trade your equity for the equity in another property under the Tax Free Exchange provision of Section 1031, and get a new depreciation tax base on your new property, but that will not accomplish the "step-up in basis" that we described before, *i.e.*, the creation of a new cost basis for your heirs, resulting from the sale. However, an installment sale to your children, or to the trustee, for $200,000 would have the effect of creating a new tax basis of $200,000 for the new owner. Under the 80%-20% allocation rule, the improvements will now be given a new basis of $160,000 and can be depreciated again. You now enter into a management contract with the trustee and collect a management fee. Now look at what you've done:

1. The property receives a new tax basis and provides new depreciation benefits for the trust.
2. You retain management control of the property under the management agreement.
3. You can receive income directly from the management of the property, in addition to the payments on the installment note. You have income and control, the kids have the property, and the tax man is thwarted.

314

One Disadvantage

The principal disadvantage of an installment sale is that it does force you to pay some capital gains on the downpayment and principal installment payments as they are made or "forgiven." The promissory note could be reduced by tax free gifts to your children, up to $15,000 each year, but additional forgiveness of debt does create a taxable event. The problem can be solved in part by providing for low, current installment payments, or making it "interest only," with a large balloon payment sometime in the distant future. Most of the gain is deferred in favor of the utilization of the tax dollars now, in exchange for a bigger tax in the future, when the money is worth much less, which it will be.

Summing Up

The installment sale concept adds up as follows:
1. The seller has a taxable gain, but only on an installment basis.
2. The trustee or the children, as buyers, may deduct the interest they pay and can treat the transferred property as having a new tax basis.
3. The trustee or children can resell the purchase property after two years without any adverse tax consequences.
4. Upon your death, the fair market value of the promissory note is an asset of your estate subject to estate taxation, but one that can be minimized.

This chapter is not meant to be a Do-It-Yourself Brain Surgery Kit. Use attorneys and estate planners who understand these concepts. I have painted with broad brush strokes, as each tactic really requires a lot of "howevers" and "be carefuls." All I really wanted to do is to open your eyes to the possibilities. With foresight and proper planning, you can declare an end to inflation as far as your estate is concerned and avoid and defer taxes for the benefit of the Ryans of the world.

In mid 1981, I introduced a program to train and certify financial planners in the Taxflation planning techniques pioneered by Bill Anderson and me. We will be developing hard-money-oriented tax shelters and closed-end and open-end mutual funds consistent with the strategies in this book. There also will be other products and services available to financial planners and investment managers (see the Appendix under "Financial Planning Services" and "Tax Shelters").

CHAPTER 18

Using Pre-1965 U.S. "Silver Coins" as Legal Tender!

Under the IRS Code, Section 1031, you are allowed to make certain tax free exchanges of investment property. Actually, the taxes are not forgiven, nor do they disappear, but are merely deferred. The properties to be traded must be of "like kind," held for productive use in a trade or business, or for investment. Investment or income-producing real estate, whether improved or unimproved, is considered "property of like kind." Even a ranch in the United States and a ranch in a foreign country are like-kind properties.

The most common form of the tax free exchange is in real estate, and is used effectively by investors such as Al Lowry, author of *How You Can Become Financially Independent by Investing in Real Estate*, to pyramid assets.

Other examples of "like-kind" exchanges are: a used automobile or truck for a new one to be used for the same purpose; trades of major league baseball or football player

317

contracts; and bullion-type gold coins minted by one country, exchanged for bullion-type gold coins minted by another, where the coins are no longer a circulating medium of exchange within their respective countries, and hence, not "money."

An exchange of numismatic gold coins (for instance, U.S. $20 gold pieces) for bullion gold coins (like Krugerrands) would not be tax free as those coins are not "like kind." The value of numismatic coins is determined by factors such as rarity and condition, while bullion coin values are established solely by metal content, so they are not of the same nature or character.

Pre-1965 American silver coins, however, may offer a unique tax deferment in transactions involving "unlike kinds" of property. This is not, however, a "1031" exchange. It's a sale.

Pre-1965 silver coins are unique. They are still considered legal tender by the United States government at face value, despite the fact that they have a silver bullion value far in excess of face value. They are bought by the "bag" from coin dealers.

To refresh your memory, a bag consists of $1,000 face value of circulated 90% silver dimes, quarters, halves, or dollars, minted in or before 1964, which was the last year we minted such coins. The price is generally about the same as the silver bullion in the coins on any given day. The bag, about the size of a bowling ball, and weighing 55 pounds, has 720 ounces of silver. As previously explained, because of the number of coins melted down for bullion in the Hunt silver panic of 1979-80, there will probably someday be an additional numismatic premium on these coins.

Silver is a highly desirable long-term investment for the 1980s. That prospect, plus the unique Constitutional dilemma those coins present to the IRS, makes the ploy described in this chapter worth a try.

Let's assume you own a building which has inflated in market value to $100,000, and it has a present "tax basis" (cost, less depreciation, plus capital improvements) of $15,000. If the property were sold for cash, and you received $100,000 in Federal Reserve Notes, you would get slugged with a capital gains tax on a profit of $85,000. If, however, you asked the buyer to pay, not in Federal Reserve Notes (cash) with a face value of $100,000, but in pre-1965 silver coins with a silver bullion market value of $100,000, and a face value, for example, of $7,500, depending on the price of silver at the time, then you would report a sale of real property at the face value of $7,500, which is $7,500 less than your basis, giving you a paper loss of $7,500. Any gain that you might have realized would be deferred. The tax basis of the coins you now own would be $7,500. If and when the coins are sold, you would then have a taxable profit on the difference between $7,500 and the sale price of the coins. If you are smart, however, you will hold the coins until inflation peaks in the mid- or late eighties.

We don't know for sure how the courts would interpret the transaction if the IRS chose to challenge it. Reporting a sale at a loss, and at an unreasonable price to boot, would probably trigger an audit, but there are reasons why the IRS might back down from challenging the transaction, after a lot of bluffing. First, the tax is merely deferred, not wiped out. Second, the IRS has been very cautiously tiptoeing around the "legal tender" issue, for reasons you will see in a moment.

The Case Against This Strategy

My attorneys haven't found any court precedent directly on point, but the IRS has issued a ruling on a specific fact situation in 1976. Revenue Ruling 76-249 holds that a taxpayer exchanging real property for silver coins realizes a taxable gain based on the difference between the fair market value of the coins and the adjusted basis of the real property. The IRS gave no discussion of the issue of the coins being legal tender, but considered coins to be "property." Even so, I think they will be most reluctant to litigate if the ruling is challenged in court, which it has not been to date.

Section 61 of the IRS Code provides that "gross income means all income from whatever source derived, including ... gains derived from dealing in property." There is no doubt that the IRS views the silver coins in our example as "property" within the meaning of Section 1001 (b) of the IRS Code, which would cause the recognition of a gain on the exchange. Furthermore, this position has been published for a number of years as Rev. Rul. 68-634 without yet being tested in the courts. Therein lies the case against this strategy.

The Case for This Strategy

On the other hand, the most direct authority for deferment lies with the United States Constitution and various laws passed by Congress.

Article 1, Section 10 of the Constitution provides that "no state shall ... make anything but gold and silver coin legal tender in payment of debts. ..." The power of Congress to establish a uniform legal tender and prohibit all other forms of currency exchange has been long established under Article 1, Section 8.

Under these Constitutional powers, Congress passed the Coinage Act of 1965. That section states:

All coins and currencies of the United States (including Federal Reserve Notes and circulating notes of Federal Reserve banks and national banking associations), regardless of when cointed or issued, shall be legal tender for all debts, public and private, public charges, public taxes, duties and dues.

320

Legal tender of the United States still includes pre-1965 silver coins at face value. Even the legislative history of this law states that:

It is of critical importance to the public and to the economy that there be a smooth transition from our present coinage system to a new system. . . . To this end, it is important that there be no incentive for the withdrawal from circulation of the existing subsidiary silver coins or of the new ones. The official agencies of the Treasury Department will continue to exchange lawfully held coins and currencies of the United States, dollar for dollar, for other coins and currencies which may be lawfully acquired and are legal tender for public and private debts.

The argument can then be made that by statute and regulation, the value of a coin for tax purposes is determined by its face value. The fact that a coin is a circulating "silver" coin does not make that coin worth more than its face value in tax transactions with the U.S. government. Moreover, the IRS said in a 1976 Revenue Ruling that "currency in its usual and ordinary acceptation means gold, silver, other metals or paper used as a circulating medium of exchange. . . ."

Under legislation sponsored by Senator Jesse Helms, signed into law on October 28, 1977, it is perfectly legal to specify gold or silver coins in payment of obligations. Inasmuch as the courts have consistently held that the Constitution leaves to Congress the power to define "legal tender," the pronouncement of Congress should be the final word. If you sell property, receiving payment with pre-1965 silver coins, and you report the sale price at the "face" and not the "silver" value of the coins, you are acting only in accordance with the Constitution, Federal law, and public policy.

If you took some silver dimes to the U.S. Treasury and requested Federal Reserve Notes computed on the silver bullion value, they would laugh in your face. Under the Federal Reserve Act, the U.S. Treasury is only required to give you Federal Reserve Notes at the face value. Likewise, if you tried to pay your Federal Income Tax with pre-1965 coins, you would be given credit only for the face value of the coins.

A letter from the Board of Governors of the Federal Reserve System stated that the term "lawful money" is generally regarded as meaning any medium of exchange which freely circulates from hand to hand as money under sanction of law.

When you take a Federal Reserve Note to the U.S. Treasury and demand payment in gold or silver, the U.S. Treasury has the right to pay you either in paper reserve notes, or other standard coins or coinage, or whatever currency they wish. One brave soul recently challenged this and demanded that his $50 Federal Reserve Bank Note be redeemed in "lawful money" of the United States which, he said, must be gold or silver. The ninth Circuit Court of Appeals disagreed (improperly, I believe), and poetically observed:

> While we agree that golden eagles, double eagles and silver dollars were lovely to look at and delightful to hold, we must at the same time recognize that time marches on, and that even the time-honored silver dollar is no longer available in its last bastion of defense, the brilliant casinos of the houses of chance in the State of Nevada. Appellant is entitled to redeem his precious note, but not in precious metal. (See *Milan* v. *U.S.*, 524 F. 2d. 629 [9th Cir. 1974, memo dec.])

The government tries to have its cake and eat it too. It will accept tax payments from you in pre-1965 silver coins at no more than face value, and will pay you only in Federal Reserve Notes, again at face value. On the other hand, if you receive payment in silver coins, they claim that you have received property at market value, and demand the taxes be computed on that basis.

The central question remains: Are pre-1965 U.S. silver coins legal tender at face value? In their efforts to prevent tax rebels from refusing to pay taxes on the "Constitutional" grounds that Federal Reserve Notes are not legal tender (lawful money), the IRS, Congress, and the court have gone to great pains to claim that such paper dollars are equal to gold or silver coins. Yet, when they see a possible tax advantage for you in using silver coins as legal tender, the IRS doesn't hesitate to reverse its previous position, and conclude that such coins are "property" for income reporting purposes but, "legal tender" for purposes of payment of taxes. The rationale is clear only to the IRS. The rest of us (including the courts and Congress) assume that any U.S. coin or paper currency that is still in circulation, regardless of any intrinsic or metal value, is legal tender.

It is significant that these coins remain in circulation and are accepted at banks, pay telephones, candy machines, and government offices as legal tender.

At present, silver coins are the only form of legal tender that have a market melt value in excess of their face value. When copper prices climb above $1.46 a pound (where the metal and face value of a penny are equal), it may be possible to demand payment of obligations in pennies, provided you have several bathtubs to store them in, as $1,000 in pennies weighs over 650 pounds and takes up a lot of room. Obviously, that limits their usefulness.

The possible tax advantage of using silver coins is limited only to tax deferral. It is not a scheme to evade taxes. It is a great way to convert property to silver, without losing investment seed money to Uncle Sam in the form of capital gains taxes. And who knows how the "revenooers" would cope with the future tax computation if you bought gas, food, and clothing with those coins later on during the nationwide barter economy.

One IRS agent, with whom this idea was discussed, cautioned that, to enjoy any tax deferral, the coins received in an exchange must be legal tender (American pre-1965 coins), and that as soon as they are sold or further exchanged for any consideration whose value exceeds the tax basis of the coins, a gain is realized and should be reported. As with any deferral, the payment of taxes is postponed to a later, more convenient date, and you get to own more silver than you could have if you had paid the taxes now.

On balance, I think you can get away with this unusual tax deferral, because, although they will bluster, I doubt if they will take up the challenge in court. If you should lose, however, you pay only the taxes you would have paid anyway, plus 12% interest, a reasonable rate for these strange times. You can drag out the case for several years, so you would have a tax deferral anyway. The coins will have appreciated by then, and the tax would be assessed only on the market value of the coins at the time of the original transaction, which would also be the next tax basis of the coins.

The tax authorities I have consulted, even those highly conservative ones who are dubious about the technique, agree that there would be no tax fraud involved. I think it's well worth a chance, unless you have something else to hide from the IRS, because you will probably be audited. If you're clean, and are a high audit risk anyway, why not? The odds favor you, because I don't think they will take you to tax court if you challenge an adverse ruling.

If the IRS plugs this small loophole, it would open a much bigger tax revolt loophole for the tax rebels. It would be a Pyrrhic victory, and they know it. And if I'm wrong about that, the consequences of losing are far less than the benefits to be gained by holding the coins in the Inflationary Eighties.

PART III

Free the Eagle

CHAPTER 19

National Survival
in the
Inflationary Eighties

Recently, Robert Ringer, best-selling author of *Restoring the American Dream*, spent some time vigorously debating with me over the great issues of the day. In his fascinating book, in reference to whether America could be saved, he had written, "It's a 100 to 1 shot, but at least it's a shot." That was gloomy enough, but this time he was so discouraged about how far we have gone down the road to ruin that he seemed to feel there is now simply no chance. He says, "The revolution is over, the redistribution-of-the-wealth advocates have won."

If we do not develop some effective national Failure Avoidance strategies, Bob could be right. If we do not take decisive action starting now, our Democratic Republic could become something entirely different—something we might not like very much. The ultimate result of the liquidation of America, the collapse of the currency from inflation, and the continued growth of regulatory government could be a dictatorship of the Left or the Right. Historical precedents are clear and unequivocal. Inflation creates increasing public demands to "Do something," usually totalitarian in nature. The history of inflation is the history of changes of government, each usually with less freedom than the one being replaced. Hitler got his first good press in 1923, the last year of the great German inflation. Brazil, Germany, Chile, Argentina, China, Rome, and Russia all ended up with military dictatorships. Teddy Kennedy's demand for wage and price controls is a mild case in point. You can't control prices without controlling people and property. This is a totalitarian measure, directly attributable to inflation.

The forces described in Part I are creating a fertile environment for such leaders to arise. The next four to seven years (the classic span of most modern hyperinflations) will bring our greatest test since the Civil War. If we can't arrest these trends, and bring about real political and legislative changes which reinforce and extend personal freedom, we will fail the test, and your personal financial victories will be like ashes in your hands. You won't have the freedom, the markets, or the safety to enjoy your wealth. I want to enlist you as an active and supportive member of a coalition of informed, concerned Americans to launch a direct and massive political assault against the evils which have brought us to this precipice.

Freedom can win. This system is eminently worth saving, and it can still be saved by working within the system, even though the day is late, and the odds are against us.

We are approaching a point that reminds me of those spikes at the entrance to parking lots, where you can drive in but you can't get out without puncturing your tires. If we drive across a no-return line into a dead-end lot and try to get out the way we came in, we will tear the tires off our economic, social, and political machine. We must go back before we have passed that point.

In *How to Prosper*, I expressed confidence that we could survive the inflationary problems ahead as merely another

328

crisis, similar to those that we have faced before, such as the great banking panic of the 1830s, the Civil War, the Depression of the 1930s, etc., and I still think so, but this sickness is very deep and getting deeper. Inflation is rotting away the fundamental institutions of our society, while at the same time we are losing the moral, ethical, and social strength and stability that in that past has gotten us through such crises.

During past crises, certain critical basic structures of society provided a supportive framework for the system, so it could withstand and recover from all assaults. Gold was universally recognized as the standard of the nation's wealth, and even though the paper currency self-destructed more than once, the fundamental monetary asset was carefully protected. Also, in the middle 1800s, we opened up the great gold mines of the West. We had a vast unexploited nation, rich in apparently inexhaustible resources. There was hope and unlimited opportunity for the pioneer who could go West and carve his own future out of those resources, and he had the total freedom to do just that. The "rugged individualist" (and his success) was honored and imitated by the next generation, and success was not "fined" by punitive, confiscatory taxes.

These things are no longer true.

The concepts of patriotism and individual responsibility to the nation were generally honored by the most influential segments of society.

We had not yet discovered that we could vote ourselves benefits from the public treasury, and we were not clumsily destroying the business geese that laid the golden eggs. We were not raping the producing members of society with confiscatory taxes in order to transfer their wealth to the "consumers." Our government was not subsidizing our enemies abroad with technology, money, and food, and propping up soul-destroying philosophies and regimes that were sworn to our destruction.

These things are no longer true.

The family unit, the basic structural unit of society, was

329

held sacred by most everyone. Parents took seriously their responsibility to pass on their values to their children. Children were taught religion, discipline, respect for institutions and people, self-control, and the virtues of hard work and productivity. There was no all-encompassing social "safety net" to protect everyone from the consequences of laziness, bad judgment, unwise speculation, or financial irresponsibility.

These things are no longer true.

Of course, there has always been sin, greed, dishonesty, and corruption. We haven't invented many nifty new sins, but the difference is that in the past they were not all-pervasive, socially acceptable, and epidemic and pounded at you in the movies, in magazines, and on TV. These sicknesses were not honored by influential professors, politicians, and clergymen teaching "situational ethics."

In our long, turbulent, and imperfect history, the unifying thread that ran through society was a generally accepted patriotic conviction that we had responsibilities to contribute to the common welfare, not privileges and "entitlements" which could be extracted from others by political power.

We still had heroes, admirable people that we looked up to and admired. We would hold up our children so they could look over the heads of the crowd to see Lindbergh, Admiral Byrd, or Sergeant York.

These things are no longer true.

When the law was violated, justice in our courts was swift, even if imperfect. Today justice is still imperfect, but something less than swift, and the bias has shifted from the protection of society to the technical interpretation of the law, too often twisted and manipulated for the benefit of the criminal.

As a nation self-sufficient in resources, it was not necessary for us to walk on eggs when a two-bit minor sheikh seized our citizens. That happened once in our past, and the simple threat of American power freed the prisoners. We were far less vulnerable to the hatred or envy of the rest of the world.

Heaven knows, this is no longer true.

Most of these old-fashioned values were still basically intact only twenty-five or thirty years ago. The extent of the changes in attitudes and values in this short time is breathtaking in its magnitude.

Since then, almost every value that has made this nation what it is has come under assault. The internal rot is publicly obvious and rapidly becoming the destabilizing norm.

What can we do to arrest these trends? Is it already too late? Have we passed that spiked point of no return?

I don't think so. I don't know for sure, but we have to try anyway. This nation has blessed us with so much that it deserves no less than our best effort.

So where do we start?

Before I invite you to jump on my bandwagon, it's only fair to let you in on my basic political philosophy. I don't want to sail under false colors.

In the 1980 general election, the issues were oversimplified, misrepresented, and misunderstood. Political labels like "conservative," "moderate," and "liberal" were thrown around, as though we all know what they mean.

I've spent five years avoiding political labels, mostly because there is no classification for me. I would like you to know what I really am—and am not.

Am I a conservative? Am I a liberal? Am I a libertarian? The answer to all three questions is "yes" and "no." At times I'm every one of these, but because labeling leads to polarized, simplistic thinking, in my opinion, every one of these philosophical groupings can justly be blamed for some of the things that are wrong with America. That which follows will probably have something to offend everyone.

When I listen to a conservative politician such as Ronald Reagan, Barry Goldwater, Jesse Helms, or my good friend Orrin Hatch, I tend to agree with what they have to say far more than I would agree with a Jimmy Carter, an Alan Cranston, or a Tip O'Neill. In a choice between those two groups, it's obvious I would generally go with the conservative, but in some critical areas they are too much alike to suit me, and they share some basic political philosophies that I think are bad for America.

For example, both the conservatives and the liberals claim they want to cut government spending to balance the budget, at least most of the time. And in all fairness, the conservatives fight for it a lot harder than the liberals. But in the final analysis, they both want more government spending in some areas.

The conservatives would like more money spent on the CIA and defense. They want big cuts in the "transfer payments," where money is taken from one segment of society and given to another—"the welfare bums," usually the poor. But the National Association of Manufacturers and the Chamber of Commerce, although quite conservative, fight for business contracts and subsidies and bailouts of the corporate welfare bums, such as Chrysler.

The liberals sometimes would like budget cuts, but they usually want to take them out of the defense budget, and would like to see further transfers of wealth. In fact, the Democratic Party platform of 1976 came right out and said there should be a "fairer and more equitable distribution of wealth." Although very few take political platforms seriously, that is a fair summation of a crucial liberal philosophical point. But when you get right down to it, they all have areas where they want more spending. Their goals are different, but the net effect is the same—spend more money on someone, and each bloc has been powerful enough to neutralize the other's version of government economy.

The bottom line? More taxes, more inflation, and more bondage from an exploding bureaucracy.

The liberals and the conservatives are also pretty much agreed on one other principle, besides cutting the other guy's government benefits. They don't hesitate to use the law to impose on society their views of social justice, economics, morality, ethics, or whatever. They tend to agree that it is perfectly moral to use the coercive force of government to tax away from people their hard-earned money to achieve whatever objectives they think are desirable.

The liberals want more laws regulating business, industry, and the marketplace. They instinctively call for coercive wage and price controls when inflation breaks out, and would like to put shackles on American business with more antitrust laws and business taxes. They generally distrust free enterprise.

The conservatives want more laws regulating crime and sexual behavior.

Liberals and conservatives have different goals, but they agree on the use of law to achieve them.

The libertarian, now a minor but growing philosophical and political force, as witness the popularity of Harry Browne and Robert Ringer, says, "Nobody has the right to make laws regulating anybody." In fact, the pure libertarian is an anarchist. He believes that government has no right to tax anybody for anything, that we have no right to make any laws that regulate anything other than aggression by one person against another. He believes that government has no legitimate function that cannot be handled by private enterprise. In fact, when you get right down to it, the pure libertarian, if given a test on the principles of the Constitution without revealing their source, would probably oppose many of them. But the libertarian does stand for freedom. He wants man to be left free to regulate himself, based on the assumption that the free marketplace of ideas, money, and competing human desires is all the regulation that man needs.

Philosophically, when it comes to government and the marketplace, I'm probably a lot closer to being a libertarian than anything else.

But there comes a point where most libertarians and I part company. Ayn Rand and other objectivist or libertarian philosophers base their philosophy around the unifying concept

333

of "natural law." This concept assumes that there is no Divinely given law, no absolute right or wrong, and that even if there was, no one, individually or collectively, has the right to enact laws saying, "Here is a standard of morality or behavior for this nation, this community, or the world."

And that's where we go our separate ways. I believe there is a higher Divine Law. I believe that a just and loving Heavenly Father has established and revealed appropriate standards for human behavior that are for the best good of the most people; and in fact, that these standards are absolutely essential for the proper functioning of a society, and that some of these standards should be the law of the land. Most libertarians don't think so. The Libertarian Party, for example, found itself publicly on the side of the Mitchell brothers, owners of a pornographic live sex show emporium in San Francisco, when they and the girls were busted for prostitution and pandering, on the pure libertarian ground that no one has the right to regulate people's standards of morality. I would abandon the Libertarian Party on this ground alone—their unseemly rush to aid these slimy people just to make an extreme philosophical point.

Yet here I stand, with my libertarian instincts hanging out all over the place saying, "Yes, but . . ." If I were to become an all-out libertarian, their public support of the Mitchell brothers' public flouting of one of God's "Top Ten" would make it a bit difficult for me to explain to my children why such behavior is wrong when society condones these actions by permission, while my party is fighting for their right to morally pollute the city. The sexual rules which have been common to most great religions over the centuries are also essential to the cohesiveness of a properly functioning society. So, I part company with the libertarians. I know that you can't legislate morality, but communities have the right to set standards for public places and to enforce them, as long as people who don't like those standards are free to choose a community that has standards which they like. I am uncomfortable with the imposition of my morals on others by force, but I could never support an effort to defend scum like the Mitchell brothers. I'm not sure I know how to resolve this dilemma, but I am uncomfortable with both the conservative and libertarian positions on this issue.

So, I guess I'm half a libertarian, which is about as easy as being half pregnant.

Conservative Half-Truths

President Reagan stands for many things I like, such as the need to cut government spending, to balance the budget, to cut taxes, to get the government out of our pockets, to reduce regulation of business and individuals, and to strengthen our national defense. Bravo! However, I have one serious gripe about the whole conservative attack on government, and this may sound a bit bizarre coming from one who yields to no one in his distaste for government.

Conservative rhetoric says that all of our economic troubles are caused by power-crazy politicians in Washington, acting in opposition to "the real will of the people," running the printing presses day and night to inflate our currency, despite the cries of the people to "balance the budget" and "stop those presses."

Inflation is caused by creation of money, and Washington is creating the money. But I have one modest question: "Why is Washington creating the money?"

Congress spends money the people want spent, more money than it has the guts to take in taxes, and the Fed and the Treasury have to create money to fund the difference. Washington has deficits because people want programs and benefits from government and do not perceive the program or benefit they want as being part of the cause of inflation problems, and they don't want to pay the full bill.

Every Federal program has a logic of its own which is supported by a significant constituency. As soon as the program is launched, it benefits someone at the cost of someone else. First, it benefits the Senators and Congressmen who voted for the program. They are rewarded with votes. No one ever lost an election because of supporting some regulatory procedure. Then comes the bureaucracy which will administer the program. Finally, there are those to whom the final benefits will filter down—the industry protected from competition, the college student who gets food stamps, the government contractor and his employees who can plan on making a living, the bureaucratic "public servant," the minority businessman who gets the SBA guaranteed loan, etc. Obviously, someone is helped by every government program. But the cost—always there is the cost. Regulatory bondage, confiscatory taxes, inflation, mounting debt (with debt service, the second largest budget item), and a growing cancer on the national character. Those printing presses are running because, politically, they can't stop.

Over two-thirds of the inflation process, however, does not result directly from Washington budget deficits. Even if we balance the Federal budget, inflation would still be uncaged. The printing presses are financing all of the deficit spenders of America, and Federal deficits are responsible for only about one-third of the deficit spending. The rest of it is caused by you consumers who make $20,000 a year and spend $25,000, borrowing the difference, either by choice or by necessity because of the inflationary squeeze in purchasing power. As long as you perceive a need to borrow, the Fed, Uncle Sam's franchised counterfeiter, will see that there is plenty of money available in the economy through the banking system so that you can borrow, otherwise you can't buy, and someone will be laid off work. People out of work get jealous of legislators who are working, and tend to retire them prematurely at the polls. Attacking the politicians in Washington for creating the problem is simply shifting the blame away from those who are telling them what to do and toward those who are doing what they are told.

I have another hang-up with the conservatives. Many of them, to put it charitably, are somewhat lacking in compassion. Most of them have never been hopelessly poor. I have. We have seduced many of the "welfare bums" into dependence on government, and it is intellectually dishonest to label only the poor as "welfare bums," without including corporate and municipal welfare bums, such as Chrysler, and all the cities who fight for Federal handouts.

Here's another example. Although I am passionately opposed to abortion, an impeccable conservative position, I have been very close to a conservative who was also passionately anti-abortion and, to his dismay, had an unwanted teenage pregnancy in his own home. He agonized over this child that he loved going through the stress, pain, humiliation, and premature end to childhood that such a pregnancy brings. Although he didn't compromise his principles, and this particular pregnancy was ended in its early stages by a miscarriage, he will never again think of an unwanted pregnancy in anything but compassionate terms. To him, abortion still remains a horrible evil, a moral wrong, and a very special kind of murder. But no longer can he label all those who wish abortions as heartless, evil killers. They are, more often than not, frightened children with a horrible dilemma, trying to make a decision in a social environment where the moral issues are anything but clear to them. The conservative anti-abortion zealots, in their crusade for a good cause, too often show little love and concern for the real anguish of the abortion dilemma, even though they are dead right on the main principle.

The liberal, on the other hand, is so consumed by "compassion" that he's willing to jettison sound principles of economics, morality, and human behavior in the interest of "tolerance" and "liberality." In his putty-minded effort to pose as "compassionate," he perpetuates more evil than the most heartless single-interest conservative. And he is usually "compassionate" with my money!

Fundamental conservative philosophy says, "Let's not change those things that worked in the past. There are standards and absolutes which mankind is best served by obeying. Let's be very careful about major change."

Three cheers for that!

The conservative also says, "Government interferes too much in our lives and it is transferring too large a percentage of our national wealth to those who did not produce it. This is wrong. Let's stop it."

Three cheers for that, as well!

Further, the conservative says, "Let's strengthen our national defense so that we can act and speak from a position of strength and security."

Three cheers for that, also!

The conservative says, "All of our problems are made in Washington. If we just change the politicians we'll change the country."

Only one cheer for that!

We get precisely the kind of government we deserve and truly want. We express that opinion at the polls every two years. In 1980, we changed the cast of characters in Washington. If we truly want change, we must not only change the politicians, we must change their marching orders.

In November, 1980, I supported the election of those who I believed advocated and understood free market principles and who would be more likely to say, "No, no, no!" to the political pressure groups who demand Federal money. I didn't care whether they were Democrats, Republicans, Libertarians, or Whigs. My expectation was a President and Congress who have the guts to tell the people that they themselves are responsible for the mess we are in and that they are going to have to change their attitudes and rediscover some very outdated principles of thrift, self-denial, and self-sufficiency. Without that transformation of public attitudes, even if every politician in Washington became, down deep in his soul, a born-again, free-market-oriented libertarian, nothing will really change, unless he has the moral and financial support of the people who elected him. The real change must first occur in the minds and hearts of America before it can occur in the halls of Congress. And it will take years for such a change of heart to bear fruit in the inflation fight. Financially, you can continue to invest on the assumption that the inflation virus is still politically incurable.

The Single-Interest Groups

What about the single-interest groups, mostly on the political Right, and mostly conservative, who fight passionately for their causes and make their sole judgment about a man's political qualifications based on whether or not he's on the right side of that particular cause? If you have strong feelings about abortion, or the Panama Canal giveaway, or the ERA, *etc.*, and judge your representatives solely on the basis of that one issue, you may be doing both yourself and the country a disservice. There are some very fine men and women in office or running for office who are on the wrong side of one or more of those issues, but economically are sound thinkers and can help bring the nation through the problems that threaten our very existence. In applying my political litmus test to a candidate, I try to look at him in totality. I'm not going to find anyone with whom I will agree 100%. If I can get 80%, I'm thrilled to death, as even that's hard to find. If it's 50%, but he's right on the key economic issues, and he is significantly better than his opponent, he gets my support. If you vote against someone who is on the wrong side of the abortion issue, for example, but who is a true free-market type who battles against the growth of government, confiscatory taxation, deficit spending, and inflation, have you thrown the baby out with the bath water? If the free enterprise system folds, taking the Constitution with it, will you still be free to fight for or against ERA? Will anyone have any rights, let alone women? Single issue fanaticism can be dangerous and divisive, as it gets things out of perspective. A fanatic is one who, having lost sight of his goals, redoubles his speed.

Every political marriage has within it the seeds of divorce if you concentrate on all of those things that are wrong. Don't reject the forest because you are mad at two trees. If the whole forest is sick, or beyond saving, that's another case entirely. Many good men will vote their conscience differently than you might have on some issue. Balance and perspective are the keys to selecting a political candidate.

The New Captain of the *Titanic*

When Ronald Reagan became President of the United States, he inherited an impossible job that could break his heart. If you elected the Archangel Gabriel President of the United States, he couldn't get an honest, sound, beat-inflation program through Congress, even as it is now constituted, without a sacrificial attitude on the part of the people.

Even the relatively minor cuts in the rate of growth of taxes and spending won by President Reagan in 1981 have caused tremendous fear and dismay among huge and diverse groups of Americans. What's it going to be like when he really gets serious and people are really stung by genuine budget cuts?

Even if I'm wrong, and Congress suddenly does its duty, any positive changes will take years to have an effect, but the pain and fear of those adversely affected will be felt almost immediately. We have to start yesterday, and even that might be too late. In the meantime, hang onto your gold, silver, diamonds, colored stones, your collectibles, and any other inflation hedges. You're going to need them.

Where Do We Go from Here?

Our immediate objectives are quite modest. At the present time, the most we can realistically achieve is to arrest the rate at which we're sliding into an economic Hell by saying, "This far and no farther."

We must practice the art of the possible. President Reagan and his friends in Congress must zero in on those things which are truly achievable and be satisfied at first with small victories, while increasing their power base to the point where they can take on the big sensitive issues. His conservative and libertarian supporters must not reject him as a traitor if he has to postpone their pet cause in the interest of some compromise that will move us a short distance in the right economic direction.

For example, we can't realistically create immediate budget surpluses and pay off the national debt. The forces that would be mortally wounded by such actions are too powerful. But we can put ceilings on spending programs which are now open-ended and force a public political review of increases in such programs.

We can't force the government to go back on the gold standard immediately, but I do have some "art of the possible" proposals which will make it easier to go back on the gold standard later on when we have created the proper political environment.

We can't abolish regulatory government over the weekend, but we can clip its wings with some politically sexy legislation.

In 1982 and 1984, we can make a difference in some very close Senate and House races between a big spender who wants to buy your vote, and a free market, constitutionally oriented challenger or incumbent. A shift of about twenty-five more votes in the House of Representatives could make an incredible difference in the legislative environment.

How to Free the Eagle

My associates and I have created actual mechanisms to enable you to exercise real political influence. They are already organized. We are functioning effectively. We have already made a significant difference in the 1980 elections and in the halls of Congress.

I first stuck my neck out politically in March, 1980. We projected that, as a result, *The Ruff Times* would lose roughly a million dollars in renewal revenues in the first year because of subscriber resentment over that action. We were right, but it was worth it!

The Birth of Ruff-PAC

I formed a political action committee called Ruff-PAC and hired Neal Blair, a genius in his political insights. We raised money and opened up a Washington office, and we targeted those Senate and House races where we knew our guy was an underdog, but the race was winnable. We concentrated especially on Senate and House races where the liberal was coming on fast or had taken a lead. We spent $125,000 ourselves, but raised more than $300,000 for candidates through direct appeals, and we got a lot more leverage by persuading other PACs to help these same races.

We gave Chuck Grassley early money in the Iowa Senate primaries because we felt he was the best man to run against Senator John Culver. We gave him late money when Culver had come from behind. Grassley is now the Senator from Iowa.

We went to work on the Steve Symms–Frank Church race in Idaho. Church had gained momentum, partly because Congressman Gunn McKay of Utah, a Mormon, who had a twenty-six point lead in the polls in his own Utah race, felt secure enough to campaign for Church to get him the Idaho Mormon vote, so we jumped into the race to help Gunn McKay's opponent, Jim Hansen. I spent a day taping spots and making personal and TV appearances. We raised $35,000 and Hansen jumped nine points in the polls overnight, and Gunn McKay had to go home to fight for his political life.

Church began hammering at Symms' supporters saying,

"These carpetbagging PACs outside Idaho are trying to run Idaho politics," and he leaped in the polls. We did our homework and Ruff-PAC ran ads in every major newspaper in Idaho, listing all of the $1,000 out-of-state contributors to Church's campaign. It took a full page to do it. And Church plunged in the polls. With six days to go, Symms was still trailing by 9%. We bought time on thirty-two radio stations and two TV stations for a last minute blitz. Symms won by 40,000 votes!

Not only that, Hansen whipped McKay in Utah.

We jumped into the Florida Senate race behind Paula Hawkins. She won by an eyelash.

A lot of people gave up on East in North Carolina, but we fought on, and he won.

Everybody gave up on Bob Kosten in Wisconsin, but we stayed in there and fought and we dragged other PAC money in also, and he also won by an eyelash.

In addition to that, I went down to Houston for incumbent Congressman Ron Paul, who was losing ground. We had a fund raiser at which 250 *Ruff Times* subscribers showed up at $100 a head, and Ron Paul won by an eyelash. Ron recently introduced a bill to back the currency with gold, and he is one of my personal heroes.

Now I'm not saying that I personally won the 1980 election. What I'm trying to show you is that we demonstrated that if we really want to, together we can make a difference. Ruff-PAC may have provided the winning margin in three Senate and two House races, maybe more. We have demonstrated we don't have to be impotent.

When you become financially involved in politics, you find that Senators and Congressmen return your phone calls. They cannot safely ignore you. If we want to have a say about regulation and legislation, if we want a gold-backed currency, we have to help the good guys, and make sure we know they know it, and remind them when their courage falters. I'm not asking for improper influence. I just want to be listened to in high places when I feel strongly about something. I want to testify on important legislation. That's consistent with the letter and the spirit of this Constitutional Democratic Republic. We must reward politicians at the polls and with financial support when they do right, just as we must punish them by supporting their opponents when they desert sound principles.

Intimidation

I also jumped into the Presidential race. I was National Fund-raising Co-Chairman for Americans for Change, which raised $1.5 million dollars to expend independently for Reagan. I taped radio spots which ran on radio stations that carry my show. If you think politics is a wholesome sport, how about this?

On one of my own regular radio commentaries, I had criticized the President's hostage rescue effort, and raised some questions about our military strength.

Apparently, the Carter-Mondale committee picked this up and, knowing of my support for Reagan, decided I was too critical of the President, so they contacted every radio station in our network that they could identify, and demanded "equal time." Our attorneys informed us that they had no case for such equal time, but it panicked a lot of stations, and we estimate twenty of them cancelled from our network as a result of this intimidation. There is nothing a radio station fears more than the possible revocation of its license by the FCC, and that tacit implied threat scared the wits out of a lot of stations. I was told, in no uncertain terms, that I had to avoid criticism of the President until after the election. I argued that I had been criticizing him for four years and I found no reason to temper that criticism now just because of the election. We were partly neutered by the equal time regulation, at least in those twenty markets where my show was dropped. Some stations now had an excuse to drop my commentary for ideological reasons. I am sure that some stations have dropped my show for reasons other than ideology or fear, but the fact remains that, as a result of the intimidation of the Carter-Mondale committee, I am no longer being heard in twenty markets.

Such intimidation is scary, and not just because it's my show. I would be almost as upset if it happened to Nicholas Von Hoffman, Jack Anderson, or Jane Bryant Quinn.

If there were more of us working together unitedly, these new legislators would probably all be publicly calling for gold-backed money. They need to know we are a united cause, that we, despite our differences, all agree that we need honest money. We may be small in comparison to the total population, but financially and in the business community, we have influence all out of proportion to our numbers if we get together. You and I are the middle class and the affluent upper middle class of America. We can and should hold our national legislators' feet to the fire and demand that they do what has to be done. You can't do that just sitting on your tail growling at the six o'clock news. You must get involved.

I have two political priorities. My first priority is a strong national defense, because if we have to knuckle under to the Soviet Union, freedom is lost. Even if the cost is temporarily more inflation, we must survive first.

My second priority is to elect people who understand the capitalist free enterprise system and the real cause of inflation, people who are business oriented and won't give up on the system when the going gets tough.

Candidates for Ruff-PAC support were and will be selected on the basis of the following criteria:

1. How we think they will vote, relative to the philosophy in this book.
2. Their past records.
3. Our estimate of their personal character and reputation.
4. Their talent and drive.

345

5. Whether or not we feel they can win. We won't pour money and time into lost causes.
6. Whether or not our contribution can make a difference.

Free the Eagle

We have also formed a Washington-based lobbying organization called Free the Eagle. Free the Eagle first tested its wings when the so-called Domestic Violence Bill, an unacceptable government intrusion into families, was working its way through Congress. Two weeks before a Senate vote, there were only thirteen votes against it. I made an announcement of opposition to the bill through *The Ruff Times*. Our subscribers' calls and letters, along with intensive lobbying efforts by our Washington office, alerted a lot of Senators about the implications of the bill. When it finally came to a vote on the floor of the Senate, it passed, but there were now forty-one votes against it. When the bill, which had passed the House, came to the Conference Committee, we discouraged them from bringing it to the floor to a vote, so the bill died.

Free the Eagle is a nonprofit organization, funded entirely with contributions, mostly from *Ruff Times* subscribers, and will need your help. But before you decide to contribute, you really ought to know some of the things we are for and against, and a lot about our strategy.

We will take as our pattern the most successful, political pressure groups in Washington. Why reinvent the wheel, if it still works?

Ralph Nader has been able to coalesce around him all of the anti-business, anti-free enterprise forces in America under the guise of "protecting the consumer."

"Consumer" is a nastily appropriate word. One who consumes, rather than contributes. One who takes, rather than gives. One who gobbles up, rather than grows, or adds to, or builds. One who uses up, rather than provides.

The "consumer" is Nader's natural constituency. He has achieved great influence because he is personally dedicated to the principles he espouses, extracts no apparent tangible personal benefit from his efforts, other than power and influence, and always seems to be arrayed against some easy-to-hate, big business interest such as General Motors or Big Oil. The people who oppose him in testimony before Congressional committees are generally those whose statements can be kissed off with the assumption that they are financial "special interests" who will lose money because of Nader's "high-minded" proposals, so everything they say can be discounted.

Common Cause, founded by John Gardner, basically uses the same technique. They are "pure," so the press loves them.

There is no effective equivalent on the free market, free enterprise side of the fence that has money, the public clout, the ears of the media, and a long-range program for offsetting the malicious influence of the Naderites. The Chamber of Commerce and the National Association of Manufacturers are not likely to excite the eager support of a troubled nation in their behalf, as they give the appearance of reacting only to protect their pocketbooks.

Free the Eagle has been formed to effectively fight, within the spirit and the letter of Constitutional government, to preserve that spirit and that letter. And like Nader, our ideological opposite, we can act from a financially disinterested point of view, except to the extent, of course, that every American has a financial stake in the outcome of this great battle. I also have the attention of the media because of my radio and TV shows, and because *How to Prosper* was such a big best-seller. All we need is enough money, and one million grass-roots supporters.

The objectives of Free the Eagle are (1) to oppose legislation that accelerates our national demise, (2) to press for legislation that can stabilize the country so that the Ship of State will not sink as it sails through the Inflationary Eighties, and (3) to be sure that the Senators and Congressmen we helped to elect know we are around *between* elections, and (4) to make sure no legislative roadblocks are placed in the way of the financial strategies outlined in this book.

Free the Eagle maintains Washington offices and topflight legislative and regulatory legal counsel, and has already established close working relationships with political leaders, Congressmen, Senators, and their key staff members.

Neal Blair, who is running Free the Eagle, brilliantly masterminded the efforts of Ruff-PAC during the last election and knows where the bodies are buried in Disneyland-on-the-Potomac as well as anyone there.

I will represent Free the Eagle in testimony before committees of both houses of Congress when we feel a piece of legislation is dangerous or important, accompanied by the same press exposure Nader gets when he shows up. The 1980 election has made the task much easier, as many of the new chairmen of the various Senate committees are my friends.

Free The Eagle's first successful skirmish was in the Money Fund War which began to rage in late 1980.

The money market funds are viewed by the banks and savings and loans of this country as a threat to their very survival. Since short-term interest rates have risen above long-term rates, money has fled the banks to the funds, seeking higher yields with liquidity. Money seeks higher interest rates, just as water seeks lower elevations.

The phenomenon of short-term rates above long-term rates is called an interest rate "inversion." It doesn't happen very often, and it usually precedes a major recession. Ordinarily, lenders demand a premium for loaning their money long-term. Consequently, in normal stable times, the bond rate and the mortgage rate will be above the bank prime rate and the

348

T-bill rate, but 1981 was abnormal times. In its misguided attempt to control inflation by monetary policy alone, the Federal Reserve squeezed the money supply and forced the short-term rates way above the long-term rates, dragging the long-term rates higher also.

For many years, the banks have been committing the most fundamental banking error of all, in that they are "borrowing short" and "lending long." This means that while they are lending money for 20 to 30 years in mortgages, they are accepting money from depositors, either in passbook accounts paying only 5-1/4% to 5-1/2%, or in 6-month or longer CDs. When the CDs mature, the depositor has a decision to make: will he "roll over" his CD and keep it in the savings institution, or will he look for a better place to keep his money?

Now along came the money market funds offering even more liquidity than passbook accounts, and yields as high as the "Super CDs" that can be purchased by the big investors for $100,000 or more, and the little guy with $1,000 can invest.

The banks, being devastated by high interest rates, inflation, and their own industry sponsored rules (like Regulation Q, which limits the amount they can pay on passbooks) could sell plenty of the high-yielding CDs, but cheap passbook account money was leaving the banks for the money funds.

The banks and S and Ls were paying an average of 1% to 1-1/2% more than they are earning on their loan portfolios, but this average was kept down by the low 5-1/4% passbook interest earned by the ignorant who put money in passbook accounts because they were either (1) too lazy to look around for a better alternative, or (2) ignorant and didn't understand that a true yield has to be higher than the rate of inflation or they are losing money. Consequently, as money fled the passbook accounts, the average cost of money went up.

Sick financial institutions piled losses day after day, seeing the market value of their loan and bond portfolios collapse as interest rates rose, and they found a scapegoat—the money market funds and attacked them legislatively, trying to eliminate their check accounting features, and requiring reserves, etc.

Because this was a pure free market issue, and the loser would be the small investor, we fought the banking industry to a standstill in Utah, blocking them in the House by persuading four key votes to switch just before the voting occurred on a bill which would have crippled the funds. We won by 39-36.

In Kansas, when a similar law sneaked through the Senate with a sudden last minute amendment, we killed it in the House. I testified on behalf of Free the Eagle before the U.S. Senate Banking Committee.

Free The Eagle is also deeply involved in the issue of hard assets in retirement plans. Last summer Congressman James Shannon (D.-Mass.) introduced HR 1821, a bill that would eliminate the long-term gains tax treatment for "unproductive assets" such as gold, silver, rare coins, rare stamps, and even unimproved land.

This means that if you had the good judgment to have bought gold and silver a few years ago, you would be sandbagged with the highest tax rates our society reserves for punishing what it considers to be anti-social financial behavior.

What is an "unproductive asset?" In the simplistic view of the gold haters, gold is an unproductive asset because people who buy gold don't put their money into "productive investments" like CDs at your friendly Savings and Loan. This is based on the assumption that money invested in gold has disappeared forever from society.

Let's take a look at what happens when you buy that "unproductive asset."

We can safely assume that the person who sold the gold you bought would rather have paper money than the gold, so you take the money out of the bank (eliminating "productive" money from our economy) and you buy gold. What does the person do who sells you the gold? He puts his money back in the bank. The net effect is a big fat zero. The money is neither more nor less productive than it was before the transaction. The only beneficiary of this new law would be the United States Treasury, which is already plundering several times more of our national wealth than it should.

And what about that piece of undeveloped land?

Someone has to own it. There is value to society when people "bank" assets, in effect holding them until society is ready to use them, and they should be rewarded for performing that useful service. Eventually, that unproductive land will become productive, and it is in anticipation of its productivity that the price has risen, creating the taxable profit in the first place.

Not only is the above true, but it is a dirty trick to change the rules in the middle of the game. How would you like to be dealt a hand of blackjack, hit a 16 with a 5 and find out the name of the game had been changed from "21" to "17?" That's exactly what's happening here.

The so-called "hard money" movement is characterized by a bunch of unorthodox mavericks who have had the good sense to see things as they really are, not as those who live in the past, or hide their heads in the sand, or those who have a vested interest in the growth of government would like us to see the world. This brave band of hardy souls, influenced and tutored by people like Jim Dines, Harry Browne, Jim Sinclair, and many others, have done exactly what common sense dictates. They have put their money into assets which will preserve their purchasing power, based on the assumption that no one is served by the destruction of everyone's capital. Most so-called "productive assets" are guaranteed instruments of purchasing power confiscation. And what about government securities? Are they "productive assets?" Would

Mr. Shannon tax away capital gains realized by the savvy investors who buy them low and sell them high? I bet he won't! Most investments have been made based on the assumption of a certain rate of return, into which we have factored the tax considerations. Now, changing those rules would be immoral, dishonest, and a downright dirty trick, to say nothing of having zero benefit for society at large. This only serves to punish the prudent. But let's face it. Inflation is a tax, and successful inflation hedges are dirty tax dodgers, and a cause of envy.

Free The Eagle fought hard for the Reagan tax and budget cut program. We worked like the dickens to support the administration in its battle with the obstructionists in the House. Then, at the very last minute before the vote on the President's tax-cut package, and without the knowledge of nearly all the members of the House Ways and Means Committee and the Senate Finance Committee, a clause (314b) was inserted into the bill which provides that tax-advantaged money in self-directed pension plans, Keoghs and IRA plans can no longer go into gold, silver, coins, stamps, and collectibles, "as defined by the Secretary (of the treasury)" without being taxed in the calendar year they are purchased. The net effect is to prohibit collectibles from self-directed pension plans, including IRAs and Keoghs.

Again, the rationale is that a lot of money is no longer going into "traditional" investment vehicles, but into "nonproductive assets." This change in the tax law is designed to divert money from flowing into hard assets, and send it back into CDs.

Let me tell you the incredible story of how the whole thing happened.

Congressman Jim Shannon of Massachusetts met with two staff people from the National Association of Mutual Savings Banks and turned those two staffers over to a member of the staff of the Joint Finance Committee, which works for both

352

the House and the Senate. This staffer worked out the language with the representatives of the Savings Banks and inserted this clause into the bill without the knowledge of all congressmen and senators sitting on the respective tax committees. We have verified several times with each office that many of them knew nothing about it.

It is awesome that these two committees, which consist of specialists in the tax area, the men who are most knowledgeable in this field, could have a clause in the most important tax bill of the last twenty years they didn't know anything about. Just contemplate that for a moment.

Consider the fact that Shannon is the same guy who introduced the legislation to take away the capital gains tax treatment for *any* investment in hard assets.

If Jim Shannon has his way, ALL hard money investments, including those outside pension plans, would not be allowed the same capital gains tax treatment routinely allowed other investments when it comes time to take profits. You would be taxed at roughly twice the usual rate on any profits from such investments. It is a direct assault on the inflation hedger. If Shannon gets away with any part of his crusade, it will hurt the market price of our hard assets by reducing demand.

The bill specifically prohibits any work of art, rugs, antiques, metals, gems, stamps, coins, or alcoholic beverages (fine wines), or any other item of personal property specified by the Secretary of the Treasury, at his sole discretion.

Even if this Secretary of the Treasury should be quite careful in his interpretation of such a law, perhaps the next one will be a lot less free-market oriented than Mr. Regan. When you have a hammer in your hand, everything looks like a nail!

As the law now stands, hard-money, tax-advantaged, pension plan inflation hedging is now dead. That's the bad news! The good news is that it probably will be resurrected.

Free The Eagle has been working to mobilize the affected

citizens to press for immediate remedial legislation. We have commitments from several Senators and Congressmen, including some liberals, to support such a bill, and we expect support from the White House.

This is an issue of great consequence, to those of us who believe you're dead without hard asset strategies to hedge for your future. There is no reason you should not be allowed to put anything you want in your tax-advantaged retirement plan. Today, the pension plans; tomorrow, your survival coins!

This precedent is another opening wedge in an all-out assault against the ownership of gold, silver, collectibles, and even land. This anti-hard-money philosophy is now a baby snake, but it will soon be a 15-foot King Cobra if we don't kill it now.

As a result of the activities of Free The Eagle and the publicity I gave this issue in *The Ruff Times,* my subscribers inundated the Congress with letters. The responses from Senators, Congressmen, and the Treasury Department contain incredibly distorted reasoning.

Most deceitful is a form letter from Assistant Treasury Secretary John Kelly, who apparently took the position that because 314-B got sneaked into the tax bill, now the President can't disavow it, and must, after the fact, defend it. Mr. Kelly says,

"Congress included this provision because these investments work at cross purposes with the objectives of the Act. While it may be true that collectibles have provided investors with a safe hedge against inflation, Congress decided that persons should not enjoy the tax benefits accorded to IRA, plans to buy luxuries or items related to hobbies or personal tastes. These investments do not tend to generate the increased capital formation we need for improving our economy. By channeling increased retirement savings toward financial institutions, more funds will be available for housing construction, mortgages and additional plants and equipment for private industry. Investments in collectibles provide no such economic benefit.

In brief, the nation's best interests are served by encouraging economic growth through tax incentives which foster individual savings and channel those savings into financial institutions where they can foster economic recovery.

This is utter garbage. First, Congress made no such informed decision. It was dumped into the act without the knowledge of the Treasury or the White House, or most members of either the Senate Finance or House Ways and Means Committees. There were no hearings. It was not considered by the Conference Committee because it did not represent a difference which had to be reconciled between the House and Senate versions. This is hypocritical at best and dishonest at worst, which doesn't exactly give you a range of good choices—there not being a heck of a lot of difference between hypocritical and dishonest.

Incidentally, one of the most creative letters I've seen on this issue is from Congressman John Myers of Indiana, who said in reference to 314-B:

"... these provisions, which discourage but do not prohibit investments in collectibles through these retirement plans (Oh yeah? It only means that you lose your tax deductibility. HJR) are based on the rationale that such investments of retirement funds are not productive to the economy and do not stimulate business activity. *This reasoning and the provisions were not challenged or opposed when the bill was considered in the senate and the house.*" (My emphasis.)

The hypocrisy in this statement is that these bills were not considered in the senate and the house. That is precisely the point.

As I have said before, this is war! Free The Eagle must stay on top of this situation or those yahoos in Congress will simply assume that we are sleeping dogs and they can just let us lie. Actually, they did the lying—not us. We won't let them off the hook until they have repealed 314-B.

This isn't the only idiocy Free The Eagle is fighting.

Two bills have been introduced into the House of Representatives. Sponsored by Steve Solarz (D, NY), HR3008 would establish a set of employment standards for United States companies with more than 20 employees in South Africa, which would make it impossible for them to operate there. These standards are imposed in the simple-minded interest of "racial equality" in South Africa.

This bill will also ban United States bank loans to the South African government.

It will require public disclosure of all loans to South African entities.

And here's the real joker, folks. This bill will prevent the importation and sale of South African gold coins in the United States. There will be no more Krugerrands.

The second bill, HR3597, introduced by William Gary (D, PA) directs the President to issue regulations preventing all investments in South Africa by the United States or its citizens, and will ban the reinvestment of dividends.

There goes your South African gold shares, and there goes ASA, and there goes the only passive inflation hedge investment that will also produce significant income.

If you need income and buy gold, you won't get it. You have to go for capital gains, alone, which creates a whole different management problem for an older person who needs to live to live on his investments.

You can always buy real estate, of course. But what if you live in one of those big cities where real estate is now a lousy investment? What if you are old and sick, or incapacitated, and can't manage real estate investments? If you need income, you are pretty well limited to the South African gold shares, some of which have paid dividends as high as 25%. This bill will entirely prohibit such investments.

This sheer stupidity of drying up investments by the U.S. companies which have done more to contribute to racial progress in South Africa than all the efforts of the South African internal reformers combined, is a sugar-coated act of aggression against every South African black!

Those hard-headed Dutchmen who run South Africa have allowed American companies to bring equality to the work force in ways that South African companies would never be permitted, simply because they need American investment. This bill, like most laws, will have the exact opposite effect of what was intended. In addition, those South African gold mines that produce the raw materials for those Krugerrands have provided more equality for blacks, more management opportunities and more income than all of the efforts of the do-good reformers combined. African blacks have been voting with their feet as they have poured into South Africa, legally and illegally, from all over the continent, to work in the mines. What a tragedy it would be if this great force for social equality were to be crippled.

There will always be the Canadian Maple Leaf and the Austrian 100 Corona, but no coin has achieved such ready liquidity and instant recognition at every coin dealer's in America as has the Krugerrand. The free flow of the market-place should determine how many Krugerrands are wanted in America, not an ill-conceived political grandstand play, aimed at those who have no understanding of the complex issues in South Africa.

I happen to think South Africa's racial policies are stupid and unchristian, but I am also opposed to the do-gooders' "equality now" approach. Change will take time, patience and a deft touch, but these "solutions" are like treating diphtheria by amputating a leg. You can bet that if South Africa is economically disrupted, which these bills could accomplish, triggering a successful black revolution, the government that follows will be anti-capitalist, anti-American, and pro-Soviet. Whether we like them or not, the South

African white regime is capitalist, free enterprise and a friend to the U.S.

Free The Eagle was founded for the dual purpose of resisting ill-considered legislation and aggressively promoting an effective program of change. Thus far, we have some very important defensive battles. We didn't just participate in the money market fund battle—we won! Even though we were able to finance those defensive efforts, we didn't have enough money go on the attack, aggressively promoting our own legislative program. There would be considerable support in the Congress if we had the money and the staff. For example, a deep reduction in the inflation rate could be achieved by eliminating the capital gains tax, the taxes on dividends and interest, and the tax deductibility of consumer debt, with the probable exception of your principal residence and one car. That would mean that the savings rate would soar and the government would be able to borrow without squeezing out all other borrowers and would not have to monetize its deficits, while, one hopes, gradually getting those deficits under control. We can't fight that crucial battle yet because it takes *money*, staff, *money*, consistent hard work, *money*, and *money*. But we can fight if you help.

The Defensive Strategy

First let's look at some of the things that Free The Eagle will fight against.

1. We will fight against the creation of new agencies. I cannot conceive of any exceptions to this policy. I am personally convinced that each new agency is foreordained to become a bureaucratic monster, consuming money and causing trouble. There are too many already.

2. We will work for the dismantling of the Department of Energy and the new Department of Education. The President has called for their abolition but there are some incredible pressures from some of the special interest groups to keep

them intact. It's going to take a lot of effort to eliminate these two.

3. We will fight against regulatory activities that use the regulatory process to increase the power and influence of these agencies, by arousing public and Congressional opinion against such actions. We will watch the Federal Register like a hawk—or an Eagle.

4. We will publicly expose examples of bureaucratic waste, extravagance, and erosion of individual rights by intensive one-on-one effort with the appropriate people in Congress, press releases, and public relation activities.

Taking the Offensive

We will introduce specific pieces of legislation in Congress and fight for them. The following list is by no means complete, but it will give you an idea of the direction in which we intend to move.

1. We will press for a change in the deadline for filing state and Federal income tax returns, to the Monday preceding the general-election Tuesday in election years, and corresponding off-year dates. I want the voters to go to the polls mad about taxes and inflation. This will make an incumbent think twice before he votes to impose new taxes on the already overburdened taxpayer.

2. We will press for a Truth in Borrowing law, which will require institutions such as banks, savings and loans, and insurance companies to disclose prominently to the prospective depositor or investor whenever the rate of interest he is offered is less than the rate of inflation, so that the investor knows that he is getting a negative return—something like "This Certificate of Deposit could be dangerous to your financial health!" I would love to see it on every insurance premium payment coupon, on each bank deposit slip, on the door of the bank right under the FDIC sticker, and on each TV commercial pitching U.S. Savings bonds—especially U.S. Savings bonds.

This is to reduce the ignorance of Americans who put money in 5.5% passbook accounts, not understanding about inflation, not realizing they are being liquidated.

3. We will have as a long-range goal the return of America to the gold standard. As a small step in that direction, I will propose that the United States government issue U.S. Treasury Bonds, fully convertible into a given number of ounces of gold.

For example, a long-term bond could be redeemed for a fixed number of ounces of gold at maturity, based on the price of gold on the date the bond was issued. If the price of gold goes up, as it will, obviously there will be substantial profit for the owner of that bond.

One of our major national problems is that interest rates on short-term securities, such as T-bills and notes, are rising so sharply that the interest on the national debt is the second largest item in the budget. It is exploding even faster than welfare, and has to be funded by more printing press money, adding immensely to the rate of inflation. We end up paying interest on interest, ad infinitum.

Our national gold reserve, at $700 an ounce, has a fair market value of about $185 billion. If the government issued gold-backed securities, it would be able to sell new long-term bonds, perhaps yielding as low as 5% or 6%, because there are enough gold-oriented investors who understand that the interest is not the important thing, but rather the capital appreciation.

This plan has some dangers. It could make it easier for the government to borrow, and might stimulate even looser fiscal practices; however, if it were limited to a rollover of present debt as it comes due, coupled with debt limits with teeth in them, the government could convert its expensive (12% to 14%) short-term Treasury bills into long-term, low-interest, gold-backed securities.

This is something short of remonetizing gold, which I don't think we are ready to accept yet. However, I think it could have at least a salutary effect on the budget by sharply reducing the interest expense, while at the same time, at least psychologically, laying the foundation for the inevitable day when our currency will have to be backed by gold in order to save our way of life. It would also stop the sale of our gold, which would be committed to backing of this new debt. It would also strenthen the dollar.

4. We will press for legislation flat-out preventing the sale of our national patrimony, our gold, which would require a complete audit by an outside independent auditor as to the amount of our present gold reserves.

5. We will press for legislation requiring that if a Federal agency brings an action against a citizen or corporation, and that citizen or corporation prevails in the courts, the agency will pay all legal fees and out-of-pocket expenses of the defendant, and must advance the money for the defense, if the defendant is unable to pay for his own defense. This will reduce Federal bullying and enable people to fight when some bureaucratic government agent comes down on them unfairly. Most of the time, people cave in because they don't have the funds to fight, and even if they win, there is no recovery of damages or out-of-pocket costs. This would make the government agency think twice about bringing an action for frivolous reasons or merely to assert their bullying power. They would have to be sure that they had a case before hassling the people.

6. In order to reverse the progressive unconstitutional blurring of distinctions between the Executive, Legislative, and Judicial branches of government, which is characteristic of regulatory agencies, we will press for simple legislation that separates the trial procedures for violation of agency regulations from the agencies.

Under the present system, the agency decides whether to bring action, acts as a grand jury, then prosecutes and tries the merits of its own case, before its own administrative judges. The hearing examiners (judges) are subordinate to the heads of the agencies who are bringing the action. The potential for mischief and the built-in bias should be obvious to anyone. Let's remove the administrative judges from the agencies and combine them into a Regulatory Hearing department of the Federal courts. This would not add a new agency, but would merely shift this already existing function. We need to clearly establish by statute that all Constitutional guarantees, including freedom of the press and of speech, and the right to a jury trial, are applicable, just as they are in actions brought by a law enforcement agency.

7. We will press for legislation that would prevent Congress from insulating itself against the evil effect of its own actions, such as being able to avoid the unsound Social Security System with their own pension plan, and having their own salaries and retirement benefits indexed against the rate of inflation caused by their irresponsible legislation.

8. We will fight to reduce the size and power of government. One fascinating proposal from a *Ruff Times* subscriber, F. F. McClatchie of Costa Mesa, California, would lower the cost of Federal government with the full and enthusiastic support of Federal employees. That's sort of like enlisting the enthusiastic support of the coyotes for a vegetarian diet. But to quote Professor Higgins in *My Fair Lady*, "I think he's got it."

Here's how it works.

No more new hiring of Federal employees.

Lay off 10% of all existing Federal employees each year, selecting those to be laid off by lottery. That's no different from the military draft. This ensures that the layoffs will be "fair," that is, the bureaucrats can't play with the deck. That way, those who are part of the fat are not in charge of cutting the fat.

Continue to pay the laid off bureaucrats at their wages as of the layoff date. This would insure their full cooperation; in fact, their full-time vacations would no doubt thrill them. This would save billions of dollars since they would no longer occupy office space or waste paper, to say nothing of working mischief. They could no longer interfere with business, saving countless billions for productive uses.

Reduce each laid-off Federal employee's paycheck by 10% per year. This would ensure that sooner or later he would seek productive employment. In the meantime, he will spend the money on hobbies, travel, etc., and keep the economy roaring along with no additional tax burden and no requirement for a big bureaucracy to administer welfare.

Continue this process until the government is operating efficiently at whatever fraction of the current payroll would make for the most efficiency.

McClatchie suggests that the military would be exempt from this plan.

9. We will press for the elimination of the capital gains tax. This will revitalize the stock markets and make tremendous amounts of capital available for expansion, modernization, and innovation in American industry. This alone could transform the economy. President Reagan made an important first step by lowering the maximum rate, but it was only a first step. The tax should be repealed.

10. We will press for immediate deregulation of the natural gas industry. Let's not worry about "excess profits." We need the energy. Those profits will flow back into the economy in the form of dividends to the stockholders, pension funds, and institutions that own that stock, and will be recycled for the good of all of us.

11. We will press for a national food reserve policy to provide tax incentives for home food storage. In times of food surpluses, especially surplus grains, any American who buys wheat or corn for emergency storage would be given a tax credit equal to what he paid for the grain. This would take big surpluses off the back of the American farmer, would make him less likely to press for sales to our enemies, such as the Soviet Union, and this reserve in the homes of Americans would be a stabilizing factor in times of distribution disrup-

tion, labor troubles, or panic. It would also require no bureaucracy to administer, and would be cheaper than existing government commodity programs. You would simply take it as a credit against your bottom-line tax on your Form 1040.

If significant numbers of Americans had an emergency supply of food within their own homes to draw on in emergencies or in periods of shortage or excessive high prices, it would be a self-regulating factor in the markets. For example, if the price of bread rose too high, a lot of people would consider breaking into their canned wheat, grinding their own flour, and making their own bread. If bread is cheap, they would simply save their wheat for when they need it.

12. We will press for abolition of the Federal Election Commission. The FEC represents a severe threat to the American free electoral process. In its overreaction to Watergate, they have made it infinitely more difficult for a challenger to take on an incumbent and win. The FEC has made it paradoxically easy for a rich candidate to buy an election by spending $1,000,000 of his own money, while a less affluent challenger will find it very difficult to raise money from his friends, because they cannot legally contribute more than $1,000 each to his campaign. Abolition is the best solution, but we would also support an appropriate overhaul of the FEC.

That's just a sampling of the kind of things we will work for and against.

We are not just another Don Quixote tilting at windmills. If you will look back over most of these proposals, you will find that they could be politically acceptable, and that they strike deep. Henry David Thoreau said, "There are a thousand hacking away at the branches of evil to one who is striking at the root." Each of these proposals is designed to go for the throat, so to speak, and get the Controllocrats where they hurt.

Free The Eagle needs millions to do its job. Any contributor to Free The Eagle will receive a monthly *State of the Nation* newsletter, written by Neal Blair and edited by me. You will be kept abreast of the status of our legislative efforts and where we are winning and where we are losing. The newsletter is free to all contributors, but bear in mind when you make a contribution, that it costs us at least $25 a year to produce and mail this letter to you, so be generous. There are several interesting additional benefits we can offer to contributors of $1,000 or more. Write to:

Free The Eagle
1835 S. South State
Suite 150
Orem, UT 84057

Our objective is to have at least 1 million supporters and contributors so that when I walk into a hearing room on Capitol Hill, they will know that behind me are 1 million concerned, affluent Americans, who vote and contribute to candidates.

Maintaining the Pressure

Over the next several years, we must hold those politicians' feet to the fire. As we approach the 1982 elections, there is a very good chance that the problems that were inherited by this Republican Administration and Senate will have created a climate of political revolt where the people will have said to themselves, "We voted against inflation, but we didn't want you to refuse to bail out my city. I'm out of work." Even the bravest conservative thinks twice at a time like that. These people need to know that if they have the courage to stick to their guns in the face of mounting political pressures and protests, that we will reward them with our financial support, our votes, and with grass-roots activities to help them win the election. And at the appropriate time, Ruff-PAC will swing into action to both reward and punish at the polls.

This is being done openly and candidly within the spirit and letter of the law, as the system is too precious to endanger it by acting as badly as those who hate the system. We cannot be like those who tried to save Vietnamese villages by burning them down. We must work within the system to let those people in Washington know that we can be generous friends or implacable enemies.

In the meantime I make the following pledges to you.

1. I will never accept a salary or compensation for my time or effort in behalf of *Free The Eagle* or Ruff-PAC, except for legitimate out-of-pocket expenses prudently incurred in the course of activities in their behalf.

2. We will not waste time or money in lost causes. We will practice the art of the politically possible. We will, however, devote some effort to long-range objectives, such as the restoration of the gold standard, which we know is not feasible now. Someone must hold aloft the banner until such time as it does become feasible.

3. Everything we do will be consistent with the philosophy in this book.

4. We will keep all contributors fully informed about our actions. You will receive regular financial reports.

5. We will make a difference, as we have already demonstrated that we can, and we believe that between now and 1984, our actions could make the difference between failure and success in a close case as this nation undergoes its greatest Constitutional test since the Civil War. Someone must fight to *Free The Eagle*.

APPENDIX

Goods and Services
For Your Consideration

In several instances, you will note a "Recommended" firm and a list of others which are "Also Reputable."

The recommended firms are those which I have personally researched, where I have negotiated favorable arrangements for those who choose to take my advice, and which I monitor on a regular basis. As my recommendation provides a substantial portion of the total business of these recommended firms, this gives me considerable clout if any problems arise.

The "Also Reputable" firms have been investigated, but time limitations preclude my monitoring them as closely. These are dependable people who have good business reputations.

In some instances there is only one recommended firm, and none are listed as "Also Reputable" because I have not had time to dig deeper.

This list is subject to change, and I accept no responsi-

bility for any trouble you might have with a firm we have dropped from the list.

Prices are subject to inflationary change.

NEWSLETTERS AND ADVISORY SERVICES

Recommended

The Ruff Times, P. O. Box 2000, San Ramon, CA 94583; $145 per year; call (USA) 800-227-0703 or (CA) 800-642-0204 or collect 415-837-1566 (AK, Canada, HI).

B. Ray Anderson's Taxflation Fighter, New Capital Publications, P.O. Box 870, Mahopac, NY 10541; annual subscription rate—$195, introductory annual rate, $145.

Douglas R. Casey's Investing in Crisis, New Capital Publications, P.O. Box 879, Mahopac, N.Y. 10541; annual subscription rate—$195, introductory annual rate, $145.

Albert J. Lowry's Winning With Real Estate, New Capital Publications, P.O. Box 869, Mahopac, N.Y. 10541; annual subscription rate—$195, introductory annual rate, $145.

Kravitz and Wright's Commodities Insider, New Capital Publications, P.O. Box 880, Mahopac, NY 10541; annual subscription rate—$195, introductory annual rate, $145.

Richard Russell's Dow Theory Letters, P.O. Box 1759, La Jolla, CA 92038; 26 letters per year—$185, 6 months, $105.

Gary North's Remnant Review, P.O. Box 7999, Tyler, TX 75711; Phone: 602-252-4477; $95 per year—22 issues.

The Reaper, P.O. Box 39026, Phoenix, AZ 85069; Phone: 602-993-1626; $225 per year, 5 issues trial—$25.00.

Daily News Digest, P.O. Box 39027, Phoenix, AZ 85069; $150 per year, 5-week trial—$19.

Personal Finance Letter, P.O. Box 974, Farmingdale, NY 11737; 24 issues—$78.

Gold Newsletter, 4425 West Napoleon Avenue, Metairie, LA 70001; $39 per year in U.S., overseas $65.

Harry Browne Special Reports, 207 Jefferson Square, Austin TX 78731; Phone: 512-453-7313; $195 per year.

Mark Skousen's Forecasts & Strategies, Phillips Publishing, 7315 Wisconsin Avenue, Suite 1200 N. Bethesda, MD 20814; $135 per year.

Robert Kinsman's Low Risk Advisory Letter, 1700 South El Camino Real, Suite 408, San Mateo CA 94402; Phone: 415-574-7174; Published 17 times annually at $125.

McKeever's Misl, Contact—Omega Services, P.O. Box 4130, Medford, OR 97501; Phone: 503-773-8575; $165 per year, 6-months $90.

Tax Angles, 901 North Washington Street, Suite 605, Alexandria, VA 22314; 12 issues—$60.

The Retirement Letter, 7315 Wisconsin Avenue, Suite 1200 N. Bethesda, MD 20814; $49 per year.

Myers' Finance and Energy, 642 Payton Bldg., Suite 418, Spokane, WA 99201; Phone: 509-747-9371; 14 issues—$200, 3 issues—$25.

World Money Analyst, 927 S. Walter Reed Dr., Arlington, VA 22204 or 1914 Asian House, One Hennessy, Hong Kong; $135 per year.

World Market Perspective, P.O. Box 91491, West Vancouver, B.C., Canada V7V 3P2; $96 per year, 3-months' trial—$36.

The International Harry Schultz, In care of XEBEX, P.O. Box 134, Princeton, NJ 08540; $258 per year.

Precioustones Newsletter, P.O. Box 4649, Thousand Oaks, CA 91359; Phone: 213-889-4367; $177 per year (12 issues) USA, $200 Canada, $219 out of USA and Canada.

Creative Real Estate Magazine, Box 2446, Leucadia, CA 92024; Phone: 714-438-2446; $40 per year.

Personal Survival Letter, P.O. Box 598, Rogue River, OR 97537; Phone: USA 800-547-5995, Ext. 215, in Oregon 800-452-8847, Ext. 215; $125 per year.

OTHER PUBLICATIONS

Acres, USA, 10008 East 60th Terrace, P.O. Box 9547, Raytown, MO 64133; Phone: 816-737-0064; $9 per year.

Small Town, USA, Woods Creek Press, Box 339, Ridgecrest, CA 93555; Phone: 714-375-1988; $30 for 10 issues, sample copy—$2.

The Mother Earth News, P.O. Box 70, Hendersonville, NC 28739; Phone: 704-693-0211; $15 for 6 issues.

Organic Gardening and Farming, Rodale Press, Inc., 33 East Minor Street, Emmaus, PA 18049; Phone: 215-967-5171; $11 per year.

Prevention Magazine, Rodale Press, Inc., 33 East Minor Street, Emmaus, PA 18049; Phone: 215-967-5171; $10.97 per year.

Let's Live Magazine, 444 North Larchmont Blvd., Los Angeles, CA 90004; Phone: 213-469-3901; $9 per year.

Dads Only, P.O. Box 340, Julian, CA 92036; Phone: 714-765-1815; $14.50 per year for 12 issues.

HOME STUDY COURSES

Financial Planning Services—A Do-It-Yourself Financial Planning Home Study Kit, 1835 S. State Street, Suite 330, Orem, UT 84057; Phone: collect 801-224-5000.

FOOD STORAGE

Recommended

Martens Health and Survival Products, Inc., P.O. Box 5969 Tahoe City, CA 95730; Phone: USA 800-824-7861, CA 800-822-5984, Local 916-583-1511.

Also Reputable

Rainy Day Foods, P.O. Box 71, Provo, UT 84603; Phone: 801-377-3093.

The Grover Company, 2111 South Industrial Park Avenue, Tempe, AZ 85282; Phone; USA 800-528-1406; 602-967-8738.

Intermountain Freeze-Dried Foods, 3025 Washington Boulevard, Ogden, UT 84401; Phone: USA 800-453-2441 or 801-627-1490.

The Simpler Life (Arrowhead Mills), P.O. Box 671, Hereford, TX 79045; Phone: 806-364-0730.

Oregon Freeze-Dry Food, P.O. Box 1048, Albany, OR 97321; Phone: 503-926-6001.

Sam Andy Foods, 1660 Chicago Avenue, Building P-1, Riverside, CA 92507; Phone: 714-684-9003.

Frontier Food Association, Inc., 7263 Envoy Court, P.O. Box 47088, Dallas, TX 75247; Phone: 214-630-6221.

SI Outdoor Food & Equipment by Mail, 17019 Kingsview, Carson, CA 90746; Phone: USA 800-421-2179 or 213-631-6197.

Survival Center, 5555 Newton Falls Road, Ravenna, OH 44266; Phone: USA 800-321-2900 or 216-678-4000.

In Canada

Scott's Perma Storage Foods, LTD., 21 Water Street, Aylmer, Ontario N5H 1G8; Phone: 519-773-2462.

Gary Bikman Distributing, Box 428, Lethbridge, Alberta, T1J 3Z1; Phone: 403-327-5734.

COIN DEALERS

Recommended

Investment Rarities, 1 Appletree Square, Minneapolis, MN 55420; Phone: USA 800-328-1860 or call collect 612-853-0700 (MN, AK, Canada, HI).

Deak-Perera, 1800 K Street NW, Washington, DC 20006; Phone: USA 800-424-1186 or 202-872-1233, (202-872-1630 —recorded exchange rates and precious metals quotes).

Also Reputable

Camino Coin Company, 851 Burlway Road, Suite 105 (P.O. Box 4292), Burlingame, CA 94010; Phone: 415-348-3000.

C. Rhyne and Associates, 110 Cherry Street, Suite 202, Seattle, WA 98104; Phone: USA 800-426-7835 or 206-623-6900, WA 800-542-0824.

Joel D. Coen, Inc., 39 W. 55th Street, New York, NY 10019; Phone: USA 800-223-0868 or 212-246-5025.

Lee Numismatics International, Executive Place, 60 Mall Road, Burlington, MA 01803; Phone: USA 800-343-8564 or 617-273-3680.

Numisco, 1423 W. Fullerton, Chicago, IL 60614; Phone: USA 800-621-1339 or 800-621-1030, 312-528-8800.

North American Coin and Currency, Ltd., 34 W. Monroe, Phoenix, AZ 85003; Phone: USA 800-528-5346 or 602-256-5200.

James U. Blanchard & Co., Inc., 4425 W. Napoleon, Metairie, LA 70001; Phone: USA 800-535-7633, LA 504-456-9034.

Sidney W. Smith & Sons, 2510 Biscayne Blvd., Miami, FL 33137; Phone: 305-573-1200, or 6639 S. Dixie Hwy., Miami, FL 33137; Phone: 305-665-1300.

Bramble Coins, P.O. Box 10026, Lansing, MI 48901; Phone: 800-248-0490 or 517-321-6650.

Manfra, Tordella & Brookes, Inc., Numismatic Department, 30 Rockefeller Plaza, New York, NY 10020; Phone: USA 800-223-5818 EXT. 621 or 619 (NY, AK, HI), 212-621-9500 EXT 621 or 619.

SURVIVAL PRODUCTS (MAIL ORDER)

Recommended

Martens Health & Survival Products, Inc., P.O. Box 5969, Tahoe City, CA 95730; Phone: USA 800-824-7861, CA 800-822-5984, Local 916-583-1511

Also Reputable

SI Outdoor Food & Equipment by Mail, 17019 Kingsview, Carson, CA 90746; Phone: USA 800-421-2179 or 213-631-6197.

The Grover Company, 2111 South Industrial Park Avenue,

Tempe, AZ 85282; Phone: USA 800-528-1406 or 602-967-8738.

The Survival Center, 5555 Newton Falls Road, Ravenna, OH 44266; Phone: USA 800-321-2900 or 216-678-4000.

MONEY MARKET FUNDS

Capital Preservation Fund, 755 Page Mill Road, Palo Alto, CA 94304; Phone: USA 800-227-8380, CA 800-982-6150 or collect 415-858-2400 (AK, Canada, HI); for information packet USA 800-227-8996 or CA 800-982-5873; Also an office at 1900 Avenue of the Stars, Suite 715, Century City, CA 90067; Phone: 213-277-7500.

National Retired Teachers Association/American Association Retired Persons U.S. Government Money Market Trust: 421 7th Avenue, Pittsburgh, PA 15219; Phone: USA 800-245-4770, PA 800-892-1040.

Merrill Lynch Cash Management Account, call your local Merrill Lynch office.

DIAMONDS

Recommended

Newcastle Financial Group, 1815 S. State, Suite 1800, Orem, UT 84057; Phone: 800-453-1466 or 801-224-9800.

Reliance Diamonds, 1911 San Miguel, Suite 203, Walnut Creek, CA 94596; Phone: USA 800-227-1590, CA 800-642-2406, Collect 415-938-6510 (CA, AK, Canada, HI).

Also Reputable

Gemstone Trading Corp., 309 5th Avenue, New York, NY 10016; Phone: 800-223-0490.

La Jolla Diamond Company, 7911 Herschel Avenue, Suite 206, La Jolla, CA 92037 (P.O. Box 2603, La Jolla, CA 92038); Phone: USA 800-854-1049 or 714-454-8806.

COLORED GEMSTONES

Recommended

Investment Rarities, 1 Appletree Square, Minneapolis, MN 55420; Phone: USA 800-328-1928 or collect 612-853-0700 (MN, AK, Canada, HI).

H. Stern Jewelers, Inc. 645 Fifth Avenue, New York, NY 10022; Phone: USA 800-221-4768 or 212-688-0300.

Newcastle Financial Group, 1815 S. State Street, Suite 1800, Orem, UT 84057; Phone: 800-453-1466 or 801-224-9800.

Also Reputable

· *Precision Gems,* 265 Santa Helena Financial Square, P.O. Box 1047, Solana Beach, CA 92075; Phone: Call Collect 714-481-1101.

REAL ESTATE
(Real Estate Investment Training)

Recommended

Dr. Albert J. Lowry, Education Advancement Institute, 50 Washington Street, Reno, NV 89303; Phone: 702-322-1923.

Also Reputable

Professional Educational Foundation, Box 2446, Leucadia, CA 92024; Phone: 714-438-2446.

Robert Allen, Investment Seminars, 3707 N. Canyon Rd., Suite 8-F, Provo, UT 84601; Phone: 801-226-2167.

Complete information on various types of real estate seminars listed monthly in *Creative Real Estate Magazine,* Box 2446, Leucadia, CA 92024; Phone: 714-438-2446.

REAL ESTATE INVESTMENTS

Newcastle Financial Group, 1815 S. State, Suite 1800, Orem, UT 84057; Phone: 800-453-1466 or 801-224-9800.

COMMODITY BROKERS (MANAGED ACCOUNTS)

Sandner Kravitz Wright, Inc., 222 S. Riverside Plaza, Suite 546, Chicago, IL 60606; Phone: USA 800-621-3053 or 312-648-0131 (Contact Maury Kravitz or Marshall Wright).

GOLD SHARE BROKERS AND/OR ADVISORS

Not Monitored

Rotan Mosle, Inc., Gold Specialist—Barry Downs, 10 E. 53rd Street, New York, NY 10022; Phone: 212-750-0813.

Rauscher, Pierce, Refsnes, Inc., 2 Houston Center, Suite 3400, Houston, TX 77002; Phone: 713-652-3033 (Mr. Douglas Johnston).

National Securities Corp., Jerry Pogue (North American Penny Shares, $3,000 minimum), 500 Union St., Seattle, WA 98101; Phone: USA 800-426-1608 or 206-622-7200 (AK, HI, WA).

T. E. Slanker Company, 9450 SW Commerce Circle, 300 AGC Center, Wilsonville, OR 97070; Phone: 503-682-4000, 800-547-2018 or HI, AK 800-547-4510.

Jon M. Bloodworth, Jack Saunders of Dean Witter Reynolds, 1 Kaiser Plaza, Suite 350, Oakland, CA 94612; Phone: collect 415-839-8080.

IRA, KEOGH AND SELF-DIRECTED RETIREMENT AND PENSION PLANS

Recommended

Newcastle Financial Group, 1815 S. State Street, Suite 1800, Orem, UT 84057; Phone: 800-453-1466 or 801-224-9800.

Retirement Consultants, Inc., Ron Holland, President, Route 2, Darby Bridge Road, P. O. Box 314, Taylors, SC 29687; Phone: 800-845-3970 or 803-895-4300.

First State Bank of Oregon Trust Group, 520 SW Sixth Avenue, Suite 400, Portland OR 97207; Phone: 503-243-3517.

Jon M. Bloodworth, Jack Saunders of Dean Witter Reynolds, 1 Kaiser Plaza, Suite 350, Oakland, CA 94612; Phone: Collect 415-839-8080.

Merrill Lynch, call your local Merrill Lynch office.

TAX SHELTERS

Newcastle Financial Group, 1815 S. State Street, Suite 1800, Orem, UT 84057; Phone: 800-453-1466 or 801-224-9800. NEWCASTLE products include real estate, gas and oil, equipment leasing, research and development, energy related programs, livestock breeding and mining tax shelters.

FINANCIAL PLANNING

Financial Planning Services—Education, Seminars and Home Study; 1835 S. State Street, Suite 330, Orem, UT 84057; Phone: collect 801-224-5000. Howard Ruff is a major stockholder of this company.

Newcastle Financial Group—Providing financial planning services; 1815 S. State Street, Suite 1800, Orem, UT 84057; Phone: 800-453-1466 or 801-224-9800.

MUTUAL FUNDS

Not Monitored

The following recommendations are subject to changes—depending on the economy.

Fidelity Select Portfolios: Energy Portfolio, Precious Metals Portfolio, 82 Devonshire Street, Boston, MA 02109; Phone: 800-225-6190.

Bull & Bear Group: Golconda (gold stock), 11 Hanover Square, New York, NY 19005; Phone: 800-942-6911.

United Services Fund, Inc., 110 East Byrd Boulevard, P.O. Box 2098, Universal City, TX 78148; Phone: 512-658-3562 or 800-531-7510.

Energy Fund, 522 Fifth Avenue, New York, NY 10036; Phone: 212-790-9800.

Rowe Price: New Era (Natural Resources), 100 East Pratt Street, Baltimore, MD 21202; Phone: 800-638-1527.

Newcastle Hard Asset Fund, 1815 S. State Street, Suite 1800, Orem, UT 84057; Phone: 800-453-1466 or 801-224-9800.

STRATEGIC METALS INVESTMENT COUNSELORS

(Not Monitored)

Kearney Metals and Minerals, Ltd., P.O. Box 784, Novato, CA 94948; Phone: 415-892-8441, TLX 172176; Bermuda Office: P.O. Box 1629, Hamilton 5 Bermuda; Phone: 809-295-6009, TLX 3292 SMLBA.

Strategic Metals Corporation, 500 Chesham House, 150 Regent Street, London W1R 5FA, England.

Strategic Metals and Critical Materials Inc. (James Sinclair Group Companies), 90 Broad Street, New York, NY 10004; Phone: 800-221-4120 or NY 212-425-2360.

PRECIOUS METALS CERTIFICATES

Deak-Perera, 1800 K Street, NW, Washington, DC 20006; Phone: USA 800-424-1186 or 202-872-1233.

Dreyfus Gold Deposits, Inc., 600 Madison Avenue, New York, NY 10022; Phone: USA 800-223-7750, call collect 212-935-6666.

Citibank, NA. Gold Center, 399 Park Avenue, New York, NY 10043; Phone: USA 800-223-1080 or NY 212-559-6041.

Merrill Lynch, Sharebuilder Marketing, One Liberty Plaza, 5th Floor, 165 Broadway, New York, NY 10080; Phone: USA 800-221-2856 or 800-221-2857, NY 800-522-8882 or 212-637-2849.

SWISS BANK PRECIOUS METALS ACCUMULATION PROGRAM
(Not Monitored)

Goldplan A.G., P.O. Box 213-K, 8033 Zurich, Switzerland.

RETREAT AND SURVIVAL COUNSELING AND SURVIVAL HOMES

Joel Skousen Survival Homes, Inc., 903 State Street, Hood River, OR 97031; Phone: 503-386-6553.

Don Stephens, Drawer 1441, Spokane, WA 99210; Phone: 509-838-8222.

WATER PURIFIERS
Recommended

American Diversified Industries (Water Washer), 115 Mason Circle, Concord, CA 94520; Phone: 415-825-9100.

STORED FUEL PRESERVATIVES
Recommended

Bob Hinrichs, Fuel-Mate, P.O. Box 3471, Santa Barbara, CA 93105; Phone: 805-682-6919 or 805-967-7914.

SECURITY STORAGE VAULTS

Perpetual Storage, Inc., 3322 South 3rd East, Salt Lake City, UT 84115; Phone: 801-486-3563.

James U. Blanchard & Co., Inc., The Security Center, 147

Carondelet Street, New Orleans, LA 70130; Phone: 504-456-9034.

SAFES

Southern Securities, 207 Center Park Drive, Knoxville, TN 37922; Phone: USA 800-251-9992 or 615-966-2300.

Survival Vaults, P.O. Box 462, Fillmore, CA 93015; Phone: 805-524-0286.

Adesco Safe, 16720 S. Garfield Avenue, Paramount, CA 90723; Phone: 213-774-0081 or 213-630-1503.

Warman Safe Co., 1545 Broadway, San Francisco, CA 94109; Phone: 415-776-5350.

Tennessee Business Systems, 1200 Dodds Avenue, Chattanooga, TN 37404; Phone: 615-265-3884.

J. Goodman Company, 29 Arden Road, Livingston, NJ 07039; Phone: 201-994-3079.

Boston Lock and Safe Company, Inc., 30 Lincoln Street, Boston, MA 02135; Phone: 617-787-3421.

FINE ARTS

Fine Arts, Ltd. (Investment Quality Prints), 1854 Vallejo Street, Suite B, San Francisco, CA 94123; Phone: 415-775-2722.

Dr. Wesley M. Burnside (Consulting & Acquisition—American Painting & Sculpture), Art Department, Brigham Young University, Provo, UT 84602; Phone: 801-378-2281 or 801-378-6204.

GOLD AND SILVER JEWELRY

Ounce o' Gold (14 carat gold jewelry), 6 D 88 Apparel Mart, 2300 Stemmons Freeway, Dallas, TX 75207; Phone: USA 800-527-9846 or TX 800-442-7789, 214-631-2655.

The Bullion Collection (one of the Deak-Perera group), (23.5 carat gold jewelry), 1800 K Street, NW, Washington, DC 20006; Phone: 800-424-1186 or 202-872-1233.

Texas Mint (silver gift items), 4503 Sunbelt, Dallas, TX 75248; Phone: 214-931-1233.

BOOKS

All available from Target Publishers, P. O. Box 2000, San Ramon, CA 94583. Add $1.00 postage/handling for each item ordered, California residents add 6.5% sales tax.

BOOKS BY HOWARD J. RUFF

Survive and Win in the Inflationary '80s, Times Books, 1981. Hardcover $12.50; paperback $6.50.

How to Prosper During the Coming Bad Years: A Crash Course in Personal Survival, Times Books, 1979. Hardcover $8.95; softcover $2.95.

MISCELLANEOUS BY HOWARD J. RUFF

Travel With Howard J. Ruff—Ruff Times Seminars at home and abroad. Contact Target Travel International, Inc., One Crow Canyon Court, Suite 200, San Ramon, CA 94583 or P.O. Box 2500, San Ramon, CA 94583; Phone: USA 800-227-2446 or 415-838-8150.

Howard Ruff Sings—Howard Ruff's record album featuring the Osmond Brothers and the Brigham Young University Philharmonic Orchestra and A Cappella Choir. Songs of country, money, family love and inspiration. Stereo record or cassette tape $9.95.

Ruff Times National Convention Tapes, available following *Ruff Times* Convention each March.

Life is Ruff, a board game using inflation beating strategies. $14.95 plus $2.00 shipping.

OTHER BOOKS

How You Can Use Inflation to Beat The IRS, B. Ray Anderson, Warner Books. Paperback $6.50.

Crisis Investing: Opportunities and Profits in the Coming Great Depression, Douglas R. Casey, Stratford Press, 1980. $14.95.

Successful Investing In An Age of Envy, Dr. Gary North, Steadman Press, IN, 1981. $14.95.

How You Can Profit From The Coming Price Controls, Dr. Gary North, American Bureau of Economic Research. $14.50.

How to Become Financially Successful by Owning Your Own Business. Albert J. Lowry, Simon and Schuster, NY. Price $14.95.

How You Can Become Financially Independent By Investing In Real Estate, Albert J. Lowry, Simon & Schuster, 1977. $15.95.

How to Successfully Manage Real Estate in Your Spare Time, Albert J. Lowry, Simon & Schuster, 1979. $24.95.

Nothing Down, Robert G. Allen, Simon & Schuster, 1980. $12.95.

A Fortune at Your Feet, A. D. Kessler, Harcourt Brace Jovanovich, NY. $10.95.

Retirement Edens, Peter Dickenson, E. P. Dutton, NY, 1981. $9.25.

The Coming Currency Collapse, Jerome Smith, Books in Focus, 1981. $13.95.

Inflation Proofing Your Investments, Harry Browne, William Morrow & Co., 1981. $14.95.

Alpha Strategy, John Pugsley, The Common Sense Press, Inc., CA, 1980. $13.95.

Common Sense Economics, John Pugsley, Common Sense Press, 1976. $14.95.

William E. Donoghue's Complete Money Market Guide—The

Simple Low Risk Way You Can Profit From Inflation and Fluctuating Interest Rates, William E. Donoghue, Harper Row. $12.95.

Invisible Crash, James Dines, Ballantine, 1975. $10 (paperback) (out of print).

Silver Bulls, Paul Sarnoff, Arlington House Publishers, CT., 1980. $12.95.

The New Money Dynamics, Venita Van Caspel, Reston, 1978. $15.00.

The Kingdom of Moltz, Irwin Schiff, Freedom Books, Hamden, CT. $3.95.

The Great Inflation, Nathan Guttman and Patricia Meechan, Clifford Frost, Ltd., Great Britain, 1976. Paperback $4.95.

The Swiss Banking Handbook, Robert Roethenmund, Harper & Row, NY. $19.95.

Wealth & Poverty, George Gilder, Basic Books, Inc., NY. $16.95.

The Penniless Billionaire, Max Shapiro, Baker & Taylor Dist. $15.00.

Dow Jones Irwin Guide to Commodities Trading, Dow Jones, Irwin, IL. $27.95.

The Commodity Futures Game, Tewles, Harlow, Stone, McGraw-Hill Book Company, NY. $5.95.

How To Use Interest Rate Futures Contracts, Edward W. Schwartz, Dow Jones, Irwin, IL. $19.95.

The Diamond Book, Michael Freedman, Dow Jones, 1981. $14.95.

The World of Diamonds, Timothy Green, William Morrow & Co., $19.95.

The World of Gold, Timothy Green, Walker & Co., NY. $15.00.

How To Buy and Sell Gems—Everyone's Guide to Rubies, Sapphires, Emeralds and Diamonds, Benjamin Zucker, Times Books. $12.95.

High Profits From Rare Coin Investment, Q. David Bowers, Bowers & Ruddy Galleries, Inc., paperback $7.95.

The Last Days of America, Paul Erdman, Simon & Schuster, NY. $13.95.

High Finance On A Low Budget, Mark Skouser, $10.

Mark Skouser's Guide to Financial Privacy, Mark Skouser, Alexandria House, $14.95.

Tax Free, Mark Skouser, $12.95.

The Spike, Arnaud de Borchgrave and Robert Moss, Crown Publishing, Inc. $12.95.

Project Readiness: A Guide to Family Emergency Preparedness, Louise E. Nelson, Horizon, 1975. $8.95.

Skills For Survival, Esther Dickey, Horizon, 1978. $9.95.

Survival Home Manual, Joel M. Skousen, Survival Homes, OR, 1977. $25.00.

Survival Food Storage, Mark Thomason, TSI Publishers, CA, 1980. $4.95.

Food Drying At Home The Natural Way, Bee Beyer, J. P. Tarcher, Inc., CA. $5.95.

The ABC's Of Home Dehydration, Barbara Densley, Horizon, 1975. $4.50.

Just In Case—A Manual of Home Preparedness, Barbara G. Salsbury, Bookcraft. $4.95.

INDEX

385

392

HELP YOURSELF AND YOUR CAREER

INC. YOURSELF
How to Profit by Setting *(large format paperback)*
Up Your Own Corporation *(K97-817, $5.95, U.S.A.)*
by Judith H. McQuown *(K97-855, $6.95, Canada)*
In easy-to-understand terms, Judith H. McQuown, an expert in the field of money management, explains the dollars-and-cents advantages of incorporating yourself; getting "Free" life and disability insurance; setting up your own tax-sheltered pension and profit-sharing plans; obtaining greater benefits than you get through the Keogh plan; generating legitimate "cashless" tax deductions; and incorporate without a lawyer.

WORKING SMART
How to accomplish more in half the time.
by Michael LeBoeuf *(K33-147, $2.95)*
In his lively, humorous style, Michael LeBoeuf will teach you how to set specific goals on a daily, intermediate and lifetime basis and how to analyze and revise your present use of time accordingly.

TELEPHONE TECHNIQUES THAT SELL *(large format*
by Charles Bury *paperback)*
(K37-215, $5.95)
An estimated $50 billion a year is spent on goods and services marketed on the telephone. But despite its paramount importance in today's economy, few business people know how to use the telephone to its full potential. Charles Bury, head of Modern Communications, explores the entire spectrum of telephone sales techniques.

HERE ARE MORE WARNER BOOKS...
A MUST FOR YOUR CAREER GROWTH

STOCK MARKET PRIMER *(hardcover)*
by Claude N. Rosenberg, Jr. *(K51-226, $14.95)*
Lucidly written, Mr. Rosenberg shares with you the fundamental facts about investing: buying stocks and bonds, how the stock market works, spotting bull and bear markets, how to tell which industries have the greatest growth potential. Mr. Rosenberg takes the mystery out of the stock market and puts valuable, profit-making ideas at your disposal.

To order, use the coupon below. If you prefer to use your own stationery, please include complete title as well as book number and price. Allow 4 weeks for delivery.